CAMBRIDGE TEXTS IN THE
HISTORY OF POLITICAL THOUGHT

—

MARX
Later Political Writings

CAMBRIDGE TEXTS IN THE
HISTORY OF POLITICAL THOUGHT

Series editors

RAYMOND GEUSS
Reader in Philosophy, University of Cambridge

QUENTIN SKINNER
Regius Professor of Modern History, University of Cambridge

Cambridge Texts in the History of Political Thought is now firmly established as the major student textbook series in political theory. It aims to make available to students all the most important texts in the history of western political thought, from ancient Greece to the early twentieth century. All the familiar classic texts will be included but the series seeks at the same time to enlarge the conventional canon by incorporating an extensive range of less well-known works, many of them never before available in a modern English edition. Wherever possible, texts are published in complete and unabridged form, and translations are specially commissioned for the series. Each volume contains a critical introduction together with chronologies, biographical sketches, a guide to further reading and any necessary glossaries and textual apparatus. When completed, the series will aim to offer an outline of the entire evolution of western political thought.

For a list of titles published in the series, please see end of book.

MARX

Later Political Writings

EDITED AND TRANSLATED BY
TERRELL CARVER
University of Bristol

CAMBRIDGE
UNIVERSITY PRESS

CAMBRIDGE UNIVERSITY PRESS
Cambridge, New York, Melbourne, Madrid, Cape Town, Singapore, São Paulo

Cambridge University Press
The Edinburgh Building, Cambridge CB2 8RU, UK

Published in the United States of America by Cambridge University Press, New York

www.cambridge.org
Information on this title: www.cambridge.org/9780521367394

In the translations, introduction and editorial matter
© Cambridge University Press 1996

First published 1996
Seventh printing 2007

Printed in the United Kingdom at the University Press, Cambridge

A catalogue record for this publication is available from the British Library

Library of Congress Cataloguing in Publication data
Marx, Karl, 1818–1883.
[Selections. English. 1996]
Karl Marx: later political writings / edited and translated by Terrell Carver.
p.   cm. – (Cambridge texts in the history of political thought)
Includes bibliographical references and index.
Contents: Manifesto of the Communist Party (with Friedrich Engels)
- The eighteenth Brumaire of Louis Bonaparte - Introduction (1857)
to the Grundrisse - Preface to a contribution to the critique of
political economy - The Civil War in France - Critique of the
Gotha programme - Notes on Adolph Wagner.
ISBN 0 521 36504 x (hardback) – ISBN 0 521 36739 5 (paperback)
1. State, The.   2. Communist state.   3. Political science.
I. Carver, Terrell.   II. Title.   III. Series.
JC233.M29213 1996   335.4 - dc20   95-6515   CIP

ISBN 978-0-521-36739-4 paperback

for

Laurie Michael Carver

Contents

Acknowledgements   *page* viii
Editor's introduction   ix
Chronology of Marx's Life and Career, 1848–1883   xxi
Bibliography   xxiii
Editor's note on texts and translations   xxvi
Glossary of major historical figures   xxviii

Manifesto of the Communist Party
  (with Friedrich Engels)   1
The Eighteenth Brumaire of Louis Bonaparte   31
'Introduction' to the *Grundrisse*   128
'Preface' to *A Contribution to the Critique*
  of Political Economy   158
The Civil War in France   163
Critique of the Gotha Programme   208
'Notes' on Adolph Wagner   227

Index   258

Acknowledgements

In preparing these translations I have consulted actual and facsimile first editions, as well as the texts established in the first and second versions of the *Marx-Engels Gesamtausgabe*. I have also made use of the *Marx-Engels Werke*, the Marx and Engels *Collected Works*, the Pelican *Marx Library* editions, and the annotated edition of the *Communist Manifesto* edited by Frederic L. Bender (New York: Norton, 1988) and I am indebted to the scholarly work in all of these.

I am grateful to the History of Ideas Unit of the Australian National University, Research School of Social Sciences, for a sabbatical grant from the History of Ideas Unit, and to the Department of Politics, University of Bristol, for the invaluable gift of time off teaching and administration. I am also indebted to the library staff at ANU for assistance, as well as to colleagues so easily accessible in the Coombes Building on campus in Canberra. I should also like to express my thanks to staff at the University of Bristol Arts and Social Sciences Library, and the British Library.

For materials, suggestions and encouragement I should like to acknowledge help from Joseph O'Malley, editor of the companion volume in this series *Marx: Early Political Writings*; from James Farr (University of Minnesota), Lawrence Wilde (Nottingham Trent University), and James Martin (Queen's University, Belfast); and from the Marx-Haus in Trier.

Editor's introduction

Karl Marx (1818–83) did not write a comprehensive or even exemplary work of political theory. Instead he addressed himself as a political agent to a politics of democratic constitutionalism and revolutionary communism, and to a detailed critique of the economics of the day. It is from those works that his contributions to political theory can be constructed and assessed.

Manifesto of the Communist Party

Marx has left us one work that outlines his views – *Manifesto of the Communist Party*, first published in 1848. This small pamphlet appeared quite fortuitously on the very eve of democratic upheaval and constitutional revolution. His previous writings, largely unavailable to the nineteenth-century audience, play a role in our reading of the *Manifesto* today, and they amplify, as well as explain, some of the arguments made in its pages. For Marx's political writings before 1848, the reader should consult the companion volume in this series, *Marx: Early Political Writings*, edited and introduced by Joseph O'Malley with Richard A. Davis. The *Manifesto* is particularly useful in structuring a reading of Marx's later writings, such as those contained in the present volume, since it introduces and develops a perspective without which the detailed propositions that may be abstracted from Marx's subsequent works are of little use.

Ostensibly the *Manifesto* was written for a small group of self-styled communists who considered themselves representative of discontented workers. Marx and his friend the journalist and businessman Friedrich Engels (1820–95) saw political possibilities in the Communist League, successor to an even more shadowy League of the Just, and they wanted its international imprimatur for their ideas. They manœuvred its two 'congresses' of 1847 into giving them responsibility for a manifesto, which Engels duly drafted (twice) and Marx ultimately produced – late for the printers, as was his habit – in January 1848.

Although very much a joint composition, Marx had the text last and took responsibility for its production. It was published in London in German for distribution throughout western Europe, and, as the document proudly boasts, for immediate translation into other European languages. Such early translations as were undertaken, including an English one of 1850, were not widely circulated, nor did the Communist League play an important role as such in the national revolutions of 1848 and 1849.

Communist politics, in the *Manifesto* and in practice, was conceived in national terms and left to 'members' in local circumstances. Some were so conventionally democratic as to stand for the Frankfurt parliament, which sat as a constituent assembly for all of Germany. Others pursued armed action against monarchical armies, who sought to restore the old regime of kingdoms and principalities, almost all non-constitutional in character. Marx and Engels edited a liberal newspaper in the Rhineland which supported constitutional democracy until, in the teeth of political reaction, they as editors advised communists and other readers to fight on alone. The *Manifesto* achieved its widest circulation as the source for a flysheet of demands posted throughout Germany, which Marx and Engels signed. The original document, incidentally, was published anonymously as a statement by the 'party'.

Marx placed social class at the centre of his conception of politics, but did not venture a comprehensive definition or thorough-going analysis of the term. Generally he argued that classes are defined by differential modes of access to productive resources, and that any given *distribution* of goods and services to individuals is a necessary result of arrangements in the sphere of *production*. In his view, the division of society into classes has been a central feature of human existence, and it is the major problem of modern times. A class-divided society is in a state of 'more or less veiled civil war'.

Intriguingly Marx suggests in the *Manifesto* that this is true whether political participants acknowledge it or not, and whether or not there is any overt struggle to be observed. Property relations are the key to the way that productive resources are controlled, and the *Manifesto* provides examples of different types. One of Marx's most important claims is that property relations, forms of the state and politics, indeed social institutions in general, are highly variable and have changed from one epoch to another. Thus there can be no timeless and universal deductive account of human society, most particularly one that presumes or argues the necessity of private property as a universal phenomenon. For Marx civilisation is built on the shifting sands of class struggle, and government has been a device employed by the well-off and powerful to contain the poor and exploited.

Marx argued that there is no credible and democratic solution to the problem of class-society that is exclusively political, rather than substantially economic. Abolition of private property, or 'bourgeois property' as he styled it, was the communist slogan that he proudly announced in the *Manifesto*. Specifically it was private property as capital – 'property which exploits wage-labour' – that communists should aim to replace with public control of productive resources.

The *Manifesto* argues that an analysis of property must precede, perhaps even supersede, an analysis of authority, legitimacy and other traditional concepts, and that a change to communism could only be the result of mass action and democratic politics. Fuller accounts of democratic institutions, political leadership, revolutionary organisation and communist social relations appeared in later works.

The Eighteenth Brumaire of Louis Bonaparte

The Eighteenth Brumaire helps to fill out the views outlined in the *Manifesto*. It was also an attempt at consolation – a major theme in the later Marx – for the failure of even democratic constitutionalism, to say nothing of the communist movement. Of more theoretical interest today is the way that Marx handled the indeterminacy of human actions, arguing an overall structure of economic motivation in individuals, and of economic crisis in the social system, whilst sketching in the varied complexity of French political life.

In the early 1850s Marx published a series of articles in German on contemporary French politics for the *Neue Rheinische Zeitung-Revue*, a short-lived left-liberal newspaper that he and Engels edited in London, and *The Eighteenth Brumaire* was written as a follow-up. The paper was intended for German-speaking readers at home and in exile. *The Eighteenth Brumaire* was first published by an emigrant '48er in New York, and it represents Marx's most sustained mature effort at satire, parody and invective. It must count as the best argued defence ever of the view that 'history is the history of class struggles', even if in it not all action in politics is traceable to social class, nor all outcomes to revolutionary action presented as advances towards communism.

For Marx a political theory was supposed to have an overtly self-fulfilling quality, as it was no mere reflection of what was supposed to be the case. In his view no theorist can really be just a theorist, all theorists are participants in some political process, and denials of political intent merely disguise an inevitable political content.

The Louis Bonaparte of the title was a nephew of the great emperor, sometime soldier and president of the republic established in 1848 after the overthrow of the 'July Monarchy' of Louis Philippe, king of the French. Marx was furious that Bonaparte was elected head of state in a national vote, and even more enraged when he mounted a *coup d'état* in December 1851 and suspended the republic indefinitely. The 'eighteenth Brumaire' of the title is a reference to the date (according to the revolutionary calendar) of the coup executed by the first Bonaparte against the Directory.

Behind the scorn and invective heaped on the admittedly somewhat comic Louis Bonaparte, Marx traced a process of liberal regression. As the democratic left and authoritarian right disagreed on 'the property question', so elements in the political centre were forced to choose. The 'party of order' figures large in Marx's account and represents a broad coalition of middle-class or 'bourgeois' forces, with the peasantry as a crucial ally. In striking language Marx dramatised the way that democrats, advocating redistributive economic policies, were smeared as communists and extremists. Conversely those democrats who feared for their economic interests were attracted by the wily Bonaparte, and Marx chronicles their ruin when a military dictatorship was declared.

In the light of *The Eighteenth Brumaire* it cannot be said that Marx's understanding of politics was reductionist and determinist. His more abstract theorisations of politics, as in the texts which follow, need to be interpreted in conjunction with the detailed analyses that he actually undertook.

'Introduction' to the *Grundrisse*

The 'Introduction' (1857) to the *Grundrisse* shows Marx enquiring into the specifics of how to study the property relations of modern society. This is an uncorrected manuscript that has had extensive attention only since the 1970s, but it has been widely read since then as a key link between the Marx's 'philosophical' methods and his 'economic' analysis. A number of important methodological problems are discussed there in novel ways.

Having argued that politics must be analysed in an economic setting, Marx strove to find the best way of doing this for the economic order that was displacing all others globally. That, of course, was 'the capitalist mode of production', or 'modern bourgeois society', so vividly described in the *Manifesto*.

The 1857 'Introduction' demonstrates a linkage between specialist works of political economy and the ordinary concepts and behaviour that occur in real life. The linkage is one of mutual reflection: the inequalities and exploitation of real life are mirrored in economic science, and the 'market' behaviour traced abstractly in works of political economy emerges eventually in the reality of wages, employment and property. Thus a close philosophical dissection of leading political economists, and a refutation of their doctrines, was politically crucial to the communist project.

In the 'Introduction' (1857) Marx recorded a decision to focus on the concept 'capital' in his analysis, making it his implied point of departure and actual point of completion. 'Capital', he wrote, 'was the power ruling over everything.' Though when he came to publish his 'critique of the economic categories' as *A Contribution to the Critique of Political Economy*, he omitted the 'Introduction' (1857), the work is notable for revealing that wide-ranging explorations of method and substance preceded the more dogmatic summary statements he offered to the public two years later.

'Preface' to *A Contribution to the Critique of Political Economy*

The 'Preface' of 1859 to *A Contribution to the Critique of Political Economy* represents a very brief introduction to the first instalment of Marx's political analysis of capitalist society, but it does this in a curiously de-politicised form. Indeed the choice of title reveals an interesting strategic ploy, in that Marx aimed to address a specialist audience in political economy. His overarching project was to reveal to them, through unimpeachable argument, that class struggle was serious, worsening and yet the bearer of its own resolution in the 'classless' society of communism. All three of those claims, so he argued, had been denied by the galaxy of respected authors whom he termed collectively 'the political economists'.

The propositions of the 'guide for my studies' that Marx included in the 'Preface' are amongst the most enigmatic passages that he ever wrote. As a statement of his 'outlook' they reappeared in a footnote to the first volume of *Capital* at its publication in 1867, and there they might have rested. The little critique of 1859 was never widely circulated, and most of the material in it was incorporated into the later opening volume of Marx's *magnum opus*.

One person, though, was gripped by Marx's text, and used it extensively at the time in reviews and in later years in explicating Marx. That was Engels, whose own presentation of Marx and his work was founded in part on the propositional generalisations that feature uniquely in the 'Preface'. Engels' reading of them as scientific laws, or law-like tendencies, became authoritative for both pro- and anti-Marxists. When in the twentieth century Marx was selected and collected as an academic writer, the 1859 'Preface' became in that context the centrepiece for inquiry. How were these propositions to be understood and tested? Their role in introducing Marx's detailed inquiries took second place, and metonymically they came to stand for his thought as a whole. The better-illustrated discussions of the *Manifesto*, the more intensely political analysis in *The Eighteenth Brumaire*, and the more exploratory conceptual studies in the economic works, from the *Grundrisse* through the various drafts and published volumes of *Capital*, were then 'rigorously' judged against Marx's 'guiding' insights.

'Guiding' these insights may have been, but what Marx actually wrote and published contradicts them in detail often enough to put paid to any notion that they were supposed to be true in some necessary or invariable sense. Indeed the propositions themselves display an ambiguity that reflects haste and inattention – Marx was late to the press as usual. Reading the supposedly central 'Preface' in the light of the other materials collected in the present volume, and in the companion volume of earlier writings, will make it easier to make some sense of the mixed metaphors Marx employs. These are now world famous, but are arguably confused even in the original. Marx did not seem to see these propositions as the foundations for a doctrine, but even if he did, he would surely have expected readers to move well beyond them in seeking to understand what he had to say.

However, it must be said that the 1859 'Preface' represents the traditional and by far the most influential and familiar way of approaching Marx. That text can be read as the doctrinal foundation for Marxism, a science of law-like tendencies in economic and political life guaranteed by abstractly formulated 'materialist premises' or concretely perceived 'class struggle'. The traditional Marxist reading, however, is not the only one. The same propositions can also be examined as 'empirical' propositions in social science, or as attempts at such. Thus they have been criticised as unfalsifiable, and so unworthy of scientific notice (by Sir Karl Popper); or as falsifiable, but proven false through close investigation of historical and contemporary circumstances (by G.A. Cohen). Both readings are at the heart of the academic enterprise that Marxology has become, and both have generated intensely interesting intellectual debate. Neither puts Marx into perspective as a political theorist, particularly one who expected to contribute to contemporary accounts of 'the social question' in the context of both industrially developed, and newly industrialising countries.

The Civil War in France

In *The Civil War in France* Marx reluctantly brought his work on French politics up to date in the 1870s. The occasion was another unhappy setback for democratic forces, socialists and communists amongst them. Consolation and inspiration were major themes again, as in *The Eighteenth Brumaire*. *The Civil War in France* represents a kind of sequel.

The French defeat in the Franco-Prussian War of 1870 had been followed by an insurrection in Paris. Resistance to the Prussians, and to a Prussian-imposed settlement, marked the uprising as a nationalist one. This rebellion arose out of disgust with the politicians who spoke for the French after the capture of the Emperor Napoleon III (the Louis Bonaparte of Marx's earlier broadside) at the humiliating battle of Sedan.

The form of domestic government that was to succeed the defunct Second Empire was of necessity an issue in the major cities, and in Paris above all, with its history of democratic revolutionary action. In his writings of the period Marx advised against a democratic rebellion, arguing rightly that forces combining liberals, who were opposed to socialist 'extremism', with the Prussians, who wanted a 'stable' France, would overpower any Parisian experiment in communal democracy and economic cooperation.

However, once the Commune was founded Marx did what he could in terms of international publicity and assistance – as always from London. *The Civil War in France* emerged as an encomium for an event that had attracted extreme notoriety in Europe. Marx's comments were published anonymously in London for distribution in Europe and the United States, and this text was his most extended attempt to write in English. It was swiftly translated into German by Engels.

Marx aimed to set the record straight, as he saw it, and to find some hope for the future – though the bloodbath visited on the Communards in 1871 was hardly inspirational. In the twentieth-century context it is his sketchy comments on communist society that have attracted attention to this text, together with his spirited defence of democratic forms of political organisation. The form of the 'ideal society' is a question familiar within political theory, and the way that representative democracy aims to bridge the gap between the individual will and collective decision-making is similarly a well-known problem.

Although Marx was an anti-utopian thinker who refused to generate detailed schemes and models for future communist society, he nonetheless vouchsafed some views on what communism was actually going to be (other than 'a historical movement that is proceeding under our own eyes', as it says in the *Manifesto*), and on how decisions would be made concerning collectively controlled resources (other than the 'free development of each is the condition for the free development of all', in the same text). Hence the interest that *The Civil War in France* has aroused centres chiefly on the view, propounded by Engels, that for Marx the Paris Commune represented the 'advancement of the proletariat to ruling class, [the] victory for democracy', mentioned in the famous pamphlet of 1848.

Many of the critical comments directed at Marx's admittedly brief account of the political 'secret' of the Commune make the economic regulation and political institutions of modern 'welfare democracy' sound impossible on any terms, let alone his. It must be said, however, that Marx's communism required the eventual abolition of the money economy altogether, as he argued in the opening chapter of *Capital*, but it is not clear under those circumstances how economic information is to be transmitted through democratic institutions to the spheres of production and consumption. Ultimately democratic institutions were to take responsibility for authoritative plans, but such plans were not to be authoritarian, precisely because they were to be the outcome of democratic decision-making. However, there are no practical clues or examples given by Marx to support these particular views.

In Marx's admittedly selective account of politics under the Commune he praised the institution of municipal councillors, chosen by universal manhood suffrage, responsible to the electorate, and revocable by them if mandated instructions were not obeyed. He envisaged a hierarchy of local and district communes, each sending representatives to a higher body, culminating in a national one handling the 'few but important' functions of central government. Unlike the 'democracies' of Marx's time or ours, these representatives and their paid officials were to be awarded only working-class wages. The standing army was to be abolished, the people were to be armed as a militia, and the police were to be responsible to their communes. Marx had no faith in an 'independent' judiciary and argued that magistrates and judges were to be made elective. The church was to be disestablished, though religious belief could evidently have survived, and free education was to be made available to all.

It takes considerable imagination to see all this in the actual Commune itself, especially given the character of the reports that Marx received in the press. Eyewitnesses, of course, may have told him a different story. The text is clearly a meditation on what he took to be the principles that emerge in democratic politics, and his 'ideal' institutions to be reasonable extrapolations that the Commune was never able to realise. How close those arrangements stand to an immediate 'dictatorship of the proletariat' (a phrase Marx only occasionally used or endorsed) or to a 'transitional socialism' preceding communism itself, are mysteries that Marx himself did not address.

Critique of the Gotha Programme

At the close of this volume are two short manuscripts. The first, Marx's *Critique of the Gotha Programme*, is by far the better known, as it was drawn from his literary legacy by Engels and published in 1891 within the context of German socialist politics. The Gotha Programme had been formulated for the unification congress of May 1875. At that venue the Social Democratic Workers' Party, whose leaders Wilhelm Liebknecht and August Bebel were in communication with Marx and Engels, and the General German Workers' Union, whose founder Ferdinand Lassalle had died in 1864, were to be unified as the Socialist Party of Germany. Marx and Engels had rejected Lassalle's brand of socialism for two reasons. First they held it to be insufficiently critical of capitalism and a money-economy. Secondly they considered it to be insufficiently suspicious of the existing German state, and too sanguine towards reformist 'solutions' to the social question. These issues were still alive in the 1890s, so that Marx's words in the *Critique* represented a posthumous intervention (by Engels) in the political scene, as the Gotha Programme was then itself up for revision at the Erfurt congress.

In twentieth-century terms, however, it is Marx's critique of liberalism that has attracted attention. Was it valid or useful to describe *all* legal 'rights' as 'bourgeois' rights? Property rights in productive resources, perhaps, but even civil rights to personal property, free expression, to equality before the law? What arrangements for the use and enjoyment of resources did he envisage, then, for communist society? How would those relations be organised? Is there any way of doing this without the mechanism of rights and the apparatus of constitutional, legal and judicial institutions of enforcement?

Marx seemed to be asserting that rights were indissolubly connected with interests construed not just individualistically but egoistically, and that under communism such a 'bourgeois' basis for behaviour would of course have been abolished. It would seem to follow that in communist society any differences or disputes would presumably be of a quite different character, and so their resolution would proceed differently, without need for 'rights'. Cooperative forms of production would make possible, and indeed would generate, a realm of individual interests in collectively beneficial relations. Marx has lately been taxed (by Jon Elster) with assuming a fallacious identification of individual with collective interests, and ignoring the dynamics of actual processes of individual and collective change. His references in the *Critique* to socialism as a transitional stage, and to differential rewards for all in society in proportion to work actually done, merely restate the problem.

'Notes' on Adolph Wagner

The final work in the present volume is the least well known, Marx's '"Notes" on Adolph Wagner', probably the last substantial work penned before his death in 1883. Wagner was a reforming economist and self-identified socialist. Marx disputed Wagner's self-identification and did not welcome the offer of support. The manuscript had no currency at the time of writing (1879–80) or for many years after. Indeed it attracted little attention till the 1970s, when the context was highly academic and theoretical. At that point the following questions were under consideration, and the 'Notes' were scrutinised for answers. Did Marx have an account of 'human nature'? If so, did it explain or predict all actions, most actions or just some actions? Or did he view individuals as determined by larger forces – economic structures, 'dialectical' laws or class interests?

The attack on Wagner has also helped somewhat in getting a grip on Marx's career as a political theorist. Had he changed his mind in any fundamental way about how theory should be done? Was his conception of the proper starting point for politically effective theory the same as in his early career? If so, what exactly was it? If not, how had it changed, and what had it become?

The 'Notes', read in that light, offer an intriguing challenge to previous concepts of 'man' in political theory. (Marx used *der Mensch*, rather than *der Mann*, so it might be argued that the term 'man' as he used it lacked at least some of the sexist overtones of the English term.) 'Man' for Marx was always a self-creation, not wholly, of course, but for political purposes Marx always looked to culture for his explanations rather than biology. Political theory, then, could not be read off 'man's' material nature. 'Man' was a conceptual and practical interpreter of the material relationship that 'he' (and, in Marx's writing, very occasionally 'she') had with nature. As 'man' altered nature in the course of that relationship, so the relationship was itself altered. In that way 'man' was never the same from era to era in any respect that was fundamental for political theory.

Thus Marx's starting point was always a fully historical and exceptionally malleable view of 'man', subject only to constraints that were themselves variable with respect to what 'man' had become and what 'he' was trying to do. As human nature was so open-textured, and so subject to reconstruction in the economic context, political theorists would have to be genuinely political in their task, as they, too, are part of the social process by which 'man' is continually re-created.

Chronology of Marx's life and career, 1848–83

1848   Feb.:   Publishes *Manifesto of the Communist Party*, jointly written with Engels, and issued anonymously in London.

1848–9   Editor of and contributor to the *Rheinische Zeitung*, daily newspaper published in Cologne.

1849   April: Publishes articles posthumously collected as *Wage Labour and Capital*.

1849   Aug.:   Moves to London.

1850   Publishes articles posthumously collected as *The Class Struggles in France* in *Neue Rheinische Zeitung*, edited with Engels and published in Hamburg.

1850   Sept.:   Death of infant son Guido.

1851–2   Writes *The Eighteenth Brumaire of Louis Bonaparte* and publishes it in German in New York.

1852   April: Death of infant daughter Franziska.

1855   April: Death of eight-year-old son Edgar.

1853–7   Publishes some hundreds of newspaper articles on current topics in world politics for European and American newspapers.

1857–8   Writes 'Introduction' and other *Grundrisse* manuscripts, posthumously edited and published.

1859   Publishes *A Contribution to the Critique of Political Economy* (with 'Preface') in Berlin.

1861–3   Writes manuscripts posthumously edited and published as *Theories of Surplus Value*, vol. I, II and III.

1864   Sept.:   Helps to found International Working-Men's Association ('First International').

1864–5	Writes manuscripts posthumously edited and published as *Capital*, vol. III.
1865	Writes English-language lectures posthumously published as *Value, Price and Profit*.
1865–7	Finishes manuscript of vol. I of *Capital*.
1867	Publishes vol. I of *Capital* in Hamburg.
1869	Publishes 2nd edn of *The Eighteenth Brumaire of Louis Bonaparte* in Hamburg.
1867–79	Writes manuscripts posthumously edited and published as *Capital*, vol. II.
1871	Publishes *The Civil War in France* in London as an 'Address of the General Council of the International Working Men's Association'.
1872	Publishes 2nd edn of vol. I of *Capital* in Hamburg; and new edn of the *Manifesto*, with jointly signed preface, in Leipzig.
1872–5	Contributes to French translation of vol. I of *Capital*, published in Paris in two parts.
1875	Writes manuscript posthumuously published as *Critique of the Gotha Programme*.
1879–80	Writes manuscript posthumously published as '*Notes*' on Adolph Wagner.
1880–1	Writes manuscripts posthumously published as *Ethnological Notebooks*.
1881	Dec.: Death of Jenny Marx (wife).
1883	Jan.: Death of Jenny Marx (daughter).
1883	March: Dies in London, aged 64, of lung disease and general ill-health.

Bibliography

Further works by Marx

The *Collected Works* of Karl Marx and Frederick Engels (begun 1975) is still in progress from Lawrence and Wishart (London) and International Publishers (New York), and it provides English versions of major works, manuscripts and letters with copious notes. The texts of this set in approximately fifty volumes are based on the scholarly work of the second series of the *Marx-Engels Gesamtausgabe* (begun by Dietz Verlag of East Berlin in 1972, and projected to comprise over a hundred volumes); this set presents all works whatsoever in the original language with considerable scholarly apparatus. The prospects for continuing the series now seem assured, as the project has passed from East German and Soviet hands to the new International Marx-Engels Foundation based in Amsterdam, and new guidelines for the edition were published in 1993.

Introductions to Marx's political thought

There are two books for students that introduce Marx's political thought, paying special attention to his activities as a political agent and to the centrality of economic issues or 'material production' throughout his work. One is *Marx: An Introduction*, by Wal Suchting (Brighton: Harvester/Wheatsheaf, 1983), and the other is my *Marx's Social Theory* (Oxford: Oxford University Press, 1982). For a somewhat more advanced level of discussion on similar premises the student is advised to consult Richard W. Miller's *Analyzing Marx: Morality, Power and History* (Princeton: Princeton University Press, 1984). A wide range of current disciplines rank Marx as an important authority and contributor, and there are original essays for students of political and moral philosophy, philosophy of science, history, sociology, aesthetics and theology (amongst others) in *The Cambridge Companion to Marx*, edited by myself (Cambridge: Cambridge University Press, 1991). There are annotated essays on the major concepts in Marx, such as class, capitalism, communism and revolution, together with detailed references to primary and secondary sources, in my *A Marx Dictionary* (Cambridge: Polity, 1987).

Biographies of Marx

The most comprehensive current biography of Marx is David McLellan's *Karl Marx: His Life and Thought* (London: Macmillan, 1973). Although the earlier works receive more attention than the later ones, the book includes considerable detail on the interrelationship between Marx's political activities and his works. For a moving evocation of historical and personal context Isaiah Berlin's *Karl Marx: His Life and Environment* is still worth reading (Oxford: Oxford University Press, 1939, 4th edn 1982; London: Fontana edn forthcoming 1995). *Karl Marx: Interviews and Recollections*, edited by David McLellan (London: Macmillan, 1981) collects numerous quite different perceptions of the man and his work. There is also an older compilation, *Reminiscences of Marx and Engels* from Progress Publishers of Moscow (n.d.).

Studies on Marx's politics and political theory

Two classic studies were produced when scholarly attention was turned to the 'early Marx', but both books set a context for the later period in Marx's life and treat the writings of that time in some detail. These are Shlomo Avineri's *The Social and Political Thought of Karl Marx* (Cambridge: Cambridge University Press, 1968 and repr.), and Allen W. Wood's *Karl Marx* (London and Boston: Routledge and Kegan Paul, 1981). Avineri situates Marx in the context of Hegelian critique and evolves the theories of alienation and revolution from philosophical origins, but his consideration of Marx's work on French politics, beginning with the Terror and continuing to the civil war of 1871, develops a controversial account of Marx's political theory. Wood's book presents a topically arranged discussion of Marx's views on various concepts relevant to political philosophy – alienation, morality, justice, explanation, etc. – and focuses particularly on the way that Marx advocates revolution but dismisses many potent arguments for it as ideological. *Marx's Theory of Politics*, by John M. Maguire (Cambridge: Cambridge University Press, 1978), does much the same job. For a detailed consideration of Marx's political involvements up to 1853, with considerable attention to the theoretical tensions and ambiguities therein, the reader should consult Alan Gilbert's *Marx's Politics: Communists and Citizens* (Oxford: Martin Robertson, 1981). Two recent examinations of Marx's relationship with and usefulness to the theory of democracy stand out: Michael Levin, *Marx, Engels and Liberal Democracy* (London, Macmillan, 1989), and Keith Graham, *The Battle of Democracy: Conflict, Consensus and the Individual*, (Brighton: Harvester/Wheatsheaf, 1986).

Editor's note on texts and translations

All translations in this volume are new and are based on first editions or reliable copy-texts of manuscripts unpublished in Marx's lifetime. Successive editors have hardly altered the 'classical' English translations, produced between the 1880s and the 1930s, of the *Manifesto of the Communist Party*, *The Eighteenth Brumaire of Louis Bonaparte*, the 'Preface' to *A Contribution to the Critique of Political Economy*, and the *Critique of the Gotha Programme*. *The Civil War in France* was written in English, and so does not pose a problem. The manuscript materials – the 'Introduction' of 1857 to the *Grundrisse* and the '"Notes" on Adolph Wagner' – appear in my own translations of 1975. I am grateful to Basil Blackwell Ltd for permission to reproduce this material from my *Texts on Method*.

It is my aim as editor of the present volume to depart substantially from the way that Marx has previously been presented in English, and in other languages, including German (which was not always the original language of his work). Marx was made responsible for a doctrine or doctrines by Engels and by subsequent Marxists, and by editors who took the view that he should be presented doctrinally in terms of what his thought *became*, according to a posthumous scheme, rather than what it arguably was, when his writings were generated in the political context that prevailed at the time of first publication or authorial production. Famously Marx commented: 'I am not a Marxist.'

I have tried to capture something of the freshness of the moment, even when this means a certain awkwardness in expression or deviation from later terminology. Interestingly the two works (other than the first volume of *Capital*) that Marx was able to see reproduced in his own lifetime – the *Manifesto of the Communist Party* (new edn 1872) and *The Eighteenth Brumaire of Louis Bonaparte* (2nd edn 1869) – were offered by him to the reader as 'historical' documents with only minimal correction and updating. He remarked that 'we have no longer any right to alter' the *Manifesto*, and that revising *The Eighteenth Brumaire* 'would have robbed it of its peculiar colouring'. Engels, by contrast, generally adopted a much more intrusive editorial policy, appending footnotes, rewriting passages and 'correcting' terminology so as to make the texts that he produced consistent with his view of Marx's 'scientific' achievements. Thus readers familiar with the traditional English versions of these *Later Political Writings* will find differences, and a number of stock terms and phrases have disappeared.

There were mistranslations and obscurities in the traditional English versions. Indeed I was consistently struck by the awkward and clumsy English through which Marx has been transmitted. I have tried at all times to adhere to the flow and tone of Marx's German, and to find appropriate expressions and metaphors in English that reflect, as much as possible, his forthright and punchy style. Every translation is an imperfect reflection, but I hope that mine is more vivid than previous renditions. I have corrected minor errors without indication. Where I have felt that editorial insertions are required to help the reader, or where the text itself is excessively abbreviated and requires amplification, I have used square brackets to enclose my insertions. For some works there are more complicated editorial notes.

Translation is inevitably interpretation, and interpretation is inevitably personal. I hope that I have been clear about what I have attempted to do in this collection: to present Marx in selected, complete writings as a political theorist who was deeply, though analytically engaged in politics. And about the way that I have tried to do it: using first editions rather than later edited versions, and striving for clarity in reaching a present-day audience.

Glossary of major historical figures

Names that are generally familiar, or are merely mentioned in passing, or are sufficiently explained in the text, are omitted from this list.

Babeuf, Gracchus (1760–97)
    Organiser of the 'conspiracy of equals' during the French revolution; executed under the Directory.

Barrot, Odilon (1791–1873)
    Leader of the liberal opposition under the 'July' monarchy, then chief minister during the second republic from December 1848 to October 1849.

Bastiat, Frédéric (1801–50)
    Political economist and author of *Economic Harmonies*.

Bismarck, Prince Otto von (1815–98)
    Minister-President of Prussia under the federal regime from 1862 to 1871, then Imperial Chancellor from 1871 to 1890.

Blanc, Louis (1811–82)
    Revolutionary socialist and member of the provisional government in early 1848; emigrated to London in August, and returned to France in 1871, when he was elected to the national assembly; favoured state-sponsored workers' cooperatives.

Blanqui, August (1805–81)
    Revolutionary communist during the 1848–9 revolution, and leader of an insurrection against the Government of National Defence in October 1870.

Brentano, Lujo (1844–1931)
    German economist and advocate of an 'academic' socialism.

Buchez, Philippe Joseph Benjamin (1796–1865)
Theorist and propagandist for state-aided workers' cooperatives in France, chiefly during the 1830s and 1840s.

Carey, Henry Charles (1793–1879)
American political economist and author of a three-volume *Principles of Political Economy*.

Cassagnac, Bertrand Granier de (1806–80)
Journalist and editor; proponent of authoritarian rule; thought to have been the author of or major contributor to the proposed revision of the constitution favouring Bonaparte in 1849.

Cato (95–46 BC)
Stoic politician and republican opponent of Julius Caesar; committed suicide when Caesar won the civil war and thus came to be considered a martyr to the republican cause.

Caussidière, Marc (1808–61)
Democrat and participant in the Lyons uprising of 1834 against the 'July' monarchy; prefect of the Paris police from February to June 1848; part of the mid-1848 emigration of democratic politicians to England.

Cavaignac, Louis-Eugène (1802–57)
Republican politician and general, war minister then chief executive for the second republic after May 1848.

Changarnier, Nicolas Anne Théodule (1793–1877)
Monarchist politician and general; commander of the Paris national guard.

Constant, Benjamin (1767–1830)
Liberal political figure under the restoration, in opposition to the reactionary King Charles X.

Cousin, Victor (1792–1867)
Philosopher and Minister of Education for Thiers in 1840 under the 'July' monarchy.

Cromwell, Oliver (1599–1658)
Leader of the English revolution against the monarchy; Lord Protector of the Commonwealth after 1653.

Danton, Georges Jacques (1759–94)
Jacobin during the French revolution; guillotined under the terror.

Darasz, Albert (1808–52)
Participant in the Polish insurrection for national liberation in

1830–1; member of the Central Committee of European Democracy, a loose and short-lived coalition of nationalist rebels in exile in London 1850–2.

Desmoulins, Camille (1760–94)
Jacobin during the French revolution; a moderate.

Dufaure, Jules Armand Stanislas (1798–1881)
Minister of the Interior during the second republic 1848–9 and Minister of Justice in 1871 for the Versailles regime.

Falloux, Alfred (1811–86)
Legitimist politician and Minister of Education in 1848; dissolved the national workshops, provoking riots.

Favre, Jules (1809–80)
Republican politician and Foreign Minister for the Government of National Defence, September 1870 to January 1871.

Flourens, Gustave (1838–71)
Organiser of the second Blanquist insurrection while Blanqui was still imprisoned; member of the Paris Commune; killed during the repression.

Fourier, Charles (1772–1837)
Utopian socialist and theorist of the 'phalansteries', cooperatives in which work and play were 'harmonised'.

Gambetta, Léon (1838–82)
Republican politician and minister in the government of national defence; dispatched by balloon over German lines during the siege of Paris to establish a government first at Tours, then Bordeaux.

Guizot, François Pierre Guillaume (1787–1874)
Prime Minister for King Louis Philippe, and symbol of the venality of the era of the 'July' monarchy for his advice to the French, 'enrich yourselves'.

Hegel, Georg Wilhelm Friedrich (1770–1831)
Idealist philosopher of history and political theorist, overwhelmingly influential in German intellectual circles in the early nineteenth century.

Kinkel, Gottfried (1815–82)
German democrat and rebel of 1848–9; an opponent of Marx in the émigré community of '48ers.

Lange, Friedrich Albert (1828–75)
Political philosopher and publicist, neo-Kantian then neo-Darwinian.

Lassalle, Ferdinand (1825–64)
German democrat, active in the 1848–9 events, and later organiser of a working-class political union in 1863.

Ledru-Rollin, Alexandre Auguste (1807–74)
Democrat and newspaper editor; deputy in the assemblies of 1848–9, and leader of the *montagne*.

Locke, John (1632–1704)
Empiricist philosopher and political theorist of government by consent.

Malthus, Thomas Robert (1766–1834)
English economist noted for his theory that population would inevitably exceed the means of subsistence.

Marat, Jean Paul (1743–93)
Publicist during the French revolution and leader of the Jacobins until his murder.

Marrast, Armand (1801–52)
Republican politician and newspaper editor; member of the provisional government of 1848 and mayor of Paris, and president of the constituent assembly.

Metternich, Prince Klemens (1773–1859)
Austrian Foreign Minister and Chancellor; organiser of the Holy Alliance against democratic rebels of 1848–9.

Meyer, Rudolph Hermann (1839–99)
Political economist and author of a work on political corruption in Germany in the 1870s.

Mill, John Stuart (1806–73)
Philosopher and political economist, author of *Principles of Political Economy* of 1848; liberal and free-trader, tending in later years to redistributive socialism.

Millière, Jean-Baptiste (1817–71)
Journalist and follower of Proudhon in the Versailles Assembly.

Mirabeau, Honoré Gabriel (1749–91)
Revolutionary and representative of the bourgeoisie during the French revolution.

Montesquieu, Charles de (1689–1755)
Political theorist and author of *The Spirit of the Laws*, arguing that different physical and cultural circumstances in a polity require different types of constitutions.

Oudinot, Nicolas (1791–1863)
Orléanist general; commander of the expeditionary army against

the Roman republic in 1849; opposed to Louis Bonaparte's *coup d'état*.

Owen, Robert (1771–1858)

Socialist and owner-founder of 'model' industrial communities.

Pouyer-Quertier, Auguste-Thomas (1820–91)

Industrialist and Minister of Finance for the Versailles regime in 1871.

Proudhon, Pierre-Joseph (1809–65)

Political theorist and economist of cooperative socialism and 'labour-money'.

Rau, Karl Heinrich (1792–1870)

Political economist and author of textbooks on economics influential in Germany in the mid-nineteenth century.

Ricardo, David (1772–1823)

Classical political economist noted for revising Adam Smith's labour theory of value.

Robespierre, Maximilien (1758–94)

Revolutionary and leader of the Jacobins during the terror of '93.

Rodbertus, Johann Karl (Jagetzow) (1805–75)

Political economist and academic socialist; author of a number of reformist *Social Letters*.

Rousseau, Jean-Jacques (1712–78)

French political philosopher and author of the *Discourse on the Origins of Inequality* and *The Social Contract*.

Royer-Collard, Pierre-Paul (1763–1845)

Political figure under the restoration and 'July' monarchy supporting constitutional monarchy as the vehicle for middle-class interests.

Ruge, Arnold (1802–80)

Revolutionary democrat in the German '48 rising; later an émigré democrat and rival to Marx amongst the German exiles.

Saint-Just, Louis-Antoine (1767–94)

Revolutionary and leading Jacobin, guillotined during the terror.

Saint-Simon, Henri, Comte de (1760–1825)

Political philosopher and theorist of utopian socialism.

Say, Jean-Baptiste (1767–1832)

French political economist and follower of Adam Smith.

Schäffle, Albert Friedrich Eberhard (1831–1903)

Political economist and academic socialist.

Sieber, Nikolai Ivanovich (1844–88)
  Russian political economist and author of a critical study of Ricardo.

Simon, Jules (1814–96)
  Republican and Education Minister in the Government of National Defence and for the Versailles regime.

Sismondi, J.C.L. Simonde de (1773–1842)
  Historian and political economist; reformist critic of capitalism.

Smith, Adam (1723–90)
  Classical political economist, theorising that labour is the source of all value, and philosopher of 'moral sentiments'.

Steuart, Sir James (1712–80)
  Classical political economist and contemporary of Adam Smith.

Storch, Heinrich Friedrich (1766–1835)
  Political economist and author of French-language textbooks and studies of national revenue in the 1820s.

Sue, Eugène (1804–57)
  Writer and reformist politician; elected deputy 1850–1.

Sulla, Lucius Cornelius (138–78 BC)
  Roman dictator 82–79 BC.

Thiers, Adolphe (1797–1877)
  Deputy during the second republic; leading figure in the government of national defence and the Versailles regime 1870–1.

Tocqueville, Alexis de (1805–59)
  Constitutional monarchist under the Orléanist regime and a deputy during the second republic; Foreign Minister for the republic from June to October 1849.

Trochu, Louis Jules (1815–96)
  Military leader of the Government of National Defence till the armistice of January 1871, and hence commander of the armed forces in Paris during the siege; deputy under the Versailles regime.

Véron, Louis Désiré (1798–1867)
  Journalist and owner of a Bonapartist newspaper.

Wagner, Adolph (1835–1917)
  Political economist and academic socialist; author of a general treatise on economics published in a second edition in 1879.

Manifesto of the Communist Party

A spectre stalks the land of Europe – the spectre of communism. The powers that be – Pope and Tsar, Metternich and Guizot, French Radicals and German police – are in holy alliance for a witchhunt.

Where is the opposition that has not been smeared as communistic by its enemies in government? Where is the opposition that has not retaliated by slandering more progressive groups and reactionary opponents alike with the stigma of communism?

Two things follow from this fact.

I. Communism is already recognised as a force by all the European powers.

II. It is high time for communists to lay before the world their perspectives, their goals, their principles, and to counterpose to the horror stories of communism a manifesto of the party itself.

For this purpose communists of various nationalities have gathered together in London and have drawn up the following manifesto, for publication in English, French, German, Italian, Flemish and Danish.

I
Bourgeois and proletarians

The history of all society up to now is the history of class struggles.

Freeman and slave, patrician and plebeian, lord and serf, guildmaster and journeyman, in short, oppressor and oppressed stood in continual conflict with one another, conducting an unbroken, now hidden, now open struggle, a struggle that finished each time with a revolutionary transformation of society as a whole, or with the common ruin of the contending classes.

In earlier epochs of history we find almost everywhere a comprehensive division of society into different orders, a multifarious gradation of social rank. In ancient Rome we have patricians, knights, plebeians, slaves; in the middle ages feudal lords, vassals, guild-masters, journeymen, serfs, and again in almost all of these classes further fine gradations.

Modern bourgeois society, which arose from the ruins of feudal society, has not transcended class conflict. It has merely established new classes, new conditions of oppression, new forms of struggle in place of the old.

Our epoch, the epoch of the bourgeoisie, is distinguished by the fact that it has simplified class conflict. Society as a whole is tending to split into two great hostile encampments, into two great classes directly and mutually opposed – bourgeoisie and proletariat.

From the serfs of the middle ages arose the petty traders of the first towns; from this class of petty traders the first elements of the bourgeoisie developed.

The discovery of America and the voyages round Africa provided fresh territory for the rising bourgeoisie. The East Indian and Chinese market, the colonisation of America, the colonial trade, the general increase in the means of exchange and of commodities, all gave to commerce, to sea transport, to industry a boost such as never before, hence quick development to the revolutionary element in a crumbling feudal society.

The feudal or guild system in industry could no longer satisfy the increasing demand from new markets. Small-scale manufacture took its place. The guildmasters were squeezed out by the middle ranks in industry; the division of labour between different guild corporations gave way to the division of labour within the individual workshop itself.

But markets were ever growing and demand ever rising. Even small-scale manufacture no longer sufficed to supply them. So steampower and machinery revolutionised industrial production. In place of small-scale manufacture came modern large-scale industry, in place of the middle ranks of industry came industrial millionaires, the generals of whole industrial armies, the modern bourgeois.

Large-scale industry has established a world market, for which the discovery of America prepared the way. The world market has given an immeasurable stimulus to the development of trade, sea-transport and land communications. This development has produced in turn an expansion of industry, and just as industry, commerce, sea-trade and railways have expanded, so the bourgeoisie has developed, increased its capital, and pushed into the background all pre-existing classes from the middle ages onwards.

So we see how the modern bourgeoisie is itself the product of a long process of development, a series of revolutions in the modes of production and exchange.

Each of these stages of development of the bourgeoisie was accompanied by a corresponding political advance. From an oppressed class under the rule of feudal lords, to armed and self-administering associations within the medieval city, here an independent urban republic, there a third estate taxable by the monarchy, then in the era of small-scale manufacture a counterweight to the nobility in the estates-system or in an absolute monarchy, in general the mainstay of the great monarchies, the bourgeoisie – with the establishment of large-scale industry and the world market – has finally gained exclusive political control through the modern representative state. The power of the modern state is merely a device for administering the common affairs of the whole bourgeois class.

The bourgeoisie has played a highly revolutionary role in history.

Where it has come to power the bourgeoisie has obliterated all relations that were feudal, patriarchal, idyllic. It has pitilessly severed the motley bonds of feudalism that joined men to their natural superiors, and has left intact no other bond between one man and another than naked self-interest, unfeeling 'hard cash'. It has drowned the ecstasies of religious fervour, of zealous chivalry, of philistine sentiment in the icy waters of egoistic calculation. It has resolved personal worth into exchange-value, and in place of countless attested and hard-won freedoms it has established a single freedom – conscienceless free trade. In a word, for exploitation cloaked by religious and political illusions, it has substituted open, unashamed, direct, brutal exploitation.

The bourgeoisie has stripped the sanctity from all professions that were hitherto honourable and regarded with reverence. It has transformed the doctor, the lawyer, the priest, the poet, the man of science into its paid workforce.

The bourgeoisie has torn the pathetic veil of sentiment from family relations and reduced them to purely monetary ones.

The bourgeoisie has revealed how the brutal exercise of power, which reactionaries admire so much in the middle ages, was suitably complemented by the dullest indolence. Uniquely it has demonstrated what human activity can accomplish. It has executed marvels quite different from Egyptian pyramids, Roman aqueducts and Gothic cathedrals; it has carried out expeditions quite different from barbarian invasions and crusades.

The bourgeoisie cannot exist without continually revolutionising the instruments of production, hence the relations of production, and therefore social relations as a whole. By contrast the first condition of existence of all earlier manufacturing classes was the unaltered maintenance of the old mode of production. The continual transformation of production, the uninterrupted convulsion of all social conditions, a perpetual uncertainty and motion distinguish the epoch of the bourgeoisie from all earlier ones. All the settled, age-old relations with their train of time-honoured preconceptions and viewpoints are dissolved; all newly formed ones become outmoded before they can ossify. Everything feudal and fixed goes up in smoke, everything sacred is profaned, and men are finally forced to take a down-to-earth view of their circumstances, their multifarious relationships.

The need for a constantly expanding outlet for their products pursues the bourgeoisie over the whole world. It must get a foothold everywhere, settle everywhere, establish connections everywhere.

Through the exploitation of the world market the bourgeoisie has made the production and consumption of all countries cosmopolitan. It has pulled the national basis of industry right out from under the reactionaries, to their consternation. Long-established national industries have been destroyed and are still being destroyed daily. They are being displaced by new industries – the introduction of which becomes a life-and-death question for all civilised nations – industries that no longer work up indigenous raw materials but use raw materials from the ends of the earth, industries whose products are consumed not only in the country of origin but in every part of the world. In place of the old needs satisfied by home production we have new ones which demand the products of the most distant lands and climes for their satisfaction. In place of the old local and national self-sufficiency and isolation we have a universal commerce, a universal dependence of nations on one another. As in the production of material things, so also with intellectual production. The intellectual creations of individual nations become common currency. National partiality and narrowness become more and more impossible, and from the many national and local literatures a world literature arises.

Through rapid improvement in the instruments of production, through limitless ease of communication, the bourgeoisie drags all nations, even the most primitive ones, into civilisation. Cut-price commodities are the heavy artillery with which it batters down all Chinese walls, with which it forces undeveloped societies to abandon even the most intense xenophobia. It forces all nations to adopt the bourgeois mode of production or go under; it forces them to introduce so-called civilisation amongst themselves, i.e. to become bourgeois. In a phrase, it creates a world in its own image.

The bourgeoisie has subjected the country to the rule of the town. It has created enormous cities, vastly inflated the urban population as opposed to the rural, and so rescued a significant part of the population from the idiocy of living on the land. Just as it has made the country dependent on the town, so it has made the undeveloped and semi-developed nations dependent on the civilised ones, peasant societies dependent on bourgeois societies, the East on the West.

Increasingly the bourgeoisie is overcoming the dispersal of the means of production, of landed property and of the population. It has agglomerated the population, centralised the means of production, and concentrated property in a few hands. The necessary consequence of this was political centralisation. Provinces that were independent or scarcely even confederated, with different interests, laws, governments and taxes, were forced together into one nation, one government, one legal system, one class interest nationally, one customs zone.

In scarcely one hundred years of class rule the bourgeoisie has created more massive and more colossal forces of production than

5

have all preceding generations put together. The harnessing of natural forces, machinery, the application of chemistry to industry and agriculture, steamships, railways, the telegraph, clearance of whole continents for cultivation, canalisation of rivers, whole populations conjured up from the ground – what earlier century foresaw that such productive powers slumbered in the bosom of social labour.

This is what we have seen so far: the means of production and trade that formed the basis of bourgeois development were generated in feudal society. At a certain level of development of these means of production and trade, the relations in which feudal society produced and exchanged, the feudal organisation of agriculture and small-scale manufacture, in a word feudal property relations, no longer corresponded to the forces of production already developed. They impeded production instead of advancing it. They became just so many fetters. They had to be sprung open, they were sprung open.

In their place came free competition along with a complementary social and political constitution, the economic and political rule of the bourgeois class.

A similar movement is going on before our very eyes. The bourgeois relations of production and trade, bourgeois property relations, modern bourgeois society, which has conjured up such powerful means of production and trade, resembles the sorcerer who could no longer control the unearthly powers he had summoned forth. For decades the history of industry and commerce has been but the history of the revolt of modern productive forces against modern relations of production, against property relations that are essential for the bourgeoisie and its rule. It suffices to mention the commercial crises, returning periodically with ever increasing severity, that place the very existence of bourgeois society in question. In these crises a large portion of the current product as well as previously generated forces of production are regularly destroyed. During these crises an epidemic breaks out in society, one which would seem a paradox to all earlier epochs – the epidemic of overproduction. Society is suddenly thrust back into a condition of temporary barbarism; a famine, a general war of annihilation appears to have cut off all means of life; industry and commerce appear to be destroyed, and why? Because there is too much civilisation, too many goods, too much industry, too much commerce.

The forces of production available to society no longer serve for the advancement of bourgeois civilisation and the bourgeois relations of property; on the contrary, the forces of production have become too powerful for these relations, they are impeded by them, and as soon as they overturn this impediment, they bring the whole of bourgeois society into disorder and endanger the existence of bourgeois property. Bourgeois relations have become too narrow to encompass the wealth they produce. – And how does the bourgeoisie surmount these crises? On the one hand through the enforced destruction of a mass of productive forces; on the other through the capture of new markets and a more thoroughgoing exploitation of old ones. How exactly? By preparing more comprehensive and devastating crises and diminishing the means for preventing them.

The weapons used by the bourgeoisie to strike down feudalism are now turned against the bourgeoisie itself.

But the bourgeoisie has not only forged the weapons which bring it death; it has also produced the men who will wield these weapons – modern workers, *proletarians*.

As the bourgeoisie, i.e. capital, develops, so in direct proportion does the proletariat, the class of modern workers who live only so long as they find work, and who find work only so long as their labour increases capital. These workers, who must sell themselves piecemeal, are a commodity like any other article of commerce and equally exposed to all the vicissitudes of competition, to all the fluctuations of the market.

Because of the extensive use of machinery and the division of labour, the work of the proletarians has lost all the characteristics of autonomy and hence all attraction for the workers. The worker becomes a mere appendage to the machine, and only the simplest, most monotonous, most reflex-like manual motion is required. The costs occasioned by the worker are limited almost entirely to the subsistence which he requires for his maintenance and the reproduction of his race. The price of a commodity, and therefore of labour, is equal to its costs of production. As the repulsiveness of a task increases, so the wage declines proportionately. Moreover as machinery and the division of labour become more widespread, the amount of work rises proportionately, whether through lengthening working-hours, or increasing the work demanded in a given time, or accelerating the speed of machines, etc.

Modern industry has transformed the small workshop of the patriarchal master craftsman into the huge factory of the industrial capitalist. Workers, pressed together *en masse* in a factory, are organised like an army. They become the common footsoldiers of industry under the command of a full hierarchy of officers and commanders. They are not only the chattel servants of the bourgeois class and the bourgeois state, they are hourly and daily enslaved by the machine, by the overseer, and above all by the individual bourgeois manufacturer himself. The more openly this despotism proclaims gain to be its ultimate aim, the more petty, hateful and embittering it is.

As manual work requires fewer skills and less exertion, that is, the more modern industry has developed, so the labour of men is more and more displaced by that of women. Differences of age and sex have no social validity any more for the working class. They are merely instruments of labour which cost more or less according to age and sex.

Once the exploitation of the worker by the factory owner comes to an end, he receives his wages in cash, and other sections of the bourgeoisie beset him in turn, the landlord, the shopkeeper, the pawnbroker, etc.

The lower middle classes, small workshop proprietors, merchants and rentiers, tradesmen and yeoman farmers of the present, all these classes will descend into the proletariat, in part because their small capital is not sufficient for the scale of large industry and so succumbs to the competition of larger capitals, in part because their skills are devalued by the new modes of production. There are recruits to the proletariat from all classes in the population.

The proletariat goes through various stages of development. Its struggle with the bourgeoisie begins with its very existence.

At the outset there are struggles mounted by individual workers, then the workers in a factory, then workers in one trade at a particular site, against the individual bourgeois who exploits them directly. They direct their assaults not only against the bourgeois relations of production but against the instruments of production themselves; they destroy imported commodities that compete with theirs, they smash up machines, they put factories to the torch, they seek to regain the lost status of the medieval workman.

At this stage the workers form a mass dispersed over the whole country and disunited through competition. The purpose behind their own unification is not yet a massive organisation of workers, rather this is a consequence of the unity of the bourgeoisie, which must set the whole proletariat in motion in order to achieve its own political purposes, and for the moment it can do so. At this stage the proletariat does not struggle against its enemies, but rather against the enemies of its enemies – the remnants of absolute monarchy, the great landowners, the non-industrial bourgeoisie, the small traders. The whole movement of history is concentrated in the hands of the bourgeoisie; every victory so gained is a victory for the bourgeoisie.

But with the development of industry the proletariat not only increases; it is forced together in greater masses, its power grows and it feels it more. The interests, the circumstances of life within the proletariat become ever more similar, while machinery increasingly obliterates different types of labour and forces wages down to an almost equally low level. The increasing competition of the bourgeois amongst themselves and the crises emerging therefrom make the worker's wage ever more fluctuating; the incessant improvement in machinery, which develops ever more quickly, makes their whole livelihood ever more uncertain; the confrontations between individual workers and individual bourgeois increasingly take on the character of confrontations between two classes. As a result the workers begin to form coalitions against the bourgeois; they unite in order to protect their wages. They establish continuing associations themselves in order to make provision in advance for these occasional rebellions. Here and there the struggle breaks out into riots.

From time to time the workers are victorious, but only temporarily. The real result of their battles is not some immediate success but a unity amongst workers that gains ever more ground. This is furthered by improved communications, which are generated by large-scale industry, and which put workers from different localities in touch with one another. But this unity is all that is needed to centralise the many local struggles of a generally similar character into a national struggle, a class struggle. Every class struggle, however, is a political struggle. And the unity, which took the burghers of the middle ages centuries with their country lanes, is being accomplished by modern proletarians in a few years with railways.

This organisation of the proletarians into a class, and hence into a political party, is disrupted time and again by competition amongst the workers themselves. But it always rises up again, stronger, more resolute, more powerful. It compels the recognition of workers' individual interests in legal form by taking advantage of divisions within the bourgeoisie itself. Thus the Ten Hours Bill in England was passed.

On the whole, clashes within the old society advance the development of the proletariat in many ways. The bourgeoisie becomes involved in a constant battle; at first against the aristocracy; later against a part of the bourgeoisie itself, those whose interests contradict the advance of industry; and always against the bourgeoisie in foreign countries. In all these struggles it finds it necessary to appeal to the proletariat, to enlist its aid, and thus to draw it into political action. Hence it supplies the proletariat with its own materials for development, i.e. weapons for use against the bourgeoisie itself.

Moreover, as we have seen, there are whole sections of the ruling class dumped into the proletariat as a result of the advance of industry, or at least threatened in their essential circumstances. These also transmit to the proletariat a mass of materials for self-development.

Finally at the time when the class struggle comes to a head, the process of dissolution within the ruling class, within the whole of the old society, takes on such a violent and striking character that a part of the ruling class renounces its role and commits itself to the revolutionary class, the class that holds the future in its hands. As in the past when a part of the nobility went over to the bourgeoisie, so now a part of the bourgeoisie goes over to the proletariat, in particular, a part of the bourgeois ideologists who have worked out a theoretical understanding of the whole historical development.

Of all the classes which today oppose the bourgeoisie, the only truly revolutionary class is the proletariat. The other classes come to the fore and then decline to extinction with large-scale industry, whereas the proletariat is its particular product.

The middle classes, the small manufacturer, the shopkeeper, the artisan, the peasant, they all struggle against the bourgeoisie in order to secure their existence as middle classes against economic ruin. Hence they are not revolutionary, but conservative. Moreover they are reactionary for they seek to turn back the tide of history. If they are revolutionary, it is because they recognise that they face a descent into the proletariat, so they defend their future interests, not just their present ones, and they abandon their own standpoint in order to adopt that of the proletariat.

The lumpenproletariat, that passive dungheap of the lowest levels of the old society, is flung into action here and there by the proletarian revolution, though by its whole situation in life it will be readier to sell itself to reactionary intrigues.

The circumstances necessary for the old society to exist are already abolished in the circumstances of the proletariat. The proletarian is without property; his relationship to his wife and children no longer has anything in common with bourgeois family relations; modern industrial labour, modern servitude to capital, which is the same in England as in France or America as in Germany, has stripped him of all national characteristics. The law, morality, religion, are for him so many bourgeois prejudices that hide just as many bourgeois interests.

Up to now all the classes that seized power for themselves have sought to assure their hard-won position by subjecting the whole of society to their own economic terms. The proletarians can only seize the productive powers of society by abolishing their own former mode of appropriation and hence all former modes of appropriation. The proletarians have nothing of their own to secure; they will have to destroy all former private security and private assurances.

All previous movements were movements of minorities or in the interest of minorities. The proletarian movement is the independent movement of the vast majority in the interests of that vast majority. The proletariat, the lowest stratum of present-day society, cannot lift itself up, cannot raise itself up, without flinging into the air.the whole superstructure of social strata which form the establishment.

The struggle of the proletariat against the bourgeoisie is at the outset a national one in form, although not in content. Naturally the proletariat of each country must first finish off its own bourgeoisie.

In outlining phases in the development of the proletariat in the most general terms, we traced the more or less hidden civil war within existing society up to the point where it breaks out into open revolution, and the proletariat establishes its rule through the forcible overthrow of the bourgeoisie.

As we have seen, all society up to now has been based on conflict between oppressing and oppressed classes. But for a class to be oppressed, there must be assured conditions within which it can at least scrape a slave-like existence. The serf rose to be a member of the medieval commune during the period of serfdom just as the petty trader rose to bourgeois status under the yoke of feudal absolutism. The modern worker, by contrast, instead of advancing with industrial progress, sinks ever deeper beneath the circumstances of his own class. The worker becomes a pauper, and pauperism develops more quickly than population and wealth. It should now be obvious that the bourgeoisie is incapable of continuing as the ruling class of society and of enforcing its own conditions of life on society as sovereign law. It is incapable of ruling because it is incapable of assuring its slave any kind of existence within his slavery, because it is forced to let him sink into a condition where it must feed him, instead of being fed by him. Society can not live under it any longer, i.e. its life is no longer compatible with society itself.

The essential condition for the existence and for the rule of the bourgeois class is the accumulation of wealth in the hands of private individuals, the formation and expansion of capital, and the essential condition for capital is wage-labour. Wage-labour rests exclusively on the competition of workers amongst themselves. Industrial progress, involuntarily and irresistibly promoted by the bourgeoisie, replaces the isolation of the workers through competition with their revolutionary unity through close association. The development of large-scale industry pulls from under the feet of the bourgeoisie the very foundations on which they produce goods and appropriate them. Above all it produces its own gravediggers. Its downfall and the victory of the proletariat are equally unavoidable.

II
Proletarians and communists

What is the general relation between communists and proletarians?

Communists are not a separate party as opposed to other workers' parties.

They have no interests apart from those of the whole proletariat.

They do not declare any special principles for shaping the proletarian movement.

Communists are distinguished from the rest of the proletarian parties only in that, on the one hand, in the various national struggles of the proletarians they raise and highlight the common interests of the whole proletariat, independent of nationality, and on the other hand, in the various stages of development through which the struggle between proletariat and bourgeoisie proceeds, they always represent the interests of the movement as a whole.

Communists are therefore in practice the most resolute and thrusting section of the working-class parties of every country; they have an advantage over the general mass of the proletariat in terms of a theoretical insight into the conditions, progress and general result of the movement.

The immediate aim of the communists is the same as that of all the other proletarian parties: formation of the proletariat into a class, overthrow of bourgeois rule, conquest of political power by the proletariat.

The theoretical propositions of the communists are in no way founded on ideas or principles invented or discovered by this or that reformist crank.

They merely express in general terms the factual relations of an existing class struggle, a historical movement that is proceeding under our own eyes. The abolition of existing property relations is not distinctively communist.

All property relations have been subject to continuous historical change, to continuous historical variation.

The French revolution, for example, abolished feudal property in favour of bourgeois property.

What is distinctively communist is not the abolition of property in general but the abolition of bourgeois property.

But modern bourgeois private property is the final and most complete expression of the production and appropriation of products which rests on class conflict, on the exploitation of individuals by others.

In that sense communists can sum up their theory in a single phrase: the transformation of private property.

We communists have been reproached with wanting to abolish property that is personally acquired or produced oneself, property that forms the basis of personal freedom, activity and independence.

Property that is hard won, dearly acquired, well deserved! Are they talking here of petty traders, small farmers and their property, which preceded the bourgeois form? We do not need to abolish it, as the development of industry has abolished it and does so daily.

Or are they talking of modern bourgeois private property?

But does wage-labour, the labour of the proletarian, create property for him? Not at all. It creates capital, i.e. property which exploits wage-labour, which can increase only on condition that it produces new wage-labour to be exploited afresh. Property in its present form develops within the essential conflict between capital and labour. Let us consider both sides of this conflict. To be a capitalist is not just to have a purely personal position in the process of production but a social one.

Capital is a social product and can only be set in motion by an activity common to many members of society, in the last instance only by the activity common to all members of it.

Capital is therefore not a personal power but a social one.

If capital is converted into social property belonging to all members of society, personal property is not therefore converted into social. Only the social character of property is converted. It loses its class character.

Now we come to wage-labour.

The average price of wage-labour is the minimum wage, i.e. the sum total of the means of life necessary for subsistence as a living worker. What the wage-labourer appropriates through his own activity merely suffices to reproduce a bare existence. We want in no way to abolish this personal appropriation of the products of labour used for the reproduction of life itself, an appropriation that leaves no pure surplus that could give power over another's labour. We want instead to transform the miserable character of this appropriation through which the worker merely lives in order to increase capital, and only in so far as it suits the interest of the ruling class.

In bourgeois society living labour is merely a means to increase accumulated labour. In communist society accumulated labour is but a means to broaden, to enrich, to promote the whole life of the worker.

Therefore in bourgeois society the past rules over the present, and in communist society the present over the past. In capitalist society it is capital that is independent and personalised, while the living individual is dependent and depersonalised.

And the bourgeoisie calls the transformation of these relationships the transformation of individuality and freedom! And rightly so. Of course this concerns a transformation of bourgeois individuality, independence and freedom.

Under the current bourgeois relations of production freedom means free trade, freedom to buy and sell.

But if bargaining disappears so does free bargaining. The expression free bargaining, like all the other boasts of freedom by our bourgeoisie, means anything only in contrast to restricted bargaining, in contrast to the suborned burgher of the middle ages, but not in contrast to the communist transformation of bargaining, the bourgeois relations of production and the bourgeoisie itself.

It horrifies you that we wish to transform private property. But in your existing society private property has been transformed for nine-tenths of its members; it exists precisely in that it does not exist for nine-tenths. You reproach us for wanting to transform a type of property which presupposes the propertylessness of the vast majority of society as a necessary condition.

In a word you reproach us for intending to transform your property. That is exactly what we want.

From the moment that labour can no longer be turned into capital, money, rent, in short, into a monopolisable power in society, i.e. from the moment that personal property can no longer be turned into bourgeois property, from that moment, clearly, the individual person is transformed.

Thus you confess that by a person you understand nothing except the bourgeois, the bourgeois property-holder. And this person is to be transformed as well.

Communism deprives no one of the power to appropriate products in society; it merely removes the power to subjugate the labour of others through this appropriation.

It has been objected that with the transformation of private property, all activity will cease and a general idleness will spread.

According to this view bourgeois society ought to have collapsed into idleness long ago; for those who work do not gain and those who gain, do not work. The whole idea amounts to the tautology that as soon as there is no more capital, there will be no more wage-labour.

All the objections which are directed at the communist mode of appropriation and production of material products have been extended to the appropriation and production of intellectual products. To the bourgeois the disappearance of class property denotes the disappearance of production itself, and in just the same way the disappearance of class-bias in education denotes the disappearance of education altogether.

The bourgeois regrets the loss of this education, but for the vast majority it is only training to act as a machine.

But do not argue with us while you judge the abolition of bourgeois property by your bourgeois conceptions of freedom, education, justice, etc. Your ideas themselves are products of the relations of bourgeois production and property, just as your justice is merely the will of your class raised to the status of law, a will whose content is established in the material circumstances of your class.

The biased conception by which you transform your relations of production and property from historical relations that emerge in the course of production into eternal laws of nature and reason is a conception you share with all the ruling classes that have previously come and gone. What you grasp in the case of ancient property, what you grasp in the case of feudal property, you will never grasp in the case of bourgeois property.

Transformation of the family! Even the most radical of the radicals flares up at this infamous proposal of the communists.

What is the basis of the contemporary bourgeois family? Capital and private gain. It is completely developed only for the bourgeoisie; but it finds its complement in the enforced dissolution of the family among the proletarians and in public prostitution.

The bourgeois family naturally declines with the decline of its complement, and the two disappear with the disappearance of capital.

Do you object that we want to transform the exploitation of children by their elders? We admit this offence. But, you say, we transform the dearest relations of all when we move child-rearing from the domestic sphere into the social.

And is your education not determined by society as well? Through the social relations with which you are brought up, through the more or less direct or indirect interference of society by means of schools, etc.? Communists did not discover the effect of society on child-rearing; they merely alter its character, rescuing it from the influence of the ruling class.

Bourgeois phrases about the family and child-rearing, about the deeply felt relationship of parent to child, become even more revolting when all proletarian family ties are severed as a consequence of large-scale industry, and children are simply transformed into articles of trade and instruments of labour.

But you communists want to introduce common access to women, protests the whole bourgeoisie in chorus.

The bourgeois sees in his wife a mere instrument of production. He hears that the instruments of production are to be utilised in common and naturally cannot think otherwise than that common use is equally applicable to women.

He does not suspect that the point here is to transform the status of women as mere instruments of production.

Anyway nothing is more laughable than the moralising dismay of our bourgeois concerning the community of women allegedly sanctioned by communists. Communists do not need to introduce the community of women; it has almost always existed.

Our bourgeois, not content with having the wives and daughters of the proletariat at their disposal, not to mention legally sanctioned prostitutes, take the greatest pleasure in reciprocal seduction of married women.

Bourgeois marriage is really the community of married women. At the very most the communists might be reproached for wanting to replace a hidden community of women with a sanctioned, openly avowed community of women. In any case it is self-evident that with the transformation of the current relations of production, the community of women emerging from those relations, i.e. sanctioned and unsanctioned prostitution, will disappear.

Communists have been further criticised for wanting to abolish the nation and nationalities.

Workers have no nation of their own. We cannot take from them what they do not have. Since the proletariat must first of all take political control, raise itself up to be the class of the nation, must constitute the nation itself, it is still nationalistic, even if not at all in the bourgeois sense of the term.

National divisions and conflicts between peoples increasingly disappear with the development of the bourgeoisie, with free trade and the world market, with the uniform character of industrial production and the corresponding circumstances of modern life.

The rule of the proletariat will make them disappear even faster. United action, at least in the civilised countries, is one of the first conditions for freeing the proletariat.

To the degree that the exploitation of one individual by another is transformed, so will the exploitation of one nation by another.

As internal class conflict within a nation declines, so does the hostility of one nation to another.

The denunciations of communism from the religious, philosophical and ideological points of view do not merit detailed discussion.

Does it require a profound insight to grasp that men's presumptions, views and conceptions alter according to their economic circumstances, their social relations, their social existence?

What else does the history of ideas demonstrate than that the products of the intellect are refashioned along with material ones? The ruling ideas of an age were always but the ideas of the ruling class.

In speaking of ideas which revolutionise the whole of society, we merely express the fact that within the old society the elements of a new one have formed, that the dissolution of the old ideas stays in step with the dissolution of the old conditions of life.

When the ancient world was in decline, the ancient religions were conquered by Christianity. When Christian concepts were defeated in the eighteenth century by the ideas of the Enlightenment, feudal society fought a life and death struggle with the then revolutionary bourgeoisie. The ideas of religious freedom and freedom of inquiry merely expressed the rule of free competition in the moral realm.

However, it may be said, religious, moral, philosophical, political and legal ideas, etc. have been modified in the course of historical development. Religion, morality, philosophy, politics, the law are always maintained through these changes.

Besides, there are eternal truths, such as freedom, justice, etc., which are common to all social circumstances. But communism abolishes eternal truths, it abolishes religion and morality, instead of maintaining them, and it therefore contradicts all historical development up to now.

What does this objection amount to? The history of all society up to now was made through class conflicts which took different forms in different epochs.

But whatever form it has taken, the exploitation of one part of society by another is a fact common to all past centuries. Hence it is no wonder that the social consciousness of all the centuries past, in spite of all its multiplicity and varying aspects, takes on certain common forms. These are forms, forms of consciousness, which finally vanish only with the total disappearance of class conflict.

The communist revolution is the most radical break with traditional property relations, so it is no wonder that in its process of development there occurs the most radical break with traditional ideas.

But let us put by the bourgeois objections to communism.

We have seen above that the first step in the workers' revolution is the advancement of the proletariat to ruling class, victory for democracy.

The proletariat will use its political power to strip all capital from the bourgeoisie piece by piece, to centralise all instruments of production in the hands of the state, i.e. the proletariat organised as ruling class, and to increase the total of productive forces as rapidly as possible.

Naturally this can only be effected at first by means of despotic incursions into the rights of private property and into bourgeois relations of production, hence through measures which appear economically inadequate and unsustainable, but which drive the course of development past that stage and are essential means for overturning the mode of production as a whole.

These measures will naturally vary according to the country.

For the most advanced countries the following could be very generally applicable:

(1) Expropriation of property in land and investment of rents in state enterprises.
(2) A sharply progressive system of taxation.
(3) Abolition of inheritance.
(4) Confiscation of the property of all emigrants and rebels.
(5) Centralisation of credit in the hands of the state through a national bank with public capital and a guaranteed monopoly.
(6) Centralisation of all means of transport in the hands of the state.
(7) Expansion of nationalised factories, instruments of production,

newly cultivated lands and improvement of agriculture according to a common plan.

(8) Equal obligation to labour for all, establishment of industrial armies, particularly for agriculture.

(9) Managerial unification for agriculture and industry, progressively eliminating the conflicting interests of town and country.

(10) Free public education for all children. Elimination of factory work for children in its present form. Associating education with material production, etc. etc.

When in the course of development class distinctions have disappeared, and all production is concentrated in the hands of associated individuals, then the public power loses its political character. Political power in its true sense is the organised power of one class for oppressing another. If the proletariat necessarily unites as a class in its struggle against the bourgeoisie, makes itself into a ruling class through revolution, and as a ruling class forcibly transforms the old relations of production, then it will transform, along with these relations of production, the underlying conditions for class conflict and for classes in general, hence its own supremacy as a class.

In place of the old bourgeois society with its classes and class conflicts there will be an association in which the free development of each is the condition for the free development of all.

III
Socialist and communist literature

(1) Reactionary socialism
(a) Feudal socialism

Because of their historical position the French and English aristocracies had the job of writing pamphlets against modern bourgeois society. In the French revolution of July 1830 and in the English reform movement these aristocracies were once more beset by the hateful upstarts. There could no longer be any question of a serious political struggle. A literary battle was the only thing left. But even in the literary domain the old phrases of the restored monarchy had become impossible. To arouse sympathy the aristocrats had to appear to forego their interests, and to formulate their indictment of the bourgeoisie only in terms of the interests of the exploited working class. Thus they prepared their revenge – daring to sing slanderous songs against their new master and to whisper more or less malign prophecies in his ear.

In this way feudal socialism arose, half lamentation, half lampoon, half echo of the past, half menace of the future, striking the bourgeoisie at its very core through bitter, witty, biting judgements that were always comic because of a total incapacity to grasp the course of modern history.

They waved the proletarian begging bowl in order to unite the people under their flag. But as often as the aristocracy succeeded, the people espied the old feudal arms on their hind quarters and deserted with loud and irreverent laughter.

A section of the French legitimists and the Young England movement gave the best exhibition of this spectacle.

When the feudalists point out that their mode of exploitation takes a form different from that of bourgeois exploitation, they still forget that they did their exploiting under wholly different and now superseded circumstances and conditions. When they demonstrate that under their rule the modern proletariat did not exist, they forget that the modern bourgeoisie was a necessary offspring of their social order.

In any case they conceal the reactionary character of their criticisms so little that their main complaint about the bourgeoisie emerges in these terms, that under their regime a class has developed, one that will explode the whole social order.

They berate the bourgeoisie more for creating a revolutionary proletariat than for merely producing a proletariat as such.

In political practice they support all the repressive legislation against the working class, and in ordinary life, in spite of all their inflated talk, they comfort themselves by picking golden apples and by swapping truth, love and honour for speculation in wool, beetroot and spirits.

The parson was always hand in glove with the feudal lord, and clerical socialism was always so with the feudalists.

Nothing is easier than to give to Christian asceticism a socialist tinge. Has not Christianity declaimed against private property, against marriage, against the state? Has it not preached their replacement by charity and poverty, celibacy and mortification of the flesh, monasticism and the organised church? Saintly socialism is but the holy water with which the priest blesses the fulminations of the aristocrat.

(b) Petty-bourgeois socialism

The feudal aristocracy is not the only class that was ruined by the bourgeoisie, not the only class whose conditions of life withered and died in modern bourgeois society. The suburban burghers of the middle ages and the small-holding peasantry were the precursors of the modern bourgeoisie. In the less industrial and commercially developed countries this class still just rubs along next to the rising bourgeoisie.

In countries where modern civilisation has developed, a new petty-bourgeoisie has formed, fluctuating between proletariat and bourgeoisie, and always renewing itself as a complement to bourgeois society, but whose members are continually being dumped into the proletariat as a result of competition, who themselves – as modern industry develops – see the time approaching when they will disappear as an independent part of modern society and will be replaced in trade, in small-scale manufacture, in agriculture by managerial classes and domestic workers.

In countries such as France where the peasant classes make up far more than half the population it was natural for writers who supported the proletariat against the bourgeoisie to use the standards of the petty-bourgeoisie and small peasantry in their criticism of the bourgeois regime and to espouse the workers' party from the standpoint of the petty-bourgeoisie. Petty-bourgeois socialism was formed in this way. Sismondi is the high point of this literature not only in France but also in England.

This type of socialism dissected with great perspicuity the conflicts inherent in modern relations of production. It exposed the hypocritical apologetics of economists. It demonstrated incontrovertibly the destructive consequences of the use of machinery and the division of labour, the concentration of capital and of land ownership, the production of surplus goods, crises, the necessary ruin of the small trader and peasant, the poverty of the proletariat, anarchy in production, flagrant disparities in the distribution of wealth, the industrial fight to the death between one nation and another, the dissolution of traditional morality, of traditional family relationships, of traditional national identities.

In its positive programme this type of socialism either wants to restore the traditional means of production and trade, and along with them traditional property relations and traditional society, or it wants to force modern means of production and trade back into the confines of traditional property relations that are now being – and must be – dismantled. In either case it is reactionary and utopian in equal measure.

Guild socialism for artisans and patriarchal relations in agriculture are the last word here.

In its later development this tendency petered out in a pusillanimous hangover.

(c) German or true socialism

The socialist and communist literature of France, which originated within the constraints imposed by the bourgeoisie in power, and which is the literary expression of the struggle against their rule, was imported into Germany at a time when the bourgeoisie had just begun its struggle against feudal absolutism.

German philosophers, semi-philosophers and wordsmiths eagerly occupied themselves with this literature and simply forgot that with the importation of these writings from France, the circumstances of French economic life were not imported into Germany at the same time. Set against German conditions, the French literature lost all immediate practical significance and took on a purely literary cast. That literature could only appear as idle speculation concerning the true society or the realisation of the human essence. Thus for the German philosophers of the eighteenth century the demands of the first French revolution only made sense as demands of 'practical reason' in general, and the public expression of the will of the French revolutionary bourgeoisie signified in their eyes the law of pure will, of will as it had to be, of the truly human will.

The definitive task of the German literati consisted in bringing the new French ideas into line with their traditional philosophical outlook, or rather in appropriating the French ideas for themselves from their own philosophical point of view.

This appropriation took place in the same way that foreign languages are learned, through translation.

It is well known how monks transcribed absurd lives of the Catholic saints over the manuscripts on which the classical works of ancient pagans were inscribed. The German literati reversed this with secular French literature. They write their philosophical nonsense under the original French. For example, under the French critique of monetary relations they wrote 'externalisation of the human essence', under the French critique of the bourgeois state they wrote 'transformation of the reign of abstract generality', etc.

This insertion of their philosophical phrases beneath the French discussions they dubbed 'philosophy of the deed', 'true socialism', 'German science of socialism', 'philosophical foundation of socialism', etc.

The literature of French socialism-communism was thus punctiliously emasculated. And since it ceased in German hands to express the struggle of one class against another, so the German 'true socialist' was conscious of superseding French one-sidedness, of having substituted for true requirements the requirement of truth, for the interests of the proletariat the interests of the human essence – of man in general, of man belonging to no class or to any actuality at all, but to the misty realm of philosophical fantasy.

This German socialism, which pursued its lumbering scholastic exercises so earnestly and solemnly and trumpeted itself so blatantly, gradually lost its pedantic innocence.

The struggle of the German, particularly the Prussian bourgeoisie against feudalism and absolute monarchy, in a word, the liberal movement, grew more earnest.

Thus the 'true socialists' were offered a much sought after opportunity to put forward socialist demands in opposition to current politics, to hurl traditional anathemas against the liberals, against the representative state, against bourgeois competition, bourgeois freedom of the press, bourgeois justice, bourgeois freedom and equality, and to preach to the masses how they had nothing to gain from this bourgeois movement and everything to lose. German socialism forgot at just the right time that French criticism, whose mindless echo it was, itself presupposed modern bourgeois society, along with the material conditions corresponding to it and the complementary political constitution, the very things for which the struggle in Germany was so earnest.

This served the absolutist regimes in Germany, with their following of clergy, schoolmasters, country squires and bureaucrats, as a welcome scarecrow to frighten off the rising bourgeoisie.

This marked a sweet revenge for the bitter whipping and buck-shot with which the same regimes belaboured the uprisings of the workers.

Though 'true socialism' formed a weapon in the hands of the governments against the German bourgeoisie, it also represented a reactionary interest directly, the interest of German philistines. In Germany the petty-bourgeoisie forms the real social basis of existing circumstances, but it is a relic of the sixteenth century, albeit one that is ever changing into different forms.

To preserve this class is to preserve existing circumstances in Germany. The industrial and political rule of the bourgeoisie threatens it with certain ruin, on the one hand as a consequence of the concentration of capital, on the other, from the rise of the revolutionary proletariat. 'True socialism' appeared to kill two birds with one stone. It spread like an epidemic.

The gown, worked from speculative cobwebs, embroidered with flowery speeches, saturated with damp, sticky sentiment, this extravagant gown, with which German socialists cover their few scraggy eternal truths, merely increased the sale of their wares to the public.

For its part German socialism recognised its vocation ever more clearly, as the highfalutin representative of petty-bourgeois philistinism.

It proclaimed the German nation to be the model nation and the German petty philistine to be the model man. To his every dirty trick it gave a hidden, higher, socialist interpretation which meant the opposite. It drew the ultimate conclusion when it directly opposed the crudely destructive programme of communism, and announced that it was impartial and above all class struggles. With very few exceptions everything that is ostensibly socialist and communist now circulating in Germany comes from this malodorous and boring domain.

(2) Conservative or bourgeois socialism

A part of the bourgeoisie wants to redress *social grievances* in order to assure the maintenance of bourgeois society.

Included in it are economists, philanthropists, humanitarians, do-gooders for the working classes, charity organisers, animal welfare enthusiasts, temperance union workers, two-a-penny reformers of multifarious kinds. This form of bourgeois socialism has been worked up into whole systems.

For example, take Proudhon's *Philosophy of Poverty*.

The socialist bourgeois want the living conditions of modern society without the struggles and dangers necessarily arising from it. They want existing society with the exception of the revolutionary elements bent on destroying it. They want the bourgeoisie without the proletariat. The bourgeoisie naturally views the world in which it rules as the best. Bourgeois socialism works this comforting conception up into a more or less complete system. By requiring the proletariat to realise this system in order to reach a new Jerusalem, bourgeois socialism requires the proletariat to remain in present-day society but to cast off its spiteful conceptions of it.

A second less systematic and more practical form of this socialism sought to discredit every revolutionary movement in the eyes of the working class by proving how only a change in the material relations of life, in economic relations, might be of use to them, not this or that political change. By change in the material relations of life this form of socialism by no means understands the abolition of bourgeois relations of production, which is only possible by revolutionary means, but rather administrative reforms presupposing the present relations of production; hence changing nothing in the relationship of capital and wage-labour, but at best reducing the costs to the bourgeoisie of their political rule and simplifying their state administration.

Bourgeois socialism only reaches a suitable expression when it turns into a mere figure of speech.

Free trade! in the interests of the working class; protective tariffs! in the interests of the working class; prison reform! in the interests of the working class, which is the final, the only sincere word of bourgeois socialism.

Ultimately its socialism consists in maintaining that the bourgeois are bourgeois – in the interests of the working class.

(3) Critical-utopian socialism and communism

We are not referring here to the literature which has expressed the demands of the proletariat in all the great modern revolutions (like the writings of Babeuf, etc.).

The first attempts by the proletariat to assert its own class interests directly were made in times of general upheaval, in the period of the overthrow of feudal society; these attempts necessarily foundered on the undeveloped condition of the proletariat itself, as well as on the lack of material conditions for its emancipation, conditions which are only the product of the bourgeois epoch. The revolutionary literature which accompanied these first stirrings of the proletariat is necessarily reactionary in content. It teaches a general asceticism and a crude egalitarianism.

Proper socialist and communist systems, the systems of Saint-Simon, Fourier, Owen, etc., emerged in the first undeveloped period of struggle between proletariat and bourgeoisie which we have outlined above. (See 'Bourgeoisie and proletariat' [sic].)

The founders of these systems, to be sure, see the conflict between classes as well as the active elements of dissolution in prevailing society itself. But they discern on the side of the proletariat no historical autonomy, no political movement of its own.

Since the development of class conflict proceeds in step with the development of industry, they discover few material conditions for the emancipation of the proletariat, and they search for a social science based on social laws in order to create these conditions.

In place of activity in society they have to introduce their personally invented forms of action, in place of historical conditions for emancipation they have to introduce fantastic ones, in place of the gradually developed organisation of the proletariat into a class they have to introduce a specially contrived organisation of society. The approaching events of world history resolve themselves into propaganda and practical execution of their plans for society.

They are indeed conscious in their plans of generally supporting the interests of the working classes as the class that suffers most. Only from the point of view of the most suffering class does the proletariat exist for them.

The undeveloped form of the class struggle, as well as their own circumstances in life, leads however to the belief that they are far above the conflicting classes. They want to improve the circumstances of all members of society, even the best placed. Hence they continually appeal to the whole of society without distinction, even by preference to the ruling class. Anyone needs but to understand their system in order to recognise it as the best possible plan for the best possible society.

Hence they reject all political action, particularly all revolutionary action; they want to reach their goal by peaceful means and seek through the power of example to pave the way for the new social Gospel through small-scale experiments, which naturally fail.

In a time when the proletariat is still highly undeveloped and hence comprehending its own position in a fantastic way, these fantastic images of future society correspond to its first deeply felt urge for a general reorganisation of society.

But the socialist and communist writings also consist of critical elements. They attack all the fundamental principles of existing society. Hence they have offered material that is very valuable for the enlightenment of the workers. Their positive proposals concerning future society, e.g. transformation of the conflict of interest between town and country, transformation of the family, of private appropriation, of wage-labour, the proclamation of social harmony, the conversion of the state into a mere agency for administering production – all these proposals merely point towards the end of class conflict which had in fact only just begun to develop, which they only knew in its first formless and undefined stage. Hence these proposals themselves still have only a purely utopian import.

The significance of critical utopian socialism and communism stands in an inverse relationship to historical development. To the extent that the class struggle develops and takes shape, this fantastic transcendence of the class struggle, this fantastic attack on the class struggle, loses all practical worth, all theoretical justification. Though the originators of these systems were revolutionary in many senses, their disciples have in every case formed reactionary sects. They adhere to the original views of their mentors in firm opposition to the historically progressive development of the proletariat. Consequently they seek to dull the class struggle further and to ameliorate conflict. They still dream of an experimental realisation of their social utopias, the establishment of individual phalansteries, the foundation of home colonies, the building of a little Icaria – pocket editions of the new Jerusalem – and to erect all these castles in the air, they must appeal to the philanthropy of the bourgeois heart and purse. Gradually they fall into the category of the reactionary or conservative socialism depicted above, and distinguish themselves only by their more systematic pedantry, by a fantastic faith in the miraculous effects of their social science.

Hence they are bitterly opposed to all political activity by the workers which could only happen through blind disbelief in the new Gospel.

The Owenites in England oppose the Chartists, the Fourierists in France oppose the *réformistes*.

IV
Relation of communists to the various opposition parties

After Section 2 the relation of the communists to the already constituted working-class parties is self-evident, hence their relation to the Chartists in England and the agrarian reformers in North America.

They struggle for the attainment of the immediate aims and interests of the working class, but within the current movement they also represent the future. In France the communists ally themselves to the social-democratic party against the conservative and radical bourgeoisie, without giving up the right to criticise the phrases and illusions flowing from the revolutionary tradition.

In Switzerland they support the radicals without losing sight of the fact that this party consists of contradictory elements, in part of democratic socialists in the French sense, in part of radical bourgeois.

In Poland the communists assist the party which works for an agrarian revolution as a precondition for national emancipation. This is the party which brought the Cracow insurrection of 1846 to life.

In Germany the communist party struggles in common with the bourgeoisie against absolute monarchy, feudal landholding classes and the petty-bourgeoisie as soon as the bourgeois revolution breaks out.

But they never cease for a moment to instil in the workers as clear a consciousness as possible concerning the mortal conflict between bourgeoisie and proletariat, so that German workers may straightaway turn the social and political conditions, which the bourgeoisie must introduce along with its rule, into so many weapons against the bourgeoisie itself, so that after the overthrow of the reactionary classes in Germany, the struggle against the bourgeoisie begins straight away.

Communists direct their attention chiefly to Germany, because Germany is on the eve of a bourgeois revolution, and because it carries out this upheaval under more advanced conditions of European civilisation in general and with a much more developed proletariat than England in the seventeenth century and France in the eighteenth; thus the bourgeois revolution in Germany can be merely the immediate prelude to a proletarian revolution.

In a word communists everywhere support every revolutionary movement against existing social and political conditions.

In all these movements they emphasise the property question, which may have taken a more or less developed form, as the basic question for the movement.

Finally communists work everywhere for the unification and mutual understanding of democratic parties of all countries.

Communists disdain to make their views and aims a secret. They openly explain that their ends can only be attained through the forcible overthrow of all social order up to now. Let the ruling classes tremble at a communist revolution. Proletarians have nothing to lose in it but their chains. They have a world to win.

Proletarians of all countries unite!

The Eighteenth Brumaire of Louis Bonaparte*

I

Hegel observes somewhere that all the great events and characters of world history occur twice, so to speak. He forgot to add: the first time as high tragedy, the second time as low farce. Caussidière after Danton, Louis Blanc after Robespierre, the *montagne* [democratic socialists] of 1848–51 after the *montagne* [Jacobin democrats] of 1793–5, and then the London constable [Louis Bonaparte], with a dozen of the best debt-ridden lieutenants, after the little corporal [Napoleon Bonaparte], with his roundtable of military marshals! The eighteenth Brumaire of the fool after the eighteenth Brumaire of the genius! And there is the same cartoon-quality in the circumstances surrounding the second imprint of the eighteenth Brumaire. The first time France was on the verge of bankruptcy, this time Bonaparte is on the brink of debtors' prison; then the coalition of the great powers was on the borders – now there is the coalition of Ruge-Darasz in England, of Kinkel-Brentano in America; then there was a St Bernard [Pass] to be surmounted [when Napoleon defeated the Austrians in 1800], now a company of policemen to be dispatched across the Jura [Mountains to demand republican refugees from the Swiss]; then there was a [battle of] Marengo to be won and a lot more, now there is a Grand Cross of the Order

---

* In the title Marx alludes to General Napoleon Bonaparte's *coup d'état* of 9 November 1799 (18 Brumaire VIII in the revolutionary calendar), overthrowing the ruling Directory and establishing a dictatorship.

of St Andrew [from the Tsar] to be gained and the esteem of the Berlin [newspaper] *National-Zeitung* to be lost.

Men make their own history, but they do not make it just as they please in circumstances they choose for themselves; rather they make it in present circumstances, given and inherited. Tradition from all the dead generations weighs like a nightmare on the brain of the living. And just when they appear to be revolutionising themselves and their circumstances, in creating something unprecedented, in just such epochs of revolutionary crisis, that is when they nervously summon up the spirits of the past, borrowing from them their names, marching orders, uniforms, in order to enact new scenes in world history, but in this time-honoured guise and with this borrowed language. Thus Luther masqueraded as the Apostle Paul, the [French] revolution of 1789–1814 draped itself alternately as Roman republic and Roman empire, and the revolution of 1848 could come up with nothing better than to parody 1789 at one point, the revolutionary inheritance of 1793–5 at another. Likewise a beginner studying a new language always translates it back into his mother tongue; but only when he can use it without referring back, and thus forsake his native language for the new, only then has he entered into the spirit of the new language, and gained the ability to speak it fluently.

Examination of this world-historical invocation of the dead reveals a further striking distinction. Camille Desmoulins, Danton, Robespierre, Saint-Just, Napoleon – these heroes of the former French revolution, as well as the political parties and massed crowds alike – accomplished the business of the day in Roman costumes and with Roman phrases: the unleashing and consolidation of modern *bourgeois* society. The one [1789–1814] harrowed up the soil of feudalism and cut down the feudal crops that were growing there. The other [1848] created within France the conditions in which free competition could be developed, land sales from estates could be exploited, the fettered industrial productive power of the nation could be utilised; and beyond French borders it swept away feudal institutions in every direction, and as far as was necessary to provide an appropriate up-to-date environment on the Continent for French bourgeois society. Once the new social formation was established, the antediluvian colossi, and along with them the resurrected Romans – the Brutuses, the Gracchuses, the Publicolas, the tribunes, the senators and Caesar himself – all vanished. Amidst a dreary realism bourgeois society produced its true interpreters and spokesmen in the Says, Cousins, Royer-Collards, Benjamin Constants and Guizots; its real commanders were in the counting houses, and the fat-head Louis XVIII was its political chief. Wholly absorbed in the production of wealth and in peaceful competitive struggle, it could no longer comprehend that the spectres of Roman times had kept watch over its cradle. But unheroic as bourgeois society is, it nevertheless required heroism, sacrifice, terror, civil war and national conflict to bring it into the world. And in the strict classical traditions of the Roman republic its gladiators found the ideals and art forms, the self-deceptions that they needed, in order to hide from themselves the constrained, bourgeois character of their struggles, and to keep themselves emotionally at the level of high historical tragedy. Thus at another stage of development, a century earlier, Cromwell and the English had borrowed Old Testament language, passions and delusions for their bourgeois revolution. When that goal was actually attained, when the bourgeois transformation of English society was complete, [the prosaic empiricist] Locke supplanted [the sorrowful prophet] Habakkuk.

Thus the resurrection of the dead in those revolutions served to glorify new struggles, not to parody the old; to magnify fantastically the given task, not to evade a real resolution; to recover the spirit of revolution, not to relaunch its spectre.

The period 1848 to 1851 saw only the spectre of the old revolution on the move, from Marrast, *Républicain en gants jaunes*, who disguised himself as the old [Jean Sylvain] Bailly [the revolutionary liberal guillotined in 1793], to the adventurer [Louis Bonaparte], who covers his low and repulsive visage with the iron death mask of Napoleon. A whole people, believing itself to have acquired a powerful revolutionary thrust, is suddenly forced back into a defunct era; and so that there is no mistake about the reversion, the old dates rise again, the old chronology, the old names, the old edicts, which had long declined to mere antiquarian interest, and the old functionaries, who had seemed long decayed. The nation is like the mad Englishman in Bedlam [asylum] who thinks he is living in the time of the pharaohs and complains every day how hard it is to work in the Ethiopian gold mines, immured in a subterranean prison, a flickering lamp fixed to his head, behind him the overseer with his long whip, and at the exits a mass of barbarian mercenaries who can understand neither the slave labourers in the mines nor one another, since they have no common language. 'And all this is demanded of me' – sighs the mad Englishman – 'me, the freeborn Briton, in order to extract gold for the ancient pharaohs.' 'In order to pay the debts of the Bonapartes' – sighs the French nation. The Englishman, so long as his mind was working, could not rid himself of his obsession with gold mining. The French, so long as they made revolutions, could not rid themselves of the memory of Napoleon, as was demonstrated by the [presidential] election of 10 December [1848]. Out of the perils of revolution they yearned for the fleshpots of Egypt, and the [*coup d'état* of the] second of December [1851] was the answer. Not only do they have the caricature of the old Napoleon, they have caricatured the old Napoleon himself as he must have looked in the middle of the nineteenth century.

The social revolution of the nineteenth century cannot create its poetry from the past but only from the future. It cannot begin till it has stripped off all superstition from the past. Previous revolutions required recollections of world history in order to dull themselves to their own content. The revolution of the nineteenth century must let the dead bury the dead in order to realise its own content. There phrase transcended content, here content transcends phrase.

The February revolution [of 1848] was a surprise attack, an *ambush* of the old society, and the people proclaimed this unexpected coup a world-historical deed inaugurating a new epoch. Then on the second of December [1851] the February revolution is conjured away by the stroke of a cheat, and now what seems to have been overthrown is not the monarchy so much as the liberal concessions wrung from it over centuries of struggle. Instead of *society* gaining for itself a new content, it seems that the *state* has merely reverted to its oldest form, to the shameless, bare-faced rule of sword and cross. So in answer to the *coup de main* of February 1848 we have the *coup de tête* of December 1851. Quickly won, quickly lost. Meanwhile the intervening years did not go to waste. During the period 1848 to 1851 French society learnt the lessons of experience – to be sure in a foreshortened, revolutionary way – that would otherwise have preceded the February revolution in its normal or textbook development, so to speak, if it were ever to do more than

ripple the surface. Society now seems to have fallen back behind
its starting point; in fact it had first to create for itself the revolutionary starting point, the situation, the relationships, the exclusive
conditions for the development of a real modern revolution.

Bourgeois revolutions, such as those of the eighteenth century,
storm along from strength to strength; their dramatic effects outdo
one another, people and events seem to have a jewel-like sparkle,
ecstasy is the feeling of the day; but they are short lived, quickly
attaining their zenith, and a lengthy hangover grips society before
it soberly absorbs the resulting lessons of such *Sturm und Drang*.
By contrast proletarian revolutions, such as those of the nineteenth
century, engage in perpetual self-criticism, always stopping in their
own tracks; they return to what is apparently complete in order to
begin it anew, and deride with savage brutality the inadequacies,
weak points and pitiful aspects of their first attempts; they seem to
strike down their adversary, only to have him draw new powers
from the earth and rise against them once more with the strength
of a giant; again and again they draw back from the prodigious
scope of their own aims, until a situation is created which makes
impossible any reversion, and circumstances themselves cry out:

> Hic Rhodus, hic salta!
> Hier ist die Rose, hier tanze!
> [There's no time like the present!]

Moreover any competent observer, even if he had not followed
all the French developments step by step, must have known that
the revolution was in for an unprecedented humiliation. It sufficed
to hear the self-satisfied yelps of victory as 'distinguished' democrats congratulated each other on the benefits to follow the 9th of
May 1852 [when President Louis Bonaparte's presidency, constitutionally limited to one term, would have lapsed]. In their heads
that day had become an obsession, a fundamentalist dogma, like the
day Christ reappears and a reign of a thousand years commences,
as in the heads of the chiliasts. As always the feeble found refuge
in a belief in miracles, believing that the enemy has been vanquished
when they have only conjured it away in a fantasy, sacrificing any
understanding of the present to an ineffectual glorification of the
future in store for them, and of deeds that they had in their hearts
but did not want to bring to fruition just yet. They are the heroes

who try to deny their proven incompetence by offering each other sympathy and banding together; they packed up their things, donned their laurel wreaths in advance of the games, and busied themselves on the financial exchanges with selling off piecemeal the republics for which they had already taken care, in their quiet and unassuming way, to nominate the government. The second of December [1851] struck them like a bolt from the blue, and the peoples that were willing enough to allow their innermost fears – in an era of cowardly dejection – to be assuaged by the most vociferous loudmouths will perhaps have convinced themselves that cackling geese can no longer save the Capitol.

The constitution, the national assembly, the dynastic parties, the blue [right-wing] and the red [left-wing] republicans, the heroes of [the Algerian wars in] Africa, the thunder from the grandstand, the sheet-lightning of the daily press, all the literature, political names and intellectual reputations, the civil law and the penal code, liberty, equality and fraternity, and the ninth of May 1852 – all that has magically vanished under the spell of a man whom even his enemies would deny was a sorcerer. Universal manhood suffrage seems to have lasted just long enough to make its own testament in the eyes of the world and to declare in the very name of the people: 'What's worth building is worth demolishing' [Goethe, *Faust*, 1].

It is not enough to say, as the French do, that their nation has been taken unawares. A nation like a woman is not forgiven the unguarded hour in which the first rake that tries can take her by force. The riddle will not be solved by mere phrases that merely state it in other terms. What needs to be explained is how a nation of 36 millions can be taken unawares by three common con-men [Louis Bonaparte, the duc de Morny his half-brother, and the Minister of Justice Rouher] and marched off unresisting into captivity.

Let us recapitulate in bold strokes the course of the French revolution in its phases from 24 February 1848 to [2] December 1851.

Three main periods are unmistakable: *the February period*; 4 May 1848 to 28 May 1849, *the period of constituting the republic* or *the constituent assembly for the nation*; 28 May 1849 to 2 December 1851, *the period of the constitutional republic* or *the legislative national assembly*.

The *first period* from 24 February, or the overthrow of [King] Louis Philippe, to 4 May 1848, the meeting of the constituent assembly, the *February period* proper, can be termed the *prologue* to the revolution. Its character was expressed officially when the improvised government declared itself *provisional*, and like the government everything that was proposed, attempted or proclaimed in this period was passed off as merely *provisional*. Neither anyone nor anything dared to claim a right to exist or to take real action. The factions which had prepared or made the revolution, the dynastic opposition [legitimists and Orléanists], the republican bourgeoisie, the democratic-republican petty-bourgeoisie, the social democratic workers, all provisionally found their place in the February *government*.

It could not have been otherwise. The original intention in the February days [of 1848] was for an electoral reform through which the circle of political privilege amongst the possessing classes was to be widened and the exclusive rule of the finance aristocracy overthrown. But when it came to actual conflict the people mounted the barricades, the national guard behaved passively, the army offered no serious opposition, and the monarchy decamped, so the republic appeared as a matter of course. Every party construed this in its own way. Once their weapons had been wrested from their hands, the proletariat set its stamp upon it and proclaimed it a *social republic*. Thus the general content of modern revolution was signalled, a content which – as is always the case in dramatic prologues – stood in the most bizarre contradiction to everything that could be put into practice there and then, given the material available, the level of popular education, present circumstances and conditions. On the other hand, the claim of all the other factions taking part in the February revolution was made good when they obtained the lion's share in government. In no period do we find a more confused mixture of superfluous phrases and practical uncertainty and helplessness, of more enthusiastic striving for innovation and of more fundamental dominance of old routine, of seeming harmony in the whole society and of deep alienation amongst the factions that compose it. While the Paris proletariat still revelled in the vision of a grand prospect opening before it, and had indulged itself collectively in earnest discussion on social problems, the old powers of society had regrouped, rallied, composed themselves and found unexpected support in the populace at large, the peasants and petty-bourgeoisie, who were all thrown onto the political stage after the fall of the July monarchy [of the Orléanist King Louis Philippe, 1830–48].

37

The *second period*, from 4 May 1848 up to the end of May 1849, is the period of *constituting, founding the bourgeois republic*. Just after the February days the dynastic opposition was surprised by the republicans, the republicans by the socialists, indeed all France by Paris. The constituent assembly, drawn from the votes of the entire nation, met on 4 May 1848 and represented the whole. It was a living protest against the aspirations of the February days and was to reduce the achievements of the revolution to bourgeois standards. Grasping at once the character of this constituent assembly, the Paris proletariat tried vainly though forcefully to negate it a few days after its meeting on 15 May [1848], to dissolve it, to shatter the organic whole into its individual constituent parts, as in it national reaction was posing a threat. The well-known result of 15 May [1848] was that Blanqui and associates, i.e. the real leaders of the proletarian party, the revolutionary communists, were removed from the public arena for the entire duration of the events we are considering.

Louis Philippe's *bourgeois monarchy* could only be followed by a *bourgeois republic*, i.e. if a limited section of the bourgeoisie has ruled in the king's name, so now the whole of the bourgeoisie rules in the name of the people. The demands of the Paris proletariat are utopian humbug which must be stopped. To this declaration of the constituent assembly the Paris proletariat replied with the *June insurrection* [of 1848], the most colossal event in the history of European civil wars. The bourgeois republic was triumphant. On its side stood the finance aristocracy, the industrial bourgeoisie, the middle classes, the petty-bourgeoisie, the army, the lumpenproletariat organised as a militia, the intellectual authorities, the church and the landowners. On the side of the Paris proletariat there was none but itself. More than 3000 insurgents were massacred after the victory, and 15,000 were transported without trial. With this defeat the proletariat moves into the *background* on the revolutionary stage. Every time events appear to take a fresh turn, it tries to press forward again, but with ever declining bursts of strength and always diminishing results. As soon as one of the higher social strata plots a revolutionary trajectory, the proletariat enters into an alliance with it and thus shares all the defeats which successive parties suffer. But these further blows are of ever diminishing force the more they are distributed over the whole surface of society. Its more important leaders in the assembly and in the press are sacrificed one after another in the courts, and ever more ambiguous figures take up leadership. Amongst other things it throws itself into *doctrinaire experiments, cooperative banks and workers' associations, hence into a movement renouncing an overthrow of the old world by means of its own great resources, and instead seeks to attain its salvation behind society's back, privately, within its own limited conditions of existence, and hence necessarily coming to naught.* It seems unable to rediscover revolutionary prowess or to renew its energy from fresh alliances, until *all the classes* it struggled with in June are lying down flat beside it. But at least it was defeated with the honours of a great world historical struggle; not only France but all Europe trembles at the June earthquake, while the ensuing defeats of the higher classes are so cheaply purchased that they require blatant exaggeration by the victorious party in order to pass as events at all, and these events become the more disgraceful the further the losing party is from the proletariat.

To be sure the defeat of the June insurgents had prepared level ground for founding and constructing the bourgeois republic; but it had demonstrated at the same time that in Europe the question of today is something other than 'republic or monarchy'. It had revealed that *bourgeois republic* means the unlimited despotism of one class over the others. It had proved that in long-civilised countries with a developed class structure, with modern conditions of production, and with an intellectual consciousness representing centuries of effort in dissolving traditional ideas, the *republic* signifies *in general only the revolutionary way to destroy bourgeois society* and not *a conservative way to develop* it, as for example in the United States, where there are already classes, to be sure, but they have not yet solidified, rather they are in constant flux, changing and switching their component parts; where modern means of production compensate for the relative paucity of heads and hands, instead of declining together with a stagnant surplus population; and where finally the feverish youth of material production, which has a new world to appropriate, left neither time nor opportunity for exorcising the spirits of the old.

During the June days [of 1848] all classes and parties that had united as the *party of order* were against the proletarian class as the *party of anarchy*, of socialism, of communism. They had 'saved' society from 'the enemies of society'. They had made the catch-phrases of the old society, *'property, family, religion, order'* into military passwords and had proclaimed to their counter-revolutionary crusaders: 'Under this sign shalt thou conquer!' From this time on, whenever one of the many parties banded together under this motto against the June insurgents seeks to claim the revolutionary high ground in its own class interest, it succumbs to the call: *'property, family, religion, order'*. Society is saved as often as its circle of rulers contracts, as a more exclusive interest is maintained against the wider one. Even the simplest demand for bourgeois financial reform, for the most ordinary liberalism, for the most formal republicanism, for the most basic democracy, is simultaneously castigated as an 'outrage to society' and stigmatised as 'socialism'. Finally the high priests of the 'religion of order' are kicked off their Pythian tripods, hauled from their beds in the dead of night, flung into prison vans, thrown into gaols or sent into exile; their temple is razed to the ground, their mouths are sealed, their pens broken, their laws torn to shreds in the name of religion, property, family, order. Bourgeois fanatics for order are shot on their balconies by mobs of drunken soldiers, their family gods are profaned, their houses are bombarded for amusement – in the name of property, family, religion and order. Finally the scum of bourgeois society forms the *holy phalanx of order* and the hero Crapulinski [Louis Bonaparte] seizes the [Palace of the] Tuileries as *'saviour of society'*.

II

Let us pick up the thread once again.

The history of the *constituent assembly* since the June days [in 1848] is the *history of the rise and fall of the republican faction of the bourgeoisie*, the faction known variously as tricolour republicans, pure republicans, political republicans, formal republicans, etc.

Under the bourgeois monarchy of [the Orléanist King] Louis Philippe they had formed the *official* republican *opposition* and hence a recognised part of the political world of the time. The faction had its representatives in the legislative chambers and an influential circle in the press. Its Paris organ, *Le National*, was considered just as respectable in its way as the [Orléanist] *Journal des Débats*. This position under the constitutional monarchy accorded with its character. It was not a faction of the bourgeoisie held together through substantial common interests and set apart by peculiar conditions of production. It was a coterie of republican-minded businessmen, writers, lawyers, officers and officials whose influence rested on the personal antipathy of the country to Louis Philippe, on recollections of the old republic [of 1789–99], on the republican faith of a number of enthusiasts, above all on *French nationalism*, a continuously awakened hatred for the Vienna treaties [of 1814–15] and the [restoration] alliance with England. A large part of the following enjoyed by the *National* under Louis Philippe was due to this hidden Napoleonic sentiment, later to emerge in the person of Louis Bonaparte as a deadly rival to the republic. It fought the financial aristocracy, as did the rest of the bourgeois opposition. Polemics against the budget, which coincided in France with the struggle against the financial aristocracy, created such a lot of cheap popularity and such rich material for puritanical 'leading articles' that exploitation of this was irresistible. The industrial bourgeoisie was grateful to it for its slavish defence of French protectionism, adopted on grounds more of national than economic interest, and the bourgeoisie as a whole for its virulent denunciations of communism and socialism. In general the party of the *National* was *purely republican*, i.e. it demanded a republican rather than a monarchical form of bourgeois rule, and above all the lion's share in power. About the conditions for this transformation it was not at all clear. What was clear as daylight, on the other hand, and was publicly clarified at the reform meetings in the last days of Louis Philippe, was its unpopularity with the democratic petty-bourgeoisie, and in particular with the revolutionary proletariat. These pure republicans, as is always the way with pure republicans, were on the point of settling for a regency of the duchess of Orléans [mother of Louis Philippe's grandson], when the February [1848] revolution erupted and appointed their best-known representatives to a place in the provisional government. At the outset they naturally had the confidence of the bourgeoisie and a majority in the constituent assembly. They at once excluded the *socialist* elements of the provisional government from the *executive commission* [which replaced the provisional government], formed when the national assembly first met, and the party of the *National* then used the outbreak of the June [1848] insurrection to dismiss the executive commission and to get rid of its nearest rivals, the *petty-bourgeois* or *democratic republicans* (Ledru-Rollin, etc.). Cavaignac, the general of the bourgeois republican party, commander for the June [1848] massacre, replaced the executive commission with a kind of dictatorship. Marrast, formerly editor-in-chief of the *National*, became the permanent president of the constituent assembly, and the cabinet posts, like all the other important appointments, came home to the pure republicans.

The republican faction of the bourgeoisie, which had long considered itself the legitimate heir of the [Orléanist] July monarchy, found its fondest hopes surpassed, but it came to power, not by means of a liberal revolt of the bourgeoisie against the throne, as it had dreamt during the time of Louis Philippe, but rather through a proletarian riot against capital, put down with grape-shot. What it had imagined as the *most revolutionary* event occurred in reality as the *most counter-revolutionary*. The fruit fell into its lap, but it fell from the tree of knowledge, not from the tree of life.

The exclusive *rule of the bourgeois republicans* lasted only from 24 June to 10 December 1848. It is summed up in the *drafting of a republican constitution* and in the *siege of Paris*.

The new *constitution* was at bottom only a republicanised version of the constitutional charter of 1830. The restricted suffrage of the July monarchy, which excluded a large portion of the bourgeoisie from political power, was incompatible with the existence of the bourgeois republic. The February revolution [of 1848] had at once proclaimed a general right to vote in place of this suffrage. The bourgeois republicans could not undo this event. They had therefore to content themselves by restricting it to include a six months residence requirement in the constituency. The old administration – local government, the judicial system, the army, etc. – was left untouched, or where altered by the constitution, the change concerned the table of contents, not the content, and the names, not the substance.

The inescapable roll call of the freedoms of 1848 – freedom of the person, press, speech, association, assembly, education and religion, etc. – obtained a constitutional guise, making them invulnerable. Each of these freedoms was proclaimed as the *absolute* right of the French citizen, but always with the marginal gloss that it is unlimited so far as it does not limit the '*equal rights of others* and the *security of the public*', or through 'laws' which were to integrate individual freedoms harmoniously with one another and with the security of the public. For example: 'Citizens have the right to associate, to assemble peaceably and unarmed, to petition and to express their opinions in the press or otherwise. *The enjoyment of these rights has no limit besides the equal rights of others and the security of the public*' (chapter II of the French constitution [of 1848], § 8) – 'Education is free. The free exercise of this right is to be *enjoyed* under conditions fixed by law and under the supervision of the state' (chapter II, § 9). – 'The home of every citizen is inviolable *except* in circumstances prescribed by law' (chapter II, § 3), etc. etc. – The constitution therefore constantly refers to future *organic* laws which are to implement these glosses and regulate the enjoyment of these unlimited freedoms so that they conflict neither with one another nor with the security of the public. Later these organic laws were promulgated by the friends of order and all those freedoms regulated so that the bourgeoisie finds no obstacle to its enjoyment of them in the equal rights of other classes. Where it denies these freedoms wholly to 'others' or permits enjoyment of them only under conditions which are just so many police traps, this always happens solely in the interest of 'public security', that is, the security of the bourgeoisie, as the constitution prescribes. Consequently both sides can appeal with perfect justice to the constitution, the friends of order, who subverted all those freedoms, just as much as the democrats, who demanded them all outright. Each paragraph of the constitution contains its own antithesis in itself, its own upper and lower house, namely freedom in general terms, and subversion of freedom in the glosses. Hence so long as freedom is *nominally* respected and only its actual exercise is hindered, in a very legal way you understand, then the constitutional existence of freedom remains undamaged, untouched, however much its *commonplace* existence is murdered.

This constitution, made inviolate in so ingenious a manner, was nevertheless vulnerable in one place, like Achilles, not in the heel, but in the head, or rather in two heads as the thing developed – the *legislative assembly*, on the one hand, and the *president*, on the other. Leafing through the constitution one finds that the paragraphs in which the relationship between the president and the legislative assembly is defined are the only absolute, positive, uncontradicted, untwistable ones that it contains. Here we see the bourgeois republicans making themselves secure. [Chapter v] §§ 45–70 of the constitution are so drafted that the national assembly can remove the president constitutionally, but the president can remove the national assembly only unconstitutionally, by removing the constitution itself. Hence it invites its own forcible destruction. Not only does it sanctify the separation of powers as under the charter of 1830, it widens this to an unendurable contradiction. *The constitutional power game*, as Guizot called the parliamentary squabble between legislative and executive power, is constantly played out in the constitution of 1848 at the highest stakes. On one side are 750 representatives of the people, elected by universal manhood suffrage and eligible for re-election, who form an uncontrollable, indissoluble, indivisible national assembly, a national assembly which enjoys legislative omnicompetence, has the final say in war, peace and trade, possesses sole right of amnesty, and as a continuing body is always at centre stage. On the other side is the president, with all the appurtenances of royal power, but augmented, in that he appoints and dismisses his ministers independent of the national assembly, and has all the tools of executive power in his hands, bestowing all offices and disposing of over $1\frac{1}{2}$ million livelihoods, for so many depend on the 500,000 officials and on officers of every rank. The whole of the armed forces are behind him, and he is possessed of the privilege of pardoning individual miscreants, of suspending the national guard, of proroguing – in conjunction with the council of state – the elected general, cantonal and municipal councils nominated and elected by the citizens, reserving to himself the initiation and negotiation of all agreements with foreign countries. Unlike the assembly, which is constantly on the boards and continuously exposed to the glare of public criticism, he leads a secluded life in the Elysian Fields [i.e. Elysée Palace], but with [chapter v] § 45 of the constitution before his eyes and in his heart, crying out to him every day [like the ascetic Trappists]: '*brother, one must die*'. 'Your power runs out on the second Sunday in the lovely month of May in the fourth year of your term! Then is power at an end, there is no second performance, and if you have debts, see to it that you pay them off in time with the 600,000 francs settled on you by the constitution, unless perhaps you prefer to wander down to Clichy [debtors' prison] on the second Monday of the lovely month of May!' – If the constitution assigns all actual power to the president, it tries to secure moral authority for the assembly. Leaving aside that it is impossible to create moral authority through legal phrases, here again the constitution subverts itself by having the president directly elected by all Frenchmen. While French votes are divided up amongst the 750 members of the national assembly, here they are concentrated on a single individual. While each individual delegate of the people merely represents this or that party, this or that city, this or that outpost, or even just the necessity of electing any old 750 where neither the man nor the matter is closely examined, *He* is the elect of the nation, and electing him is the trump card which the sovereign people plays once every four years. The elected national assembly stands in a metaphysical relation to the nation, but the elected president stands in a personal one. Through its individual members the national assembly well represents manifold aspects of the national character, but the president is the spirit of the nation incarnate. As opposed to the assembly he has a kind of divine right, he is president by the people's grace.

Thetis, the sea goddess, prophesied to Achilles that he would die in the bloom of youth. The constitution, which had its weak spot like Achilles, also had its forewarning that it would have to go to an early death. It sufficed for the pure republican constitutionalists to cast a glance from the high heavens of their republican ideals down to the base world below in order see how the morale of the royalists, of the Bonapartists, of the democrats, of the communists, and also their own discredit, increased proportionally each day as they neared completion of their great legislative masterpiece, without any need for Thetis to leave the sea and communicate this secret to them. They sought to cheat destiny through constitutional shenanigans in [chapter XI] § 111, according to which every motion for a *revision of the constitution* must be supported by at least three-quarters of the votes, not less than 500 members of the national assembly taking part, and in three successive debates, between each of which there must always be a whole month. At a time when they controlled a parliamentary majority and all the resources of governmental authority, they saw themselves prophetically as a parliamentary minority, and made only an impotent attempt to exercise a power, which was day by day slipping from their feeble grasp.

Finally in a melodramatic paragraph, the constitution entrusts itself to 'the vigilance and patriotism of the people of all France and of every single Frenchman', after it had previously entrusted 'vigilant' and 'patriotic' Frenchmen to the tender yet necessarily very painful ministrations of its own high court of justice, or '*haute cour*', in another paragraph.

Such was the constitution of 1848, overturned on 2 December 1851, not by a knockout, but felled at the mere touch of a hat; indeed the hat was a three-cornered Napoleonic one.

While the bourgeois republicans in the assembly were busy with picking over, arguing about and voting in this constitution, outside the assembly Cavaignac mounted the *siege of Paris*. The siege of Paris was midwife for the constituent assembly in the birth throes of the republic. If the constitution were later dispatched from the world with bayonets, it must not be forgotten that it had to be protected with bayonets, even in its mother's womb, and to be sure, bayonets turned against the people, and it had to be brought into the world with bayonets. The [revolutionary] forefathers of the 'honest republicans' had sent their symbol, the tricolour, on a tour [of conquest] round Europe. For their part they made a discovery which found its way over the whole Continent, but which came back to France with ever increasing affection, until it became a true citizen in half its *départements* – *the state of siege*. A splendid invention, periodically employed in each successive crisis in the course of the French revolution. But barrack and bivouac, which were periodically applied to the head of French society to compact the brain and render the body torpid; sabre and musket, which were periodically allowed to judge and administer, to tutor and to censor, to act the policeman and to do duty as night watchman; moustache and uniform, which were periodically trumpeted as the highest wisdom and saviour of society – were not barrack and bivouac, sabre and musket, moustache and uniform finally bound to hit on the idea of saving society once and for all by touting their own regime as best and setting bourgeois society free from the trouble of governing itself? Barrack and bivouac, sabre and musket, moustache and uniform were all the more bound to come to this realisation because they could then expect better cash payment for their enhanced services, while from merely periodical sieges and transitory rescues of society, at the behest of this or that faction of the bourgeoisie, there was little substantial gain, other than a few dead and wounded and some bourgeois smirks of friendship. Should not the military once and for all play out a siege in its own interest and for its own benefit, and at the same time help itself to the wallets of the bourgeoisie? One should not forget, be it noted in passing, that *Colonel Bernard*, the president of the military commission under Cavaignac who transported 15,000 insurgents [of June 1848] without trial, is again acting at this very moment [early 1852] as head of the military commission for Paris.

Though with the siege of Paris the honest, pure republicans laid the seedbed in which the praetorians of 2 December 1851 grew strong, they still deserve praise because instead of exaggerating national sentiments as they had done under Louis Philippe, now, when they had the power of the nation at their bidding, they relinquished it, and instead of conquering Italy for themselves, they let the Austrians and Neapolitans reconquer it. The election of Louis Bonaparte as president on 10 December 1848 put an end to Cavaignac's dictatorship and to the constituent assembly.

The constitution states in [chapter v] § 44: 'The president of the French republic must never have lost his status as a French citizen.' The first president of the French republic, one L.N. Bonaparte, had not simply lost his status as a French citizen, had not merely been an English special constable, he was in fact a naturalised Swiss.

I have explained elsewhere the significance of the [presidential] election of 10 December [1848]. I will not advert to this here. It suffices to say that it was a *reaction by the peasantry*, which had had to bear the costs of the February revolution [of 1848], against the other classes of the nation, a *reaction of the country against the town*. This struck a chord in the army, for which the republicans of the *National* had provided neither glory nor a pay rise, also amongst the highest of the bourgeois who hailed Bonaparte as a transition to monarchy, and amongst the proletarians and petty bourgeoisie, who hailed him as a scourge for Cavaignac. I shall find an opportunity later to go more thoroughly into the relationship between the peasantry and the French revolution.

History from 20 December 1848 [when Bonaparte's presidency succeeded Cavaignac's dictatorship] to the dissolution of the constituent assembly in May 1849 marks an epoch in the downfall of the republican bourgeoisie. After founding a republic for the bourgeoisie, driving the revolutionary proletariat from the field and reducing the democratic petty-bourgeoisie to silence for the time being, they were themselves shoved aside by the bulk of the bourgeoisie, who with some justice seized this republic as *its property*. However, this great bourgeoisie was *royalist*. One part of it, the large landowners, had held power under the *restoration* [of the Bourbons after 1815] and was therefore *legitimist*. The other, the financial aristocracy and great industrialists, had held sway under the July monarchy [1830–48] and was therefore *Orléanist*. The highest echelons of the army, the universities, the church, the legal profession, the academy and the press divided themselves between the two camps, though in varying proportions. Here in the bourgeois republic, which bore neither the name of *Bourbon* nor that of *Orléans*, but rather the name *capital*, they found a type of state through which they could rule *conjointly*. The June insurrection [of 1848] had already united them in the 'party of order'. The next business was to remove the coterie of bourgeois republicans who still held seats in the national assembly. When it was a matter of holding their republicanism and their legislative rights against the power of the executive and of the royalists, these pure republicans were just as cowardly, shamefaced, dispirited, broken down, incapable of fighting, even in retreat, as they had been brutal in using physical force against the people. There is no need to relate the ignominious tale of their disintegration. It was a fade-out, not a blow-up. Their history has ceased forever, and in subsequent times, whether inside or outside the assembly, they figure as memories, memories which seem to come to life whenever the republic is merely named and as often as revolutionary conflict threatens to sink to new depths. I note in passing that the journal which gave this party its name, the *National*, turned in subsequent years to socialism.

Therefore the period of constituting or founding the French republic falls into three periods: 4 May to 24 June 1848, a struggle of all the classes and their allies united in February under the leadership of the bourgeois republicans against the proletariat, [with a] terrible defeat of the proletariat; 25 June 1848 to 10 December 1848, rule of the bourgeois republicans, drafting of the constitution, siege of Paris, Cavaignac's dictatorship; 20 December 1848 to the end of May 1849, struggle by Bonaparte and the party of order with the republican constituent assembly, defeat of same, downfall of the bourgeois republicans.

Before we finish with this period we must cast a backward glance at two powers, one of which destroyed the other on 2 December 1851, and yet the two had lived as a happy couple from 20 December 1848 up to the departure of the constituent assembly [in May 1849]. I have in mind Louis Bonaparte, on the one hand, and the party of the royalist coalition, of order, of the great bourgeoisie, on the other. On acceding to the presidency Bonaparte at once formed a ministry of the party of order, placing Odilon Barrot at its head, the former leader, take note, of the most liberal faction of the parliamentary bourgeoisie. M. Barrot had finally bagged the cabinet which he had been stalking since 1830, and still better the premier post in that cabinet; but not, in the way that he had envisaged under Louis Philippe, as the ablest leader in the parliamentary opposition, but rather as charged with the task of putting a parliament to death, and as the confederate of all his arch-enemies, Jesuits and legitimists. He brought the bride home at last, but only after she had been prostituted. Bonaparte himself seemed completely eclipsed. This party acted for him.

The very first cabinet meeting decided on the expedition to Rome, which, so it was agreed, was to be conducted behind the back of the national assembly, and resources for which were to be wrested from it under false pretences. So they began by swindling the national assembly and conspiring secretly with absolutist powers abroad against the revolutionary Roman republic. In the same way and with the same manoeuvres Bonaparte prepared his coup of 2 December [1851] against the royalist legislature and its constitutional republic. Let us not forget that this same party which formed Bonaparte's cabinet on 20 December 1848 also formed the majority of the legislative national assembly on 2 December 1851.

In August [1848] the constituent assembly had resolved not to disband itself without debating and promulgating an array of organic laws to augment the constitution. On 6 January 1849 the party of order had its representative Rateau propose to the assembly that the organic laws should be abandoned and that it should resolve its *own dissolution* instead. At that time all the royalist representatives in the national assembly, not just the cabinet headed by M. Odilon Barrot, pestered it that its dissolution was necessary for the maintenance of credit, for the consolidation of order, for bringing provisional arrangements to an end and for establishing a definite state of affairs; it hindered the efficacy of the new government and sought to eke out its life from sheer rancour; the country was weary of it. Bonaparte noted well all this invective against the power of the legislature, learnt it by heart and showed the parliamentary royalists on 2 December 1851 that he understood it. He quoted their own catchphrases back to them.

The Barrot cabinet and the party of order went further. They drew up *petitions to the national assembly* throughout all France, in which this body was most kindly requested to dissolve itself, to disappear. Thus they led the unorganised populace into the fray against the national assembly, the voice of the people organised constitutionally. They taught Bonaparte to appeal from parliamentary assemblies to the people. Finally on 29 January 1849 the day had come on which the constituent assembly was to make a decision concerning its own dissolution. The national assembly found its chambers occupied by soldiers; Changarnier, the general of the party of order, in whose hands was united the supreme command of the national guard and regular troops, staged a grand show of force in Paris, as if a battle were in the offing, and the royalist coalition put threats to the constituent assembly that force would be used if it did not comply. It was compliant and merely bargained for a very short lease of life. What was 29 January 1849 but the *coup d'état* of 2 December 1851, only carried out by royalists together with Bonaparte against the republicans of the national assembly? These worthy men did not notice or did not want to notice that on 29 January Bonaparte had taken the opportunity to have a portion of the troops go on parade before the Tuileries and had thus seized with avidity this first proclamation of military might against parliamentary power, alluding to Caligula. Doubtless they saw only their Changarnier.

The *organic* laws augmenting the constitution, like the education bill, the bill on religion, etc., were a particular motive for the party of order to cut short the lifespan of the constituent assembly by force. For the royalist coalition everything lay in making these laws themselves, and in not letting the increasingly mistrustful republicans do it. Amongst these organic laws there was even one on the accountability of the president of the republic. In 1851 the legislative assembly was occupied with drafting such a law when Bonaparte anticipated this coup with the coup of 2 December. What would the royalist coalition not have given in their campaign in the parliamentary winter of 1851 to have found the article of accountability ready to hand, and drawn up at that by a mistrustful, hostile republican assembly!

After 29 January 1849, when the constituent assembly destroyed its last weapon itself, the Barrot cabinet and the friends of order hounded it to death, leaving nothing undone which could humiliate it, and wresting laws from its self-pitying weakness that cost it all remaining public regard. Preoccupied with his Napoleonic *idée fixe* Bonaparte was impudent enough to exploit this abasement of parliamentary power in public. On 7 May 1849, when the national assembly censured the cabinet for the occupation of Civitavecchia by [General] Oudinot and ordered the expedition to Rome to return to its original purpose, Bonaparte published a letter to Oudinot in the *Moniteur* that evening congratulating him on his heroic exploits and posing as the munificent protector of the army, in contrast to the pen-pushing parliamentarians. The royalists chuckled at this. They regarded him simply as their dupe. At last when Marrast, president of the constituent assembly, believed for a moment that the security of the national assembly was endangered, he appealed to the constitution and requisitioned a colonel and his regiment; the colonel refused, citing proper discipline and referring Marrast to [General] Changarnier, who haughtily demurred with the comment that he did not like bayonets with brains. In November 1851 when the royalist coalition wanted to mount the decisive contest with Bonaparte, they tried to go too far and to force through the direct requisition of troops by the president of the national assembly in their infamous *commissioners'* bill. One of their generals, Le Flô, had signed the proposed law. In vain did Changarnier vote for the bill and in vain did [the Orléanist politician] Thiers pay homage to the foresight of the erstwhile constituent assembly. The *Minister of War [the Bonapartist] Saint-Arnaud* answered him as Changarnier had answered Marrast – and all to the cheers of the [social-democrats of the] *montagne*.

Thus the *party of order* itself, though as yet still the cabinet, and not yet the national assembly, denounced the parliamentary regime.

And it protests when 2 December 1851 banishes the *parliamentary regime* from France!

We wish it a pleasant journey.

III

On 28 May 1849 the national assembly gathered in legislative sessions. On 2 December 1851 it was dispersed. This period comprises the lifespan of the *constitutional or parliamentary republic*. It falls into three main periods: *28 May to 13 June 1849*, conflict between democrats and the bourgeoisie, *defeat of the petty bourgeois or democratic party*; – *13 June 1849 to 31 May 1850*, parliamentary dictatorship of the bourgeoisie, i.e. of the Orléanists and legitimists in coalition, or of the party of order, a dictatorship which fulfilled itself by *abolishing universal manhood suffrage*; – *31 May 1850 to 2 December 1851*, conflict between the bourgeoisie and Bonaparte, *collapse of bourgeois rule, demise of the constitutional or parliamentary republic*.

In the first French revolution the rule of the *constitutionalists* is succeeded by the rule of the *Girondins*, and the rule of the *Girondins* by the rule of the *Jacobins*. Each party leans on the more progressive party for support. When each has led the revolution to a point where there is no going further, still less of going on ahead of it, each is pushed aside by the keener ally waiting in the background and sent to the guillotine. The revolution thus follows an ascending path.

The revolution of 1848 is just the reverse. The proletarian party appears as an annex of the petty-bourgeois democrats. The proletarians are betrayed and dropped by the democratic party on 16 April, 15 May and in the June days [of 1848]. The democratic party, for its part, rides on the shoulders of the bourgeois republican party. The bourgeois republicans no sooner believe themselves set up than they shake off their burdensome friend and support themselves on the shoulders of the party of order. The party of order hunches its shoulders, allows the bourgeois republicans to topple off and heaves itself onto the shoulders of the armed forces. It fancies that it is still sitting on those shoulders when one fine morning it realises that the shoulders have been transformed into bayonets. Each party kicks back at the one pressing from behind, and leans forward on the one pushing back. It is no wonder that in this ridiculous position each loses its balance, and after making the inevitable faces, each collapses in curious spasms. Thus the revolution follows a descending path, and it commenced retrograde motion before the last barricade of February [1848] had been cleared away and the first revolutionary authority set up.

The period unfolding before us comprises the most motley mixture of crying contradictions: constitutionalists who conspire openly against the constitution; revolutionaries who are confessedly constitutional; a national assembly which wants to be all-powerful and still remains parliamentary; a *montagne* that makes a career out of patience and parries present defeats with prophecies of future victories; royalists who are the founding fathers of the republic, and who are forced by the situation to maintain inimical royal houses, which they support, in exile abroad, and the republic, which they hate, at home in France; an executive power that finds its strength in its own weakness, and its respectability in the contempt that it provokes; a republic that is none other than the disrepute of two monarchies, the restored Bourbons and the July monarchy, combined with an imperial etiquette – alliances whose first proviso is separation; contests whose first law is indecision; wild, senseless agitation in the name of peace, and the most solemn preaching of peace in the name of revolution; passion without truth, truth without passion; heroes without exploits, history without achievements; development driven solely by the calendar and wearisome through constant repetition of the same tension and release; antagonisms which seem periodically to reach a peak only to go dull and diminish without resolution; pretentious interventions for show and smallminded terror that the world will end; and at the same time the saviours of the world play out the pettiest intrigues and high comedies, redeemers whose inaction reminds us less of the Day of Judgement than of the [confusions of the anti-absolutist] Fronde [rebellion amongst the nobility of 1648–53] – the whole genius of official France disgraced by the artful foolishness of a single individual; as often as it is voiced in a general election, the will of the whole nation seeks self-expression in superannuated enemies of the general interest, finding this at last in the self-will of a racketeer. If any episode in history has been coloured grey on grey, this is the one. Men and events appear as Schlemihls in reverse, as shadows that have lost their bodies. The revolution has paralysed its own proponents and has endowed only its enemies with passion and violence. The counter-revolutionaries continually summon, exorcise and banish the 'red spectre', and when it finally appears, it is not in the phrygian cap of anarchy but in the uniform of order, in [the soldiers'] *red breeches*.

We have observed: the cabinet, which Bonaparte installed on 20 December [1848], his Ascension Day [to the office of president], was a ministry for the party of order, the coalition of legitimists and Orléanists. This Barrot-Falloux cabinet outlasted the constituent assembly for the republic, whose lifespan it had shortened, more or less forcibly, and found itself still at the helm of state. Changarnier, the general of the united royalists, continued to unite in his person the general command of the First Army and the Paris National Guard, and the general election [of 28 May 1849] had finally secured a large majority in the national assembly for the party of order. Here the deputies and peers of Louis Philippe met up with a holy order of legitimists who emerged from hiding after great quantities of voting papers from the nation had been transformed into admission tickets to the political arena. The Bonapartist representatives of the people were sown too thinly to be able to form an independent parliamentary party. They were sufficiently to hand to make up numbers in a general call-up against the republican forces. They appeared merely as pitiful hangers-on of the party of order. Thus the party of order was in possession of the powers of government, the army and the legislative bodies, in short: the whole might of the state, bolstered morally by the general elections which made its rule appear to be the will of the people, and by the simultaneous triumph of counter-revolution on the whole of the European continent.

Never did a party inaugurate its campaign with greater resources and under more favourable auspices.

The shipwrecked *pure republicans* found that they had dwindled in the national assembly to a clique of about fifty headed by generals from the north African wars: Cavaignac, Lamoricière, Bedeau. The principal opposition party however was made up of the *montagne*. The *social-democratic party* christened itself with this parliamentary name. It commanded more than 200 of the 750 votes in the national assembly and was therefore at least as powerful as any of the other three factions of the party of order taken singly. Its relative inferiority compared to the whole of the royalist coalition seemed to be mitigated by special circumstances. It was not only the case that voting in the *départements* revealed that they had won a significant following amongst the rural population. It counted in its ranks almost all the deputies from Paris; the army had pledged a confession of faith in democracy in the election of three junior officers; and the leader of the *montagne* Ledru-Rollin, in contradistinction to all the other representatives of the party of order, had been raised to the heights of parliamentary distinction by five *départements* pooling their votes for him. Hence on 29 May 1849 the *montagne* appeared to have all the makings for success to hand, given the inevitable clashes of the royalists between themselves and of the entire party of order with Bonaparte. Fourteen days later they had lost everything, honour included.

Before going any further with this parliamentary history, a few introductory remarks are necessary to avoid widespread misconceptions concerning the overall character of the epoch which lies before us. From a democratic point of view, the period of the national assembly was concerned with what the period of the constituent assembly was concerned with, a straightforward conflict between republicans and royalists. Yet they sum up the events themselves with one word: '*reaction*', a night in which all cats are grey and which allows them to rattle off clichés like a night watchman. And indeed at first glance the party of order appeared to be a tangle of different royalist factions not only intriguing against one another to put their own pretender on the throne and exclude the pretender of the opposing party, but also uniting in a common hatred of and attacks on the 'republic'. The *montagne* for its part appears in opposition to this royalist conspiracy as a representative of the 'republic'. The party of order appears continuously occupied with a 'reaction' directed against the press, voluntary associations and the like, no more and no less than in [Prince Metternich's] Austria, and executed in a brutal police intervention into the state bureaucracy, the local constabulary and the judiciary, as in Austria. The '*montagne*' for its part is just as constantly occupied with fighting off these attacks and protecting the 'natural rights of man' as every so-called people's party has been, more or less, for a century and a half. Nevertheless on closer inspection of the situation and the parties, this superficial appearance, which veils the *class struggle* and the peculiar physiognomy of this period, disappears, and it thus becomes a gold mine for saloon bar politicians and republican-minded gents.

As we said, legitimists and Orléanists make up the two great factions of the party of order. Was what bound these factions to their pretenders and kept them mutually at odds – was it nothing but the lily and tricolour, the royal house of Bourbon and the royal house of Orléans, different shades of royalism? Was it their royalist faith at all? Under the Bourbons the *large propertied interests* governed with priests and lackeys, under Orléans rule it was high finance, large-scale industry, large commercial interests, i.e. *capital* with its retinue of lawyers, professors and smooth-talkers. The legitimate monarchy was merely the political expression of the hereditary rule of the feudal lords, and the July monarchy was likewise merely the political expression for the usurping rule of bourgeois parvenus. What kept the two factions apart was not any so-called principles, it was their material conditions of existence, two different kinds of property; it was the old opposition between town and country, the rivalry between capital and landed property. That at the same time old memories, personal antipathies, hopes and fears, prejudices and delusions, sympathies and antipathies, convictions, articles of faith and principles bound them to one or the other royal house, whoever denied this? On the different forms of property, the social conditions of existence, arises an entire superstructure of different and peculiarly formed sentiments, delusions, modes of thought and outlooks on life. The whole class creates and forms them from the material foundations on up and from the corresponding social relations. The single individual, to whom they are transmitted through tradition and upbringing, can imagine that they form the real motives and starting-point for his actions. As Orléanists, as legitimists, each faction sought to convince itself and the other that loyalty to their two royal houses separated them, yet facts later proved that it was rather their divided interests which forbade their unification. Just as in private life one distinguishes between what a man thinks and says, and what he really is and does, so one must all the more in historical conflicts distinguish between the fine words and aspirations of the parties and their real organisation and their real interests, their image from their reality. Orléanists and legitimists found themselves side by side in the republic with the same demands. If each side wanted to carry out the *restoration* of its own royal house in opposition to the other, then this signified nothing but the desire of each of the *two great interests* into which the *bourgeoisie* had split – landed property and capital – to restore its own supremacy and to subordinate the other. We are talking in terms of two interests within the bourgeoisie, for large landed property, in spite of its flirtations with feudalism and pride in its pedigree, has been thoroughly assimilated to the bourgeoisie by the development of modern society. Thus the Tories in England long fancied that they were in raptures about royalty, the church and the beauties of the ancient constitution, until a time of trial tore from them the confession that they were only in raptures about rent.

The royalist coalition pursued their intrigues against one another in the press, at Ems [in Germany amongst the Bourbons], at Claremont [in England amongst the Orléanists], outside parliamentary bounds. Behind the scenes they donned their antique Orléanist and legitimist livery once again and pursued their old tournaments. But on the public stage, in high politics and matters of state, as a grand parliamentary party, they pawned off their royal houses with token acts of reverence, and adjourned the restoration of the monarchy *ad infinitum*, and did their real business as the *party of order*, i.e. under a *social* rather than a *political* banner, as a representative of the bourgeois world order, not as knights seeking fair ladies, as the bourgeois class against other classes, not as royalists against republicans. And as the party of order they exercised a more unrestricted and sterner dominion over the other classes of society than they had been able to do under the restoration or the July monarchy, as was possible only in a parliamentary republic, for only under that form could the two great divisions of the French bourgeoisie unite and make the rule of their class the order of the day, instead of the regime of one of its privileged factions. If in spite of that as the party of order they insulted the republic and expressed aversion to it, this did not happen as the result of mere royalist recollections but rather from the instinct that the republican form made their political dominion complete and stripped it of all alien appearances, but at the same time undermining its social basis in that they have to confront the subjugated classes, and to grapple with them without a mediator, without the crown for cover, without being able to distract the interests of the nation with their secondary quarrels amongst themselves and with royalty. This results from a weakness which causes them to recoil from the pure conditions of their own class rule and to hanker after the incomplete, undeveloped and on that account less dangerous forms of dominion. On the other hand every time that the royalist coalition comes into conflict with the pretender opposing them, with Bonaparte, they believe their parliamentary might to be threatened by the power of the executive, and they have to pull out the political title to their rule; they come forward as *republicans* and not as *royalists*, from the Orléanist Thiers who warns the national assembly [on 17 January 1851] that the republic would divide them least to the legitimist Berryer, who on 2 December 1851 harangues the assembled people of the tenth arrondissement in the name of the republic as a tribune, swathed in the tricolour on the steps of the town hall. To be sure a mocking echo calls: Henri V! Henri V! [the legitimist pretender and self-styled king].

Opposed to the bourgeoisie in coalition there was a coalition between the petty-bourgeoisie and the working classes, the so-called *social-democratic* party. The party regarded themselves as badly rewarded after the June days of 1848, their material interests endangered and the democratic guarantees, which ought to have assured the exercise of these interests, called into question by the counter-revolution. Hence they drew near to the workers. On the other hand, their parliamentary representation, the *montagne*, pushed aside during the dictatorship of the republican bourgeoisie, had reconquered its lost popularity because of the struggle between Bonaparte and the royalist ministers during the second half of the constituent assembly's lifespan. It had struck an alliance with the leaders of the socialists. In February 1849 there were banquets to celebrate the event. A joint programme was produced, joint election committees were instituted and joint candidates put up. The revolutionary sting was taken from the social demands of the proletariat, and a democratic cast was given to them; the merely political form was stripped back from the democratic claims of the petty bourgeoisie and a socialist sting revealed. In that way *social-democracy* arose. The new *montagne*, the result of this combination, contained the same elements as the old *montagne* only numerically stronger, apart from a few token workers and a few socialist sectarians. But in the course of development it had altered, along with the class which it represented. The peculiar character of social-democracy is epitomised in the way that democratic and republican institutions are demanded as a means of weakening the conflict between capital and labour, and of creating a harmony between the two extremes, but not of transcending them both. Different markers for reaching this goal may be proposed, and it may be embellished with more or less revolutionary notions, but the content remains always the same. This content is the reform of society in a democratic way, but a reform within petty-bourgeois limits. Only we must not take the narrow-minded view that the petty-bourgeoisie wants on principle to pursue an egoistic class interest. Rather it believes that the particular conditions for its freedom are the only general conditions under which modern society can be safeguarded and escape the class struggle. Even less should one imagine that democratic representatives are all shopkeepers or their admirers. In respect of education and circumstances they could be as far removed from them as the heavens above. What makes them representatives of the petty-bourgeoisie is the fact that in their heads they do not transcend the limitations that others have not surmounted in life, that they are therefore driven to the same problems and solutions in theory that material interests and social life pose for others in practice. In general terms this is the relationship between the *political and literary representatives* of a class to the class that they represent.

After the exposition given above, it is self-evident that if the *montagne* continually contends with the party of order for the republic and the so-called rights of man, neither the republic nor the rights of man are its real goal, just as an army, which one wants to disarm and which mounts resistance, has not entered the field of battle in order to safeguard its own weapons.

When the national assembly met, the party of order immediately provoked the *montagne*. The bourgeoisie just then felt the necessity of getting rid of the petty-bourgeois democrats, just as a year before it had realised the necessity of putting an end to the revolutionary proletariat. Yet the situation of its adversary was different. The strength of the proletarian party lay in the streets, that of the petty-bourgeoisie in the national assembly itself. It was therefore a question of luring them from the national assembly onto the streets and making them destroy their parliamentary power themselves, before time and opportunity could consolidate it. The *montagne* sprang at full gallop into the trap.

The bombardment of Rome by French troops [in June 1849] was thrown to it as bait. It violated article V of the [preamble to the] constitution which prohibits the French republic from turning its military forces against the freedom of any other people. In addition [chapter V] § 54 forbade any declaration of war by the executive without the assent of the national assembly, and by its resolution of 8 May [1849] the constituent assembly had disavowed the expedition to Rome. On these grounds Ledru-Rollin introduced a bill of impeachment against Bonaparte and his ministers on 11 June 1849, and stung by Thiers into action, he let himself get carried away to the point of threatening that he would defend the constitution by any means, even fighting hand-to-hand. The *montagne* rose up as one man and echoed this call to arms. On 12 June [1849] the national assembly threw out the bill of impeachment, and the montagne walked out of parliament. The events of 13 June [1849] are well known: the proclamation from one part of the *montagne* by which Bonaparte and his ministers were declared 'outside the constitution'; the democratic national guard, parading weaponless in the streets, dispersed when they met up with Changarnier's troops, etc. etc. A part of the *montagne* fled abroad, another was arraigned before the high court at Bourges, and a parliamentary regulation subjected the rest to the schoolmasterly supervision of the president of the national assembly. Paris was again besieged and the democratic section of the national guard dissolved. The influence of the *montagne* in parliament and the power of the petty-bourgeoisie in Paris was thereby destroyed.

Lyons, where the signal for a bloody workers' insurrection had been given on 13 June, was besieged, along with five neighbouring *départements*, a situation which continues up to the present moment.

The bulk of the *montagne* had abandoned the avant garde, refusing to sign its proclamation. The press had deserted, only two papers daring to publish the broadside. The petty-bourgeoisie betrayed their representatives in that the national guard stayed away, or where they appeared, they obstructed the building of barricades. The representatives had duped the petty-bourgeoisie, as the alleged affiliates from the army were nowhere to be seen. Finally, instead of gaining additional strength from the proletariat, the

democratic party infected it with its own weakness, and as is generally the case with democratic heroism, the leaders took satisfaction
in being able to blame the 'people' for desertion, and the people in
charging the leaders with fraud.

Seldom had a charge been sounded with greater alarum than the
impending campaign by the *montagne*, seldom had an event been
trumpeted with greater certainty or further in advance than the
inevitable victory of democracy. This is for certain: the democrats
have faith in the trumpeting that breached the walls of Jericho. And
as often as they confront the ramparts of despotism, they try to
imitate the miracle. If the *montagne* wished to triumph in parliament, it should not have resorted to arms. If the call to arms was
in parliament, it should not have behaved in a parliamentary way
in the streets. If the peaceful demonstration was seriously intended,
then it was foolish not to foresee a violent reception. If they had a
real war in mind, then it was eccentric to put aside the weapons to
fight it. But the revolutionary threats of the petty-bourgeoisie and
their democratic representatives are mere attempts to bully the
enemy. And if they run into a cul-de-sac, if they compromise themselves enough to force them to carry out their threats, then this
will happen in an ambiguous way which avoids nothing so much
as the means to an end and which hankers after excuses for failure.
The thundering overture announcing the contest dies away to the
faintest growl as battle is commenced, the players cease to take
themselves seriously, and the affair goes flat like a burst balloon.

No party exaggerates its strength more than the democratic one,
and none deludes itself with more insouciance about the situation.
Since a part of the army had declared for it, the *montagne* was now
convinced that the army would revolt for it. And on what occasion?
On an occasion that had no meaning for the troops other than that
the revolutionaries sided with the soldiers of Rome against the
French ones. Concerning the workers, the *montagne* had to know
that the recollections of June 1848 were still too fresh for anything
but a deep aversion on the part of the proletariat for the national
guard and a thoroughgoing mistrust on the part of the chiefs of the
secret societies for the democratic chiefs. To even out these differences would require an overwhelming common interest to come
into play. The infraction of an abstract constitutional clause could
not provide this. Had not the constitution been repeatedly infringed

according to the testimony of the democrats themselves? Had the popular papers not branded it as a counter-revolutionary botch-job? But the democrat, because he represents the petty-bourgeoisie, hence a *transitional class*, in which the interests of two classes are neutralised, fancies himself above class conflict entirely. The democrats admit that a privileged class confronts them, but they together with the whole rest of the nation make up the *people*. What they represent is the *people's right to rule*; their interests are the *people's interests*. Hence at a time of impending struggle, they do not need to examine the interests and positioning of the different classes. They do not need to weigh their own resources all that critically. They have only to give the signal, and the *people* will fall on the *oppressors* with inexhaustible resources to hand. If in the course of events their interests turn out to be uninteresting and their power turns out to be impotence, then the fault lies either with damned sophists splitting the *indivisible people* into different warring camps, or the army was too brutalised and too dazzled to understand that the pure aims of democracy are in its best interests, or the whole thing has been wrecked by a mere detail in execution, or else an unforeseen accident has thwarted the party this time. In any case the democrat emerges from the most shameful defeat just as unscathed as he was when he innocently went into it, with the newly won conviction that he is bound to triumph, not that he and his party have given up their long-standing views but rather the opposite, that conditions have to ripen to suit him.

Decimated and broken down and humiliated by the new parliamentary order, the *montagne* should not be thought particularly unfortunate. The remuneration for attendance and their official position were for many of them a source of consolation that was renewed daily. If 13 June [1849] had removed its leaders, then it opened the way for lesser talents who were flattered by this new arrangement. If their impotence in parliament could no longer be doubted, then they were justified in limiting their interventions to outbursts of moral indignation and tub-thumping oratory. If the party of order pretended to see in them an embodiment of all the terrors of anarchy, as the last official representatives of the revolution, then they could in reality be all the more insipid and unassuming. They consoled themselves, however, for 13 June [1849] with this profound twist: But if any dare to attack the general suffrage, well then! Then we will show them what we are made of! We shall see!

So far as the *montagnards* who fled abroad are concerned, it suffices to note here that Ledru-Rollin, since he had succeeded in scarcely a fortnight in irretrievably ruining the powerful party that he headed, now found himself called up to form a French regime in exile; his distant figure, far from the scene of action, seemed to increase in stature proportionate to the sinking level of the revolution and the dwarfing of the great and the good of official France, so that he could figure as republican pretender for [the presidential election of May] 1852; periodically he issued circulars to the Wallachians and to other peoples whereby the despots of the Continent were threatened with his actions and the actions of his confederates. Was Proudhon wholly wrong when he called out to these men [in 1850]: 'You're nothing but braggarts'?

On 13 June [1849] the party of order had not only broken the *montagne*, it had brought about the *subordination of the constitution to the majority decisions of the national assembly.* And this is what it understood about the republic. That the bourgeoisie rules here in parliamentary form, without encountering any limitations in the veto power of the executive or in the power to dissolve parliament, as there are in a monarchy. That was the *parliamentary republic*, as Thiers had termed it [in 1851]. But on 13 June when the bourgeoisie secured its supreme power within the parliamentary chambers, did it not afflict parliament itself, as opposed to the executive power and the people, with an incurable weakness by throwing out the most popular section? By surrendering numerous deputies to the writs of the judiciary without further ceremonial, it abolished parliamentary immunity itself. The humiliating regulations to which it subjected the *montagne* denigrated the individual representatives of the people, and exalted the president of the republic in inverse proportion. By condemning the insurrection to maintain constitutional rule as anarchic and tending to the overthrow of society, it precluded an appeal to insurrection, should the executive power act against it by violating a constitutional provision. The irony of history had it that the general who bombarded Rome on Bonaparte's orders and so provided the immediate occasion for the constitutional fracas of 13 June [1849], that very same *Oudinot*, had to be the one that the party of order offered, with fruitless supplications, to the people on 2 December 1851 as a constitutional general in opposition to Bonaparte. Another hero of 13 June [1849], [General] *Vieyra*, praised from the rostrum of the national assembly for leading a gang of national guards linked to high finance to commit brutalities in the offices of the democratic press, this same Vieyra was sworn to Bonaparte and played an essential part in the death throes of the national assembly by depriving it of any protection from the national guard.

The 13th of June [1849] had still another meaning. The *montagne* had wanted Bonaparte out of the way through impeachment. Its defeat was therefore a signal victory for Bonaparte, a personal triumph over his democratic enemies. The party of order gained a victory; Bonaparte had only to cash in. And that he did. On 14 June [1849] there was a proclamation to be read on the walls of Paris whereby the president, quite without meaning to, fighting against it, forced by pressure of events to emerge from cloistered seclusion, intones the calumnies of his enemies against his misprised virtue, and in fact identifies the cause of order with his person whilst seeming to identify his person with the cause of order. Moreover the national assembly had sanctioned the expedition against Rome after the fact, but Bonaparte had taken the initiative. Having installed the high priest Samuel in the Vatican once again, he could hope to enter the Tuileries [crowned by the pope] as King David. He had won over the church.

The revolt of 13 June [1849] was limited, as we have seen, to a peaceful march through the streets. Hence there were no laurels to be won in combating it. At a time when heroes and exploits were scarce, the party of order nevertheless transformed this bloodless encounter into a second [Battle of] Austerlitz [when Napoleon defeated the Austrians and Russians on 2 December 1805]. Speechmakers and leader-writers extolled the army as the champion of order, versus the impotent anarchism of the populace at large, and praised Changarnier as the 'bulwark of society'. This was a mystification that he finally believed himself. But secretly the army corps that seemed doubtful were transferred from Paris, the regiments that had voted for the democrats were banished to Algiers, hotheads amongst the troops were consigned to punishment squads, and finally the press was systematically barred from the barracks and the barracks from civilian life.

We have now reached the turning-point in the history of the French national guard. In 1830 it was decisive in the overthrow of the restoration monarchy [of Charles X]. Under Louis Philippe, every time the national guard sided with the troops, the rebellion misfired. In the February days of 1848, when it signalled passivity to the uprising and ambiguity to Louis Philippe, he acknowledged defeat and went under. Thus the conviction took root that the revolution could not win *without* the national guard, and the army could not win *against* it. Thus the army had a superstitious belief in an almighty civilian power. That superstition was strengthened when the national guard joined forces with regular troops to put down the insurrection of the June days of 1848. When Bonaparte took office, the standing of the national guard declined somewhat owing to the unconstitutional amalgamation of its command with that of the first army in the person of Changarnier.

The national guard itself now appeared to be but an appendage to the regulars, just as its command appeared to be a department of the top brass. It was finally disposed of on 13 June [1849]: not just by the partial dissolution of the national guard, periodically re-enacted all over France, and leaving only fragments behind. The demonstration of 13 June was above all a demonstration by the democratic [elements of the] national guard. They had, to be sure, confronted the army with their uniforms, not with weapons, but the talisman was precisely in the uniform. The army satisfied itself that the uniform was a length of woollen cloth just like any other. The spell was broken. In the June days of 1848 the bourgeoisie and petty-bourgeoisie were united as national guards against the proletariat, and on 13 June 1849 the bourgeoisie let the army disperse the petty-bourgeois national guards; on 2 December 1851 the bourgeois national guard itself vanished and Bonaparte merely confirmed this fact when he signed an order of dissolution. So the bourgeoisie itself smashed its last weapon against the army, doing this the moment the petty-bourgeoisie rebelled and ceased to be its vassal, and generally destroying all its own defences against absolutism once it became absolute itself.

Meanwhile in the national assembly the party of order celebrated the reconquest of a power that seemed lost only in 1848 but was recovered in 1849 free from previous restrictions, spouting invective against the republic and the constitution, cursing all future, present, and past revolutions including the one their own leaders had made, and passing laws muzzling the press, forbidding free association and making siege controls a permanent institution. The national assembly then adjourned from the middle of August to the middle of October [1849], after naming a commission to rule in its absence. During this recess the legitimists intrigued at Ems, the Orléanists at Claremont, Bonaparte on his princely rounds, and councils of the *départements* in deliberations on constitutional revision – incidents which regularly recur in the periodic recesses of the national assembly, and which I will examine only when they turn out to be events. Here it is merely noted that the national assembly behaved in an impolitic way by disappearing for long intervals from the stage and leaving only a single figure at the head of the republic, Louis Bonaparte, even if a pitiable one, while the party of order caused a public scandal by separating into its royalist elements with mutually conflicting demands for restoration. Once the distracting din of parliament was silenced by this recess and it had dissolved bodily into the nation, it became inescapably clear that the republic required but one thing for true completion: making parliamentary recess permanent and replacing the republican motto 'liberty, equality, fraternity' with the unambiguous words 'infantry, cavalry, artillery'!

IV

In mid-October 1849 the national assembly went back into session. On 1 November Bonaparte surprised it with a communiqué announcing the dismissal of the Barrot-Falloux cabinet and the formation of a new one. Nobody has sacked his lackeys more unceremoniously than Bonaparte did his ministers. For the moment Barrot and Co. got the boot intended for the national assembly.

The Barrot cabinet, as we have seen, was composed of legitimists and Orléanists, a cabinet for the party of order. This was what Bonaparte needed in order to dissolve the constituent assembly, to mount the expedition against the republic in Rome, and to destroy the democratic party. In apparent eclipse behind this ministry, he had delivered governmental authority into the hands of the party of order and masked himself in the unassuming guise of a 'straw man', which the respectable 'guarantors' of the Paris press bore [under Louis Philippe, when the real editors were in prison]. Now he cast off his larval shell, which was no longer a light covering under which he could hide his features but rather an iron mask which prevented him from showing his true face. He had appointed the Barrot cabinet to break up the national assembly in the name of the party of order; in his own name he discharged it in order to declare his independence from the party of order and its national assembly.

There was no lack of plausible pretexts for this dismissal. The Barrot cabinet neglected even the formalities that would have let the president of the republic appear to hold power alongside the national assembly. During the recess of the national assembly Bonaparte published a letter to [his military aide] Edgar Ney in which he seemed to object to the liberal policies of the pope, just as he had published a letter in opposition to the constituent assembly praising Oudinot for his assault on the Roman republic. When the national assembly approved the budget for the Roman expedition, the liberal Victor Hugo brought this letter to attention [on 19 October 1849]. The party of order drowned out the suggestion that Bonaparte's ideas could have any political weight with exclamations of disbelieving scorn. Not one of the ministers took up the challenge to defend him. On another occasion Barrot, with his usual high seriousness, alluded from the rostrum to his indignation concerning the 'abominable intrigues' that in his opinion were going on in the immediate entourage of the president. Finally, though the cabinet obtained a widow's pension for the duchess of Orléans from the national assembly, it refused to consider an increase in presidential expenses. In Bonaparte the imperial pretender was so intimately bound up with the down-and-out mercenary that his one big idea – that his mission was to restore the empire – was always accompanied by another – that it was the mission of the French people to pay his debts.

The Barrot-Falloux cabinet was the first and last *parliamentary cabinet* that Bonaparte called into existence. Its discharge therefore marks a decisive turning-point. In it the party of order lost the lever of executive power, an indispensable position for defending a parliamentary regime, and never again recovered it. In a country like France, where the executive power has at its disposal a bureaucracy of more than half a million civil servants, so holding an immense number of individual interests and livelihoods in abject dependence; where the state restricts, controls, regulates, oversees and supervises civil life from its most all-encompassing expressions to its most insignificant stirrings, from its most universal models of existence to the private existence of individuals; where through the most extraordinary centralisation this parasite acquires an all-knowing pervasiveness, an enhanced capacity for speed and action which only finds an analogue in the helpless dependence and scatter-brained formlessness of the actual body politic – it is easy to see that in such a country the national assembly forfeits any real influence when it loses control of ministerial portfolios, if it does not at the same time simplify the state administration, reduce the bureaucracy as far as possible, and lastly allow civil life and public opinion to create their own organs of expression independent of governmental authority. But the *material interests* of the French bourgeoisie are intertwined in the most intimate way with the maintenance of just that wide-ranging and highly ramified machinery of state. Here it accommodates surplus population and makes up in the form of state maintenance what it cannot pocket in the form of profit, interest, rent and fees. On the other hand its political *interests* force it to increase state repression day by day, hence resources and personnel, while at the same time waging a continuous war on public opinion, suspecting independent movement in society, then maiming and laming its limbs where not wholly successful in amputating them. Thus the French bourgeoisie was compelled by its class position both to negate the conditions of existence for any parliamentary power, including its own, and to make the power of the executive, its adversary, irresistible.

The new cabinet was known as the d'Hautpoul ministry. Not that General d'Hautpoul had been granted the title prime minister. With Barrot's dismissal Bonaparte had also abolished this office which condemned the president of the republic to the legal nullity of a constitutional monarch, though a constitutional monarch without throne or crown, without sceptre and sword, without unilateral power, without unimpeachable possession of the highest office of state, and most fatal of all, without [expenses from] a civil list. The d'Hautpoul cabinet included only one man of parliamentary standing, the Jew *Fould*, one of the most notorious of the high financiers. The finance ministry went to him. Check the quotations on the Paris *bourse* and you will find that from 1 November 1849 onwards French government securities rose and fell with the fall and rise of Bonapartist shares. While Bonaparte was finding friends on the *bourse* he also took control of the police, appointing Carlier as prefect in Paris.

This change of cabinet had consequences that would only emerge in the ensuing train of events. At first Bonaparte seemed to take a step forward only to be driven conspicuously back again. His abrupt communiqué was followed by the most servile pledge of allegiance to the national assembly. Whenever ministers dared to make a diffident attempt to introduce his personal whims as proposed legislation, they appeared unwilling, forced by their position to fulfil comic instructions, convinced in advance of their failure. Whenever Bonaparte babbled out his intentions behind his ministers' backs and played up his 'Napoleonic ideals' [as published in a book of 1839], his own ministers disavowed him from the rostrum of the national assembly. His usurpatory lusts only seemed to come forth so that the malicious laughter of his enemies would not die away. He behaved like an unrecognised genius whom all the world takes for a simpleton. Never did he experience the contempt of all classes to a greater degree than in this period. Never did the bourgeoisie rule more unconditionally, never did it display the insignia of power with more bravado.

I do not need to tell the story of the bourgeoisie's legislative activity here, as it can be summarised for this period in two laws: the reintroduction of the *wine tax*, and the *education act* disallowing atheism. Though wine drinking was made harder for the French, they were all the more richly supplied with the water of the living truth. Though the bourgeoisie declared the old, despised tax system in France sacrosanct by reintroducing the despised tax on wine, it tried to secure the old habits of mind that helped people to bear it by passing the education law. It is astonishing to see the Orléanists, the liberal bourgeois, these votaries of Voltaire and apostles of philosophical eclecticism, entrusting the supervision of French intellectual life to their sworn enemies the Jesuits. Though Orléanists and legitimists could part company over pretenders to the throne, they both understood that their joint authority required a combination of the repressive apparatus of two eras, the July monarchy and the restoration, supplementing and strengthening the former with the latter.

Out in the *départements* the peasantry began to agitate, as they were dashed in all their hopes, oppressed more than ever by low price-levels for grain, and by increasing tax burdens and mortgage debts. They were answered with a witch hunt against school teachers, who were subjected to the clergy, a witch hunt against mayors, who were subjected to prefects, and through a system of spying, which subjected everyone. In Paris and the big cities [political] reaction bears the true character of the times and provokes more than it executes. In the countryside it is vulgar, sordid, petty, tiresome and badgering, in a word the gendarme. We know how much three years of a police state, blessed by the authority of the Church, must demoralise an unsophisticated population.

Despite all the passion and shouting from the rostrum that was directed by the party of order against the minority in the national assembly, its words were always monosyllabic, like the Christian who was to say: Yea, yea; nay, nay! Monosyllables from the rostrum, monosyllables in the press. Boring as a riddle whose solution you already know. Whether it was a question of the right of petition or of the tax on wine, of freedom of the press or free trade, incorporating societies or municipalities, protecting personal freedom or accounting for public money, the universal remedy recurs, one theme is always the same, the verdict is ever ready and is invariably a cry of: '*socialism*'! Even bourgeois liberalism is decried as *socialistic*, bourgeois enlightenment is socialistic, bourgeois financial reforms are socialistic. It was socialistic to build a railway where there was already a canal, and it was socialistic to defend oneself with a stick when attacked with a sword.

This is not mere rhetoric, fashion or party tactics. The bourgeoisie saw correctly that all the weapons it had forged against feudalism were turned back on their makers, that all the educational institutions it had supported were rebelling against its own civilisation, that all the gods it had created were forsaking them. It knew that all so-called liberty and progress threatened and strained its class-rule both at the foundations of society and at its political heights, and had therefore become '*socialistic*'. In these threats and strains it rightly discerned the secret of socialism, whose tendency and aim it judges more correctly than so-called socialism knows how to judge itself, since it cannot understand how the bourgeoisie stubbornly resists it, even though it snivels sentimentally about the suffering of mankind, or prophesies brotherly love and the millennium like the Christians, drivels humanistically about ideas, education and freedom, or concocts a doctrinaire system for the reconciliation and welfare of all classes. But what it doesn't grasp is the conclusion that its *own parliamentary regime*, its *political rule* in general, must now be condemned universally as *socialistic*. So long as the organisation of bourgeois class rule is incomplete, and has not taken on its purest political expression, the opposition of other classes cannot emerge in a pure form, and where it does emerge, it cannot take the dangerous turn of calling property, religion, the family and public order into question, and so transforming the struggle against state power into a struggle against capital. If it saw 'peace and quiet' endangered by every stirring of life in society, how could it want to retain at the head of society a *regime of unrest*, its own regime, the *parliamentary regime*, a regime that – as one of its spokesmen put it – thrives on conflict? The parliamentary regime lives by discussion, so how is it to forbid it? Every interest, every social organisation is transformed into a generality, debated as a generality, so how is an interest, any kind of institution, to transcend thinking and to impose itself as an article of faith? The war of the orators at the rostrum evokes the war of the printing presses; parliamentary debaters are necessarily supplemented by debaters in the salons and saloon bars; representatives who make constant appeals to public opinion license public opinion to express itself openly in petitions. The parliamentary regime leaves everything to majority decision, why then should the great majorities outside parliament not want to make decisions? When you call the tune at the pinnacles of power, is it a surprise when the underlings dance to it?

By branding as '*socialistic*' what it had previously extolled as '*liberal*', the bourgeoisie confesses that its own interests require it to dispense with the dangers of self-government; that in order to restore peace to the countryside the bourgeois parliament must first be laid to rest; that to retain its power in society intact its political power would have to be broken; that the individual bourgeois could continue to exploit other classes 'privately' and to continue in untroubled enjoyment of property, family, religion and public order only on condition that his class and all the others be condemned to the same political nullity; that to save its purse it must forfeit the crown, and the sword of state must be hung up like the sword of Damocles.

In the domain of bourgeois interests in general, the national assembly proved itself so unproductive that, for example, the negotiations on the Paris–Avignon railway, begun during the winter of 1850, were still not wrapped up on 2 December 1851. Where it was not repressive or reactive, it was incurably sterile.

While Bonaparte's cabinet took the initiative, in part, to put the programme of the party of order into law, and surpassed, in part, its harshness in executing and administering it, he also tried to win popularity through silly, childish proposals, to manifest his opposition to the national assembly and to hint at a secret reserve, though conditions temporarily hindered the French people from spending the hidden treasures. Such was the proposal to grant a pay increase of four sous per day to non-commissioned officers. Such was the proposal for unsecured bank loans for workers. Cash in hand and cash on tick, that was the perspective with which he hoped to lead on the populace. Gifts and loans – here we have the only economics of the lumpenproletariat, both the refined and the common sort. And here we have the only trips which Bonaparte knew how to wire. Never has a pretender speculated so stupidly on the stupidity of the populace.

The national assembly raged repeatedly at these bare-faced attempts to win popularity at its expense, at the growing danger that this shyster, goaded by debt and unrestrained by reputation, would risk a desperate coup. The discord between the party of order and the president had taken on a threatening character when an unexpected event threw him repenting into its arms. We refer to the *by-elections of 10 March 1850*. These were held to fill seats vacated by deputies exiled or imprisoned after 13 June [1849]. Only social-democrats were elected in Paris. Indeed most of the votes there were concentrated on Deflotte, an insurgent in June 1848. Thus did the Paris petty-bourgeoisie, in alliance with the proletariat, take revenge for its defeat on 13 June 1849. Though it seemed to disappear from battle at the crucial time, it regained the field on a more propitious occasion with greater forces and a bolder battle-cry. Another circumstance seemed to make this electoral victory more dangerous for Bonaparte. In Paris the army voted for one of the June [1848] insurgents against one of Bonaparte's ministers, La-hitte, and in the *départements* mostly for the *montagnards*, out-weighing the enemy there, too, though not so decisively as in Paris.

Suddenly Bonaparte saw revolution rising against him once more. On 10 March 1850, as on 29 January and 13 June 1849, he disap-peared behind the party of order. He bowed down, he humbly begged pardon, he offered to appoint any cabinet it pleased on behalf of the parliamentary majority, he even implored the Orléanist and legitimist leaders, the Thiers's, the Berryers, the Broglies, the Molés, in short the so-called grandees, to take the helm of state in person. The party of order did not know what to do with this chance of a lifetime. Instead of boldly seizing power it did not even force Bonaparte to reinstate the cabinet previously discharged on 1 November [1849]; it was satisfied to humiliate him with forgiveness and to attach *M. Baroche* to the d'Hautpoul cabinet. As public pros-ecutor, this Baroche had ranted before the high court at Bourges on two occasions, the first time against the revolutionaries of 15 May [1848] and the second against the democrats of 13 June [1849], both times because of the outrage to the national assembly. But none of Bonaparte's ministers had a bigger part in the subsequent abase-ment of the national assembly, and after [the coup of] 2 December 1851 we meet him once more, comfortably installed and highly paid as vice-president, presiding over the senate. He had spat in the revolutionists' soup so that Bonaparte could slurp it up.

The social-democratic party seemed only to snatch at pretexts for doubting its own victory and for taking the edge off it. Vidal, one of the newly elected representatives for Paris, had also been elected for Strasbourg. He was persuaded to give up the seat in Paris and take the one in Strasbourg. Instead of making its victory at the polls definitive and forcing the party of order into a parlia-mentary showdown, instead of drawing the enemy into battle at a time of popular enthusiasm and favourable disposition in the army, the democratic party wearied Paris with electoral campaigning in March and April [1850], let popular excitement wear itself out in a game of repeated provisional ballots; let revolutionary energy sate itself in constitutional successes, fizzle out in petty intrigues, hollow rhetoric and illusory actions; let the bourgeoisie rally and prepare itself; and finally, let an April [1850] by-election victory for Eugène

Sue become a sentimental commentary on the earlier March vote and weaken its significance. In a word it made 10 March [1850] into April Fool's.

The parliamentary majority knew the weakness of its adversary [the social-democrats or *montagne*]. Bonaparte had left it the job of organising an attack and taking responsibility for it; seventeen grandees worked out a new electoral law to be proposed by [the minister of the interior] Faucher, who had begged to be entrusted with that honour. On 8 May [1850] he brought in a bill to abolish universal manhood suffrage, to impose a three-year condition of residence on the electors, and finally in the case of workers to make proof of residence depend on certification by their employer.

During the electoral contest over the constitution, the democrats had fussed and blustered in a revolutionary way, but now when it was a matter of demonstrating the importance of free elections through force of arms they sermonised in a constitutional way about public order, lofty tranquillity (*calme majestueux*), legal procedure, i.e. blind subjection to the terms of the counter-revolution, which paraded itself as law. During the debate the *montagne* shamed the party of order by adopting the dispassionate mien of the honourable law-abiding man, as opposed to its passionate revolutionism, and the *montagne* cut them down with the fearful reproach that they were revolutionaries. Even the newly elected deputies took care to be respectable and discreet to show what a misperception it was to decry them as anarchists and to interpret their election as a victory for revolution. On 31 May [1850] the new electoral law went through. The *montagne* was content to go to the president of the national assembly and stick a protest in his pocket. The electoral law was followed by a new press law completely eliminating the revolutionary newspapers. They deserved their fate. After this deluge the *National* and *La Presse*, two bourgeois papers, remained behind as the most extreme outposts of revolution.

We have seen how the democratic leaders did everything to embroil the people of Paris in a sham battle during March and April [1850], and how after 8 May [1850] they did everything to hold them back from a real one. It should also not be forgotten that 1850 was one of best years of industrial and commercial prosperity, so that Paris proletariat was fully employed. But the electoral law of 31 May 1850 excluded it from any part in political power. The field of battle was barred to it. The workers were pariahs once again, as they had been before the February revolution. By allowing the democrats to lead them after such an event and by forsaking the revolutionary interests of their class for transitory comforts, they renounced the honours of conquest, surrendered to their fate, demonstrated that the defeat of June 1848 had rendered them incapable of fighting for years to come and that the historical process would once again have to go on over their heads. As for the petty-bourgeois democrats who had cried on 13 June [1849], 'just one finger on universal manhood suffrage, and then!' – they now consoled themselves with the thought that the counter-revolutionary blow which they suffered was no blow and the law of 31 May [1850] no law. On 9 May 1852 [when Bonaparte's term as president was to expire] every Frenchman would appear at the polls, ballot in one hand and sword in the other. For the petty-bourgeois democrats this prophecy was self-sufficient. Finally the army was punished by its superior officers for the elections of March and April 1850 as it had been for the one of 29 May 1849. But this time it said decidedly: 'the revolution will not cheat us a third time'.

The law of 31 May 1850 was the *coup d'état* of the bourgeoisie. All its previous victories over the revolution had had a merely provisional character. They were called into question once the national assembly had retired from the stage [for an electoral campaign]. They were dependent on the hazards of a new general election, and the history of elections since 1848 had demonstrated incontrovertibly that when the political authority of the bourgeoisie went up, its moral authority over the populace went down. On 10 March [1850] universal manhood suffrage made a declaration directly contrary to the authority of the bourgeoisie, and the bourgeoisie replied by outlawing it. Hence the law of 31 May [1850] was one of the requirements of the class struggle. On the other hand, the constitution demanded a minimum of two million votes to validate the election of the president of the republic. Should none of the presidential candidates obtain the minimum, the national assembly was to choose the president from amongst the five candidates at the top of the poll. At the time when the constituent assembly passed this law, there were ten million voters on the rolls. In its view a fifth of the electorate sufficed to validate the election of the president. The law of 31 May [1850] struck at least three million voters from the rolls, reduced the number in the electorate to seven million, and still retained the legal minimum of two million for the election of the president. It therefore raised the legal minimum from a fifth to nearly a third of the eligible voters, i.e. it did everything to wangle the election of the president from the hands of the people into the hands of the national assembly. Thus the party of order appeared to have made its rule doubly secure through the electoral law of 31 May [1850], because it put the election of the national assembly and of the president of the republic into the hands of this stable part of society.

V

The struggle between the national assembly and Bonaparte broke out again once the revolutionary crisis had blown over and universal manhood suffrage was abolished.

The constitution had set Bonaparte's salary at 600,000 francs. Scarcely six months after his installation he succeeded in doubling his money. This happened when Odilon Barrot extracted an annual supplement of 600,000 francs from the constituent assembly for so-called official expenses. After 13 June [1849] Bonaparte had similar requests put about but this time Barrot did not give them a hearing. Now after 31 May [1850] he seized an auspicious moment and got his ministers to propose a civil list of three million in the national assembly. Leading the life of an adventurous vagabond had endowed him with highly sensitive feelers for searching out the weak moments when he might squeeze money from the bourgeoisie. He was a real blackmailer. The national assembly had violated the sovereignty of the people with his cooperation and connivance. He threatened to expose this crime to the people unless it loosened the purse-strings and paid up three million a year in hush-money. It had robbed three million Frenchmen of their right to vote. For every Frenchman put out of circulation he demanded a franc in circulation, three million to be precise. Elected by six million, he demanded compensation from the assembly for subsequently cheating him of votes. The executive commission of the national assembly dismissed this upstart. The Bonapartist press grew threatening. Could the national assembly break with the president of the republic at a time when it had broken decisively with the bulk of

the nation on a matter of principle? Admittedly it had thrown out
the annual civil list but it had granted one-off supplementation of
2,160,000 francs. Thus it was guilty of a double weakness in granting the money and at the same time displaying an irritation that
revealed its reluctance to do so. We will see later what Bonaparte
used the money for. After this irritating sequel to the abolition of
universal manhood suffrage, in which Bonaparte switched from
humility during the crises of March and April [1850] to provocative
impudence when challenged by parliament, the national assembly
adjourned for three months, from 11 August to 11 November
[1850]. It left behind an executive commission of eighteen members
containing no Bonapartists but a few moderate republicans. The
executive commission of 1849 had included only gentlemen from
the party of order and Bonapartists. But at the time the party of
order had declared itself implacably opposed to the revolution. This
time the parliamentary republic declared itself implacably opposed
to the president. After the electoral law of 31 May [1850] this was
the only rival confronting the party of order.

When the national assembly came back into session in November
1850 it seemed that there would be a ruthless struggle with the
president, an inevitable battle to the death between two great
powers, instead of the previous petty skirmishing.

During this parliamentary recess, just as in the one of 1849, the
party of order broke up into factions, each busy with its restorationist intrigues, given new impetus by the death of Louis
Philippe [on 26 August 1850]. The legitimist Henri V had even
appointed a proper cabinet which met in Paris and included members of the executive commission amongst its numbers. Bonaparte
was therefore licensed for his part to progress through the *départements* of France, canvassing for votes, and airing his own plans for
a restoration, overtly or covertly, depending on the politics of the
town favoured with his presence. On this procession, necessarily
celebrated as a triumphal progress by the official gazette and Bonaparte's minor ones, he was continually accompanied by affiliates of
the Society of 10 December. This society dates from the year 1849.
Under the pretext of incorporating a benevolent association, the
Paris lumpenproletariat was organised into secret sections, each led
by a Bonapartist agent, and the whole headed by a Bonapartist general. From the aristocracy there were bankrupted roués of doubtful

means and dubious provenance, from the bourgeoisie there were degenerate wastrels on the take, vagabonds, demobbed soldiers, discharged convicts, runaway galley slaves, swindlers and cheats, thugs, pickpockets, conjurers, card-sharps, pimps, brothel keepers, porters, day-labourers, organ grinders, scrap dealers, knife grinders, tinkers and beggars, in short, the whole amorphous, jumbled mass of flotsam and jetsam that the French term bohemian; from these kindred spirits Bonaparte built up his Society of 10 December. This was a 'benevolent society' in that all its members, like Bonaparte, felt a need to benefit themselves at the expense of the nation's workers. This Bonaparte, installed as chief of the lumpenproletariat, discovering his personal interests here in popular form, perceiving in the dregs, refuse and scum of all classes the sole class that offers unconditional support, here is the real Bonaparte, the genuine article, even though when in power he paid his debt to some of his erstwhile fellow-conspirators by transporting them to [the penal colony in] Cayenne [in South America] alongside the revolutionaries. A cunning old roué, he conceives popular history and high politics and finance as comedies in the most vulgar sense, as masquerades where fine costumes, words and postures serve only to mask the most trifling pettiness. So it was [in 1830] when he processed into Strasbourg, where a trained Swiss vulture played the part of the Napoleonic eagle. For his entry into Boulogne [in 1840] he put some London lay-abouts into French uniforms. They stood in for the army. In his Society of 10 December he collected 10,000 ragamuffins who were supposed to represent the people the way that Klaus Zettel represented the lion. The bourgeoisie was playing an utter comedy, but in the most serious way in the world, without infringing even the most pedantic strictures of French dramatic etiquette, and themselves half swindled, half convinced of the solemnity of their own high politics and finance; that was a time when a swindler, who took the comedy straight, was bound to win. Only now [in early 1852] that he has removed his solemn opponent, when he has taken on the imperial role in earnest and with his Napoleonic mask means to represent the real Napoleon, does he become a victim of his own world-view, the straight comedian who no longer sees world history as a comedy but his own comedy as world history. What the nationalised workshops were for the socialist workers, what the militia was for the bourgeois republicans, the Society of 10 December, his very own fighting force, was for Bonaparte. On his journeys, detachments were to pack the trains to improvise a crowd, raise public enthusiasm, howl a salute to the Emperor, insult and beat up republicans, all under the protection of the police, of course. On his return journeys to Paris they were to form an advance guard, forestalling or breaking up counter-demonstrations. The Society of 10 December belonged to him, it was *his* work, his very own idea. Whatever else he got his hands on, came to him by force of circumstances; whatever else he did, either circumstances did for him or he was satisfied to copy the deeds of others; but he became an artist in his own right when he put official turns of phrase – like public order, religion, the family and property – before the public, but kept the secret society of racketeers and con-artists, the society of disorder, prostitution and pilfering well out of sight, and the history of the Society of 10 December is his own history. But once there was an exception, when representatives of the party of order got hammered by the December-mob. And there was worse to come. Police commissioner Yon, assigned to security at the national assembly, got a story from a certain Alais and informed the executive commission that a section of the December-mob were plotting to murder General Changarnier and Dupin, the president of the national assembly, and had already found people to carry this out. M. Dupin's panic is understandable. A parliamentary enquiry into the Society of 10 December, i.e. the profanation of the secret world of Bonapartism, seemed unavoidable. But just before the national assembly came into session, Bonaparte prudently dissolved his society, only on paper of course, for even at the end of 1851, Carlier, the prefect of police, was still pressing him in a detailed but vain memorandum to make the break-up of the December-mob a fact.

The Society of 10 December was to remain Bonaparte's private army until he could successfully transform the official army into the Society of 10 December. Shortly after the adjournment of the national assembly Bonaparte made his first attempt at this, and to be sure with the money that he had just extorted from it. As a fatalist, he lived the maxim that there are certain higher powers which a man, and particularly a soldier, cannot withstand. Amongst those powers he reckoned first of all on cigars and champagne, cold chicken and garlic sausage. Hence he began by treating officers and

79

junior officers to cigars and champagne, cold chicken and garlic sausage in his residence at the Elysée Palace. On 3 October [1850] he repeated this ploy with the massed troops reviewed at Saint-Maur and on 10 October the same thing again on a still grander scale at the army's Satory parade. His uncle Napoleon had invoked the campaigns of Alexander in Asia, the nephew the triumphs of Bacchus in the same land. Alexander was of course a demi-god, but Bacchus was a full-fledged one, and in fact the god watching over the Society of 10 December.

After the military review of 3 October [1850], the executive commission summoned the minister of war d'Hautpoul to a hearing. He promised that such breaches of discipline would not be repeated. We know how on 10 October [at Saint-Maur] Bonaparte kept to d'Hautpoul's promise. At both reviews Changarnier had been in command as head of the army in Paris. He was simultaneously a member of the executive commission, commander-in-chief of the national guard, 'saviour' of 29 January and 13 June [1849], 'bulwark of society', presidential candidate for the party of order, the presumed [General] Monk [who restored King Charles II] for two [pretending] monarchs; up to then he had never acknowledged that he was subordinate to the minister of war, had always openly scoffed at the republican constitution, and had acted as a highly placed but ambiguous protector for Bonaparte. Now he was a stickler for discipline against the minister of war and a zealot for the constitution against Bonaparte. Despite the fact that on 10 October [1850] a part of the cavalry raised the cry: 'Long live Napoleon! and the sausages!' Changarnier arranged that at least those troops under the command of his friend Neumeyer would observe an icy silence whilst parading by. At Bonaparte's instigation the minister of war punished General Neumeyer by relieving him of his post in Paris, under the pretext of making him commander of the 14th and 15th divisions. Neumeyer refused this transfer and so had to take his leave. On 2 November [1850], for his part, Changarnier posted an order forbidding the troops from engaging in political sloganising or demonstrations of any kind whilst under arms. The Elyséeist papers attacked Changarnier, the papers for the party of order attacked Bonaparte; the executive commission held numerous secret sessions repeatedly proposing a state of emergency; the army seemed divided into two warring camps with two warring general staffs, one in the Elysée with Bonaparte and the other in the

Tuileries with Changarnier. It appeared that only the recall of the national assembly was needed to sound the call to arms. The French public reacted to the dissension between Bonaparte and Changarnier rather like the English journalist who characterised it in the following way: 'Housemaids in France are clearing away the glowing lava of revolution with old brooms and bickering amongst themselves while they do their work.'

Meanwhile Bonaparte hastened to remove the minister of war, d'Hautpoul, speeding him headlong to Algiers and appointing General Schramm in his place. On 12 November [1850] he sent the national assembly a communiqué of American prolixity, overburdened with detail, redolent of order, anxious for reconciliation, acquiescing in the constitution, treating of all and sundry except the burning questions of the time. As if in passing he remarked that according to the express provisions of the constitution, the army was answerable to the president alone. The communiqué concluded with this solemn affirmation:

> *Above all France clamours for peace ... I alone am bound by an oath of office, so I shall stay within the narrow limits that the constitution has set for the president ...* Concerning myself, I have been elected by the people and owe my power solely to them, and I shall always submit to their lawful will. Should you resolve on a revision of the constitution at this session, a constituent assembly will determine the extent of executive power. If not, then the people will make their solemn decision in [May] 1852. But whatever the future may bring, let us come to an understanding so that emotion, shock or violence will never decide the fate of this great nation ... What is always at the forefront of my concern is not to know who will govern France in 1852, but rather to use the time at my disposal so that the interim passes without unrest or disorder. I have sincerely opened my heart to you, you will answer my frankness with your trust, my good endeavours with your cooperation, and God will do the rest.

In the mouth of Bonaparte – the autocrat of the Society of 10 December and the picnic hero of Saint-Maur and Satory – the language of the bourgeoisie – respectable, moderate in its hypocrisy, virtuous in its commonplaces – opened new vistas of meaning.

The grandees of the party of order did not delude themselves for a moment concerning the trust that this heartfelt effusion deserved. They had long been blasé about oaths, as they numbered in their midst veterans and virtuosi of political perjury, and they had not omitted to note the passage concerning the army. They remarked with annoyance that the communiqué, in a long-winded enumeration of the latest enactments, had passed over the most important measure, the electoral law, in studied silence, and moreover, that unless the constitution were revised, the election of the president in 1852 would be left to the people. The electoral law was a ball and chain for the party of order, hindering motion of any kind, much less forward assault! Moreover by disbanding the Society of 10 December and sacking the war minister d'Hautpoul, Bonaparte had found scapegoats to sacrifice on the altar of patriotism. He had taken the force from the impending collision. Finally the party of order itself was anxious to avert, mitigate or conceal any conflict with the executive that might be decisive. For fear of losing what it had gained in the revolution, it allowed its rivals to help themselves to the fruits of victory. 'Above all France clamours for peace.' The party of order had proclaimed this to the revolution since February [1848], and now Bonaparte's communiqué proclaimed it to the party of order. 'Above all France clamours for peace.' Bonaparte had committed acts that pointed towards usurpation, but the party of order committed 'unrest' if it raised the alarm over these acts and exposed its hypochondria. The sausages of Satory were quiet as mice when no one mentioned them. 'Above all France wants order.' Thus Bonaparte demanded to be left in peace, and the parliamentary party was doubly crippled by fear – fear of precipitating revolutionary unrest once again, and fear of appearing to its own class, the bourgeoisie, as the instigator. Since above all France clamours for peace the party of order dared not reply 'war' to Bonaparte's communiqué on 'peace'. The public, anticipating a juicy scandal at the opening of the national assembly, was cheated of this expectation. The opposition deputies, demanding the executive commission's account of the events of October [1850], were overruled by the majority. All debates that could cause an uproar were avoided on principle. The proceedings of the national assembly during November and December [1850] were entirely without interest.

At last towards the end of December [1850] guerilla warfare began over certain prerogatives of parliament. The fighting got bogged down in small-scale manœuvres over the power of the two branches of government, because the bourgeoisie had wound up the class struggle by abolishing universal manhood suffrage.

A court judgement for debt had been delivered against one of the people's representatives, Maugin. Responding to the petition from the president of the court, the minister of justice, Rouher, declared that a warrant for his arrest should be issued without further formalities. Maugin was therefore thrown into debtors' prison. The national assembly flared up at news of this outrage. Not only did it order his immediate release, but it had him forcibly sprung from Clichy that very same evening by a justice's clerk. But in order to prove its faith in the sanctity of private property – and with the ulterior motive of opening an asylum in case the *montagnards* became troublesome – it declared that the people's representatives might be imprisoned for debt on prior consent of the national assembly. It forgot to decree that the president could also be locked up for debt. It destroyed the last semblance of the immunity encompassing its own members.

It will be recalled that police commissioner Yon, acting on reports from a certain Alais, had denounced a section of the December-mob for plotting to murder Dupin and Changarnier. On this account at the very first session the commissioners proposed a parliamentary police, funded from its private budget and completely independent of the prefect of police. The minister of the interior, Baroche, protested at this encroachment on his territory. On that they reached a shabby compromise that the parliamentary police chief should be paid from the private budget [and] appointed and dismissed by parliamentary commissioners, but only on prior agreement with the minister of the interior. Meanwhile the government had taken criminal proceedings against Alais, and here it was easy to represent his information as a hoax and to make a laughing stock of Dupin, Changarnier, Yon and the whole national assembly through the speeches of the public prosecutor. Then on 29 December [1850] Baroche wrote to Dupin demanding Yon's dismissal. The officers of the national assembly decided to retain Yon in his position, but the national assembly did not approve this, as they were frightened by their own use of force in the Maugin affair and were used to double blows from the executive for every poke they took at it. As a reward for his faithful service Yon was discharged, and the national assembly robbed itself of a parliamentary privilege indispensable against a man [Louis Bonaparte] who does not decide by night and act by day, but decides by day and acts by night.

We have seen already how the national assembly met with striking opportunities during November and December [1850] in its great battle with the executive, but ducked out or went under. Now we see it compelled to take up the most trivial points. In the Maugin affair it confirmed the principle that representatives of the people may be imprisoned for debt, but reserved the right to apply this only to representatives it found obnoxious, and it haggled with the minister of justice over this dubious privilege. Instead of making the assassination plot an occasion to initiate an inquiry into the Society of 10 December and irrevocably to expose Bonaparte's real role as chief of the Paris lumpenproletariat before France and all of Europe, it let the conflict sink to a point where all that divided it from the minister of the interior was which of them had the authority to hire and fire the commissioner of police. Thus during the whole of this period we see the party of order compelled by its equivocal position to dissipate and fragment its struggle with the executive into petty disputes over authority, chicanery, legal hair-splitting and demarcation disputes with ministers, and to make the silliest questions of form into the substance of its action. It did not dare to do battle when there was a matter of principle at stake, when the executive was really compromised, and the cause of the national assembly would have been the cause of the nation. By doing that it would have given the nation its marching orders, and it feared nothing so much as that the nation should get on the move. Accordingly it rejected the motions of the *montagne* at those junctures and proceeded to the business of the day. Having put aside the broad question of principle, the executive calmly bided its time until it could take up again on trivial, insignificant matters of merely local parliamentary interest, so to speak. Then the pent-up rage of the party of order bursts out, it tears down the backdrop, denounces the president, declares the republic in danger; but then its pathos appears absurd and the occasion for battle a hypocritical pretext or hardly worth the effort. The parliamentary storm is a storm in a teacup, the battle an intrigue, the conflict a scandal. The revolutionary classes revel in the humiliation of the national assembly, for they were just as enthusiastic for parliamentary privilege as the assembly was for their civil liberties. And the bourgeoisie outside parliament cannot understand how the bourgeoisie inside parliament can waste its time on such trivial back-biting and so compromise public order through such pitiful rivalries with the president. It becomes confused and bewildered by a strategy which makes peace at a time when the whole world expects war, and attacks at a time when the whole world believes that peace has been made.

On 20 December [1850] Pascal Duprat [the Orléanist deputy] cross-examined the minister of the interior on the 'gold bars' lottery. This lottery was blessed by the Elysée, as Bonaparte and his faithful henchmen had brought it into the world, and Carlier the prefect of police had taken it under his wing, although in France all lotteries, with the exception of charitable raffles, were illegal. Seven million tickets at a franc apiece, the profits supposedly earmarked for the transportation of Parisian riff-raff to California. Partly the idea was to replace the socialist dreams of the Paris proletariat with dreams of glistering gold, and the guarantied right to employment with the seductive prospect of the grand prize draw. Of course workers in Paris did not see through the blaze of California gold to the plain old francs winkled from their pockets. But in the main it was just a straightforward swindle. The riff-raff wanting to open up the gold mines of California without the trouble of leaving Paris were Bonaparte himself and his debt-ridden cronies. They had partied through the three million authorised by the national assembly, and the cash box had to be refilled one way or another. Bonaparte had vainly launched a national subscription for so-called workers' towns, putting himself at the head for a substantial donation. Mean-minded bourgeois awaited this with grave suspicion, and when of course it was not forthcoming, the socialist 'castles in the air' crashed to earth. The gold bars were a better draw. Bonaparte & Co. were not satisfied with pocketing part of the profit from the seven million over and above the cost of the prize bullion; they fabricated false lottery tickets, issuing the same number 10 on fifteen or twenty tickets, a financial scam in keeping with the Society of 10 December. Here the national assembly was confronted with the real flesh and blood Bonaparte, and not with the fictional 'president of the republic'. Here it could catch him in open violation of the criminal law rather than of the constitution. If it passed over Duprat's cross-examination and proceeded to the business of the day, this was not just because the motion of confidence in the minister from [the republican deputy] Girardin reminded the party of order of its own systematic corruption. The bourgeois, above all the bourgeois inflated into a statesman, supplements his commonplace practicality with theoretical superfluity. As a statesman he becomes a higher form of existence, like the state power facing him, which can only be contested on an ethereal plane.

Because he was such a bohemian, and such a prince of thieves, Bonaparte had the advantage over bourgeois grafters of fighting dirty; once the national assembly itself had escorted him over the treacherous terrain of regimental dinners, army reviews, the Society of 10 December and finally the criminal law, he saw that the moment had come to go openly on the offensive. He was little troubled with the minor reversals sustained by the minister of justice, minister of war, minister for the navy and minister of finance, through which the national assembly growled its displeasure. Not only did he prevent ministers from resigning, and thus stop the executive from being accountable to parliament, but he was now able to complete what he had begun during the recess of the national assembly: the severance of military power from parliamentary control, *Changarnier's dismissal.*

An Elyséeist paper published an order, allegedly sent during May [1850] to the first army division, hence from Changarnier, in which officers were advised to give no quarter to traitors in their own ranks, should there be an insurrection, but rather to shoot them straight away and to refuse any requisition of troops by the national assembly. On 3 January 1851 questions were put to the cabinet concerning this order. To examine these circumstances it requested a stay of three months at first, then a week, and finally a mere twenty-four hours. The assembly insisted on an immediate explanation. Changarnier rose to explain that no such order had ever existed. He added that he would always hasten to comply with any demands from the national assembly and that it could rely on him in case of conflict. It received this assurance with ineffable applause and voted its confidence in him. By putting itself under the private protection of a general, the national assembly abdicated, decreed its own impotence beside the almighty army, but the general was deceiving himself when he put at the assembly's disposal a force that he held only at Bonaparte's behest, when he expected protection from the parliament which needed him to be its protector.

Changarnier, however, believed in the mysterious power that the bourgeoisie had invested in him since 29 January 1849 [when he and his troops successfully intimidated the constituent assembly]. He considered himself the third governmental power alongside the other two branches of state. He shared in the fate of the other heroes or rather saints of this era whose fame consisted in the biassed reports which their own parties put about, but who collapse into ordinary mortals as soon as they are required to perform miracles. Scepticism is the deadly enemy of these reputed heroes and real-life saints. Hence their self-righteous indignation at the dearth of enthusiasm displayed by wits and scoffers.

That same evening ministers were summoned to the Elysée Palace; Bonaparte insisted on dismissing Changarnier; five refused to sign this; the *Moniteur* announced a ministerial crisis; and the press siding with the party of order threatened to form a parliamentary army under Changarnier's command. The party of order had constitutional authority to take this step. It merely had to appoint Changarnier to the presidency of the national assembly and to requisition any number of troops it pleased for security. It could do this all the more safely as Changarnier was still heading the army and the national guard in Paris and was only waiting to be requisitioned together with the army. The Bonapartist press did not as yet even dare to question the right of the national assembly to requisition troops directly, a legal scruple that did not promise to be of any use under the circumstances. That the army would have obeyed the national assembly is probable, remembering that Bonaparte had to scour all Paris for eight days to find two generals – Baraguay d'Hilliers and Saint-Jean d'Angély – who were ready to countersign Changarnier's dismissal. That the party of order would have found in its own ranks and in parliament the votes necessary for such a resolution is much more doubtful, considering that eight days later 286 of them took their votes elsewhere, and that the *montagne* rejected a similar resolution in December 1851 in the last decisive hours [of the parliamentary regime]. Nonetheless the grandees might perhaps have succeeded in spurring the mass of their party to a heroism consisting in feeling secure behind a forest of bayonets and accepting the services of an army which had deserted in order to join their camp. Instead of doing this the grandees betook themselves to the Elysée on the evening of 6 January [1851] to make Bonaparte desist from sacking Changarnier by using states-manlike phrases and scruples. He who seeks to persuade, acknowl-edges the superiority of the other. Reassured by this, Bonaparte appointed a new cabinet on 12 January [1851], retaining Fould and Baroche, the leaders of the old one. Saint-Jean d'Angély became minister of war, the *Moniteur* published the decree discharging Changarnier, his command was divided between Baraguay d'Hilli-ers, who got the first army division, and Perrot, who got the national guard. The bulwark of society was dismissed, and while the earth did not move, prices did go up on the stock exchange.

The party of order revealed that the bourgeoisie had lost its will to rule in that it had rebuffed the army, which had been at its disposal in the person of Changarnier, and had made it incontro-vertibly accountable to the president. A parliamentary cabinet was no longer in existence. Having lost its grip on the army and the national guard, what means were left for retaining the power over the people it had usurped from parliament and its constitutional power *vis-à-vis* the president? None at all. All that was left was a nugatory appeal to principles, general rules one prescribes to others just to make one's own actions easier. With the dismissal of Chan-garnier and Bonaparte's acquisition of military power, the first part of the period we are considering, the period of conflict between the party of order and the executive power, draws to a close. War between the two authorities was now openly declared and waged, but only after the party of order had lost both weapons and soldiers. Without a cabinet, without an army, without a people, without public opinion, no longer representing the sovereign nation after its electoral law of 31 May [1850], *sans* eyes, *sans* ears, *sans* teeth, *sans* everything, the national assembly was gradually transmuted into a pre-revolutionary *parlement* which left action to the government and had to content itself with whingeing after the event.

The party of order received the new cabinet with a storm of protests. General Bedeau recalled the deference of the executive commission during the recess and the punctiliousness with which it refused publication of its proceedings. The minister of the interior himself now insists on the publication of these minutes which were of course as dull as ditchwater, uncovering nothing new and making not the slightest impression on a *blasé* public. Following a proposal from [the Orléanist] Rémusat, the national assembly retired to its quarters and appointed a 'commission for extraordinary measures'. Ordinary life was very little disturbed in Paris as trade was flourishing, factories were busy, grain prices were low, food was plentiful and savings banks took in new deposits every day. The 'extraordinary measures' which parliament had announced with such a stir then fizzled out into a vote of no-confidence in the minister on 18 January [1851] without a mention of General Changarnier. The party of order was forced to word its resolution in this way to secure the republican vote, since of all the cabinet's measures the discharge of Changarnier was the sole one that it approved of, while it could not complain about the other ministerial actions as it had in fact dictated them itself.

The vote of confidence of 18 January [1851] passed 415 to 286. Hence it was carried only through a *coalition* of staunch legitimists and Orléanists together with the pure republicans and the *montagne*. This proved that in its conflicts with Bonaparte the party of order had lost not just the cabinet and the army but its independent parliamentary majority, that a detachment of representatives had deserted out of fanaticism for compromise, fear of conflict, from boredom, nepotism, expectation of cabinet posts (Odilon Barrot), from the base egoism that always inclines the ordinary bourgeois to sacrifice the common interest of his class to this or that private benefit. From the beginning, Bonapartist representatives only belonged to the party of order to do battle against the revolution. The head of the Catholic party, Montalembert, had already thrown his influence into Bonaparte's begging bowl, because he doubted that the parliamentary party would survive. Finally the leaders of this party, Thiers the Orléanist and Berryer the legitimist, were forced to admit openly their republicanism, to acknowledge that they were royalist at heart but republican in the head, that the parliamentary republic was the only possible form for the rule of the bourgeoisie as a whole. Thus they were forced in front of the whole bourgeoisie to brand the restorationist plots, indefatigably conducted behind the back of parliament, as stupid and dangerous intrigues.

The no-confidence motion of 18 January [1851] hit the cabinet and not the president. But it was the president and not the cabinet that had discharged Changarnier. Ought not the party of order to impeach Bonaparte himself? For his restorationist sympathies?

These were only added to their own. For conspiracy in the military reviews and in the Society of 10 December? They had long ago buried these matters under business as usual. For dismissing the hero of 29 January and 13 June [1849], the man who in May 1850 threatened to set all Paris ablaze in the event of insurrection? Their allies from the *montagne* and Cavaignac did not let them re-erect the fallen bulwark of society by sending an official message of sympathy. Indeed they could not dispute the constitutional authority of the president to discharge a general. They were only fussing because he had made an unparliamentary use of a constitutional right. But had they not made repeated unconstitutional use of parliamentary prerogative, in particular abolishing universal manhood suffrage? They were therefore constrained to work within strict parliamentary limits. This was part and parcel of a peculiar malady that after 1848 spread to a whole continent, *parliamentary cretinism*, which confines its victims to an imaginary world and robs them of their senses, their recollection, all knowledge of the rude external world; it was part of this parliamentary cretinism that the party of order took their parliamentary victories to be real ones and believed they had hit the president when they struck his ministers, although they had themselves destroyed the whole basis of parliamentary power with their own hands as they were bound to in battling against other classes. They merely gave him the opportunity to humiliate the national assembly in front of the nation once again. On 20 January [1851] the *Moniteur* announced that the resignation of the entire cabinet had been accepted. Under the pretext that no parliamentary party had a majority, as was demonstrated by the vote of 18 January [1851] won by the coalition of the *montagne* and the royalists, Bonaparte appointed a so-called transition cabinet while waiting for a new majority to form; not one member of this cabinet was in parliament; it was all unknown and insignificant individuals, a cabinet of mere clerks and scribes. The party of order could now wear itself out playing with these puppets; the executive no longer thought it worthwhile to be seriously represented in the national assembly. Bonaparte concentrated the entire power of the executive in his own person all the more securely and had all the more room to exploit it for his own ends, the more his ministers were reduced to mere ciphers.

The party of order, in coalition with the *montagne*, revenged itself by throwing out a subvention of 1,800,000 francs to the president which the head of the Society of 10 December had pushed his ministerial clerks to propose. This time a majority of only 102 votes decided it; since 28 January [1851] another twenty-seven votes had departed, and the dissolution of the party of order continued apace. To leave no doubt about the nature of its coalition with the *montagne* it disdained even to consider a motion signed by 189 members of the *montagne* for a general amnesty for political offenders. It sufficed for the minister of the interior, a certain Vaïsse, to explain that the present calm was only apparent, but that hidden disorder prevailed, everywhere secret societies were being organised, the democratic papers were preparing to reappear, reports from the *départements* sounded unfavourable, Genevan exiles were directing a conspiracy beyond Lyons through the whole of southern France, France was on the brink of an industrial and commercial crisis, the factories in Roubaix were working short-time, the prisoners on Belle Isle were in revolt – a mere Vaïsse creating a red scare was all that was needed for the party of order to reject without discussion a motion that would have won immense popularity for the national assembly and thrown Bonaparte back into its arms. Instead of allowing the executive to intimidate it with prospects of renewed unrest, it should have yielded a little to the class struggle in order to preserve the dependence of the executive. But it did not feel up to the business of playing with fire.

Meanwhile the so-called transitional cabinet continued to vegetate up to the middle of April. Bonaparte tired and teased the national assembly with constant ministerial shuffles. Sometimes he seemed to want to form a republican cabinet with [the poet] Lamartine and [the Bonapartist] Billault, sometimes a parliamentary one with the inevitable Odilon Barrot, whose name never failed to come up when a dupe was needed, sometimes a legitimist one with Vatimesnil and Benoist d'Azy, sometimes an Orléanist one with Maleville. While he set the different factions of the party of order against one another and frightened them with the prospect of a republican cabinet and the inevitable reinstatement of universal manhood suffrage, he made the bourgeoisie believe that his honest efforts to form a parliamentary ministry had foundered on the intransigence

of the royalist factions. The bourgeoisie cried all the louder for
'strong government', but it found it unforgivable to leave France
'without administration', as an economic crisis appeared to be
advancing and so recruiting socialists in the cities, just as ruinously
low farm prices did in the countryside. Trade was getting slacker
by the day, unemployed hands were increasing noticeably, in Paris
there were at least 10,000 workers without food, in Rouen, Mul-
house, Lyons, Roubaix, Tourcoing, Saint-Etienne, Elbeuf, etc.
innumerable factories were idle. Under these conditions Bonaparte
could risk a restoration on 11 April [1851] of the cabinet of 18
January. Messrs Rouher, Fould, Baroche, etc. strengthened by M.
Léon Faucher, who was censured [on 11 May 1849] during the last
days of the constituent assembly for telegraphing false dispatches,
all of the deputies (save five cabinet ministers) having voted no-
confidence in him. The national assembly had therefore won a victory over the cabinet on 18 January [1851], then struggled for three
months with Bonaparte, so that on 11 April Fould and Baroche
could take on the ultra-moral Faucher as third man in their ministerial cabal.

In November 1849 Bonaparte had been satisfied with an *unparliamentary* cabinet, in January 1851 with an *extra-parliamentary*
one, on 11 April 1851 he felt strong enough to form an *anti-
parliamentary* cabinet, harmoniously combining no-confidence
votes from both assemblies, the constituent and the national,
republicans and royalists. This graded progression of cabinets
was the thermometer by which parliament could measure the
decline in its own vitality. By the end of April this had sunk so
low that [the Bonapartist deputy] Persigny could enjoin Changarnier in a personal interview to go over to the presidential
camp. He assured him that Bonaparte considered the influence
of the national assembly to be completely null and had already
perpetrated a proclamation to be published after the *coup d'état*,
continuously in mind but delayed once again for contingent
reasons. Changarnier imparted this obituary to the leaders of the
party of order, but whoever believes that such flea-bites are fatal?
And the assembly, defeated, disintegrated, rotting as it was, could
not bring itself to see the fight with the grotesque chief of the
Society of 10 December as other than a fight with a flea. But
Bonaparte answered the party of order as Agesilaus [King of

Sparta] answered King [Tachos] of Egypt: 'I may seem an ant to you but one day I shall be a lion.'

VI

In its futile endeavours to keep possession of military power and to reconquer supreme control of executive power, the party of order saw itself condemned to remain in coalition with the *montagne* and the pure republicans, proving incontrovertibly that it had lost its independent *parliamentary majority*. The mere advance of dates and ticking of the clock gave the signal on 28 May [1851] for its complete disintegration. The 28th of May marked the beginning of the last year of life for the national assembly. It had now to decide whether to keep the constitution unchanged or revise it. But constitutional revision did not only involve bourgeois rule or petty-bourgeois democracy, democracy or proletarian anarchy, parliamentary republic or Bonaparte, it also meant Orléans or Bourbon! Thus the apple of discord fell into the midst of parliament, opening up conflicts of interest and sundering the party of order into warring factions. The party of order was a conglomerate of heterogeneous social components. Constitutional revision raised the political temperature to the point where decomposition had to occur.

The Bonapartists' interest in revision was simple. They were concerned above all with the question of abolishing [chapter v] § 45, which forbade Bonaparte's re-election and any continuation of his authority. No less simple was that of the republicans. They unconditionally rejected any revision, seeing in it a comprehensive conspiracy against the republic. Since they held sway over more than a quarter of the votes in the national assembly, and constitutionally three quarters of the votes were required for a valid motion for revision and for summoning a revising convention, they needed only to tally their votes to make sure of victory. And they were.

Compared to these clear positions, the party of order found itself entangled in contradictions. If it rejected revision, it endangered the status quo by leaving Bonaparte only one way out, force, and by abandoning France to revolutionary anarchy at the deciding moment of 9 May [1852], with a president who had lost his authority, with a parliament which no longer possessed it, and with a people who thought they would conquer it again. The party of order knew that to vote for revision in accordance with the constitution would be to vote for nothing and would have to fail constitutionally because of the republican veto. If it declared a simple majority to be binding, in defiance of the constitution, then it could hope to master the revolution only if it subordinated itself unconditionally to the sovereignty of the executive and thus made Bonaparte master of the constitution, of any revision and of the party of order itself. A merely partial revision prolonging the authority of the president would pave the way for an imperial take-over. A general revision which shortened the existence of the republic would bring dynastic claims into inevitable conflict, for the conditions for a Bourbon restoration and for an Orléanist one were not merely different but mutually exclusive.

The *parliamentary republic* was more than the neutral territory where the two factions of the French bourgeoisie, legitimists and Orléanist, large-scale landed property and industry, could take up residence with an equal right. It was the inescapable condition of their *joint* rule, the sole form of state in which the claims of their particular factions and those of all other classes of society were subjected to the general interest of the bourgeois class. As royalists they relapsed into their old antagonism, a battle for supremacy between landed property and money, and the highest expression of this antagonism, the personification of it, were their kings, their dynasties. Hence the resistance of the party of order to the *recall of the Bourbons*.

In 1849, 1850 and 1851 the Orléanist deputy Creton had regularly introduced a measure to rescind the decree exiling the royal families. Parliament just as regularly presented the spectacle of an assembly barring the gate through which their exiled kings could come home. Richard III murdered Henry VI with the remark [in Shakespeare's play] that he was too good for this world and belonged in heaven. They declared that France was too bad to have the kings back again. They had become republicans through force of circumstances, and they repeatedly sanctioned the decision by the people to banish their kings from France.

A revision of the constitution – and circumstances compelled this – called into question the republic as well as the joint rule of the two bourgeois factions, and the possibility of monarchy brought back to life a rivalry between interests it had promoted in turn, and the battle for supremacy of one faction over the other. The diplomats of the party of order thought that they could settle the struggle by merging the two dynasties, a so-called *fusion* of the royalist parties and their royal houses. The real fusion of the restoration and the July monarchy was the parliamentary republic in which Orléanist and legitimist colours were extinguished and the various varieties of the type bourgeois disappeared into the bourgeois pure and simple, into the bourgeois species. But now the Orléanist was to become legitimist and the legitimist Orléanist. Royalism, which personified their antagonism, was to embody their unity, the expression of their exclusive factional interests was to become an expression of the common class interest, the monarchy was to accomplish what only the abolition of two monarchies – the republic – could do and had done. This was the philosophers' stone, and the learned doctors of the party of order racked their brains to produce it. As if the legitimate monarchy could ever become the monarchy of the industrial bourgeoisie, or the bourgeois kingdom the kingdom of the hereditary landed aristocracy. As if landed property and industry could fraternise together under a single crown, when the crown could be lowered onto a single head, the head of the elder brother or the younger one. As if industry could be reconciled at all with landed property, so long as landed property did not decide to go industrial itself. If Henri V [Bourbon] were to die tomorrow, the [Orléanist] comte de Paris [grandson of Louis Philippe] would not become the legitimist king, unless he ceased being the Orléanist king. The philosophers of fusion who achieved wide circulation as the question of constitutional revision came to prominence, who had created an official voice in the daily *Assemblée nationale*, working away at this very moment [February 1852], explained all the difficulties in terms of the conflict and rivalry between the two dynasties. The attempt to reconcile the house of Orléans with Henri V, begun after the death of Louis Philippe, was only played out, like dynastic intrigues in general, during the recesses of the national assembly, in the intervals, behind the scenes, more sentimental coquetry with ancient superstition than business in earnest; these now became high affairs of state and were performed by the party of order on the public stage instead of in amateur theatricals as before. The couriers flew from Paris to [the legitimist pretender in] Venice, from Venice to [the Orléanists at] Claremont, from Claremont to Paris.

The [Bourbon] comte de Chambord [known as King Henri V] issued a manifesto announcing not his own but the 'national restoration' 'with the help of all members of his family'. The Orléanist [politician] Salvandy threw himself at the feet of Henri V. The legitimist leaders Berryer, Benoit d'Azy, Saint-Priest, journeyed to Claremont to persuade the Orléanists but without success. Too late did the fusionists perceive that the interests of the two factions of the bourgeoisie did not lose their differences or gain in compliance when crystallised into family interests, the interests of the two royal houses. If Henri V recognised the comte de Paris as his successor – the best outcome that fusion could achieve – then the house of Orléans would not win anything that was not already assured by the childlessness of Henri V, but it would lose everything gained in the July revolution. It would abandon its original objectives, all the authority wrung from the elder branch of the Bourbons in more than a hundred years of struggle; it would have exchanged its historical prerogative, the prerogative of modern monarchy, for the prerogative of its ancestral line. Fusion was therefore nothing other than a voluntary abdication by the house of Orléans, a resignation in favour of legitimism, a penitent retreat from the Protestant state church into the Catholic one. A retreat would not bring it to the throne it had lost but to the steps of the throne from which it was born. The old Orléanist ministers Guizot, Duchâtel, etc., who had hastened to Claremont to speak up for fusion, only represented regret for the July revolution in the first place, a despair in the bourgeois monarchy and in the monarchism of the bourgeois, superstitious belief in legitimism as the last amulet to ward off anarchy. In their imagination they were mediators between Orléans and Bourbon, but were in reality only backsliding Orléanists, and the prince de Joinville [son of Louis Philippe] received them as such. On the other hand the Orléanists who were wide-awake and wanting a fight – Thiers, Baze, etc. – convinced the family of Louis Philippe all the more easily that if any direct restoration of the monarchy were the fusion of the two dynasties, presupposing the abdication of the house of Orléans, then it corresponded entirely to the tradition of its forebears to recognise the republic straight away and to await the conversion of the president's seat into a throne when events permitted. Joinville was widely touted as a candidate [for the presidency of the republic], the public curiously was kept in suspense, and a few months later after constitutional revision was rejected, his candidature was announced in September [1851].

The attempt at a royalist fusion of Orléanists and legitimists had not only foundered, it had broken up their *parliamentary fusion*, their common republican mode, and had again split the party of order into its original constituents; but as Claremont and Venice grew more estranged from each other, their working arrangements collapsed, and support for Joinville mounted, so the negotiations between Faucher, Bonaparte's minister, and the legitimists grew more pressing and serious.

The disintegration of the party of order did not stop at its original elements. Each of the two great factions underwent further fragmentation. It was as if all the old nuances that had previously jostled and conflicted within the two circles, legitimist and Orléanist, were once again brought to life like dried infusoria on contact with water, as if they had regained enough vital energy to form their own groups and take independent positions. The legitimists imagined they had returned to the disputes [during the restoration period] between the Tuileries [where Louis XVIII held court] and the Pavillon Marsan [where the reactionary comte d'Artois resided], between [the corresponding political rivals] Villèle and Polignac. The Orléanists relived the golden age of knightly tournaments between Guizot, Molé, Broglie, Thiers and Odilon Barrot.

The section of the party of order that was eager for constitutional revision, but disunited concerning the bounds of the exercise, composed of legitimists under Berryer and Falloux on the one hand and under La Rochejaquelin on the other, and the battle-weary Orléanists under Molé, Broglie, Montalembert and Odilon Barrot, agreed the following indeterminate and sweeping motion with the Bonapartist representatives: 'The undersigned representatives, aiming to restore the nation to the full exercise of its sovereignty, move that the constitution be revised.' But at the same time they unanimously declared through their rapporteur [the legitimist historian and deputy Alexis de] Tocqueville that the national assembly did not have the right to undertake the *abolition of the republic*, that this right belonged only to a constitutional convention. Otherwise the constitution could only be revised *in a 'legal' manner* when the constitutionally prescribed three-quarters of the votes were cast for revision. On 19 July [1851], after six days of stormy debate, they threw out constitutional revision, as expected. There were 446 votes in favour but 278 against. The staunch Orléanists Thiers, Changarnier, etc. voted with the republicans and the *montagne*.

A parliamentary majority had declared against the constitution, but the constitution itself had declared for *the* minority, and for its decision to be binding. But hadn't the party of order subordinated the constitution to the parliamentary majority on 31 May 1850 and 13 June 1849? Didn't its whole previous policy rest on subordinating the articles of the constitution to majority decisions in parliament? Hadn't it left an Old Testament belief in the letter of law to the democrats and punished them for it? But at this moment constitutional revision meant nothing but continuation of presidential power, just as continuation of the constitution meant nothing but the removal of Bonaparte. Parliament had declared for him, but the constitution declared against parliament. Therefore he carried out the will of parliament when he tore up the constitution, and he carried out the will of the constitution when he sent parliament packing.

Parliament had declared the constitution and perforce its own authority to be 'beyond majorities', it had abolished the constitution with its own decision and augmented the president's power, and yet was saying at the same time that the one could not die nor the other live so long as parliament itself continued. Its grave diggers were on the doorstep. While it debated the question of revision, Bonaparte relieved General Baraguay d'Hilliers, who was indecisive, from the command of the first army division and appointed General Magnan to the post, the victor [over the workers] of Lyons [on 15 June 1849], the hero of the December days [of 1848], one of his creatures who had more or less compromised himself under Louis Philippe in connection with the march from Boulogne.

By its decision on constitutional revision the party of order proved that it could neither rule nor obey, neither live nor die, neither tolerate the republic nor overthrow it, neither stick to the constitution nor throw it overboard, neither cooperate with the president nor break off with him. Who then was it expecting to resolve these contradictions? The calendar, the course of events. It stopped pretending to have any control over events. It therefore challenged events to take control, hence surrendering to that power one thing after another in battling the people until it was impotent; hence the chief executive could produce a battle plan undisturbed, strengthen the means of attack, choose the instruments for it, fortify his positions, precisely because they decided to withdraw from the stage during this critical time and to recess for three months, from 10 August until 4 November [1851].

Not only was the parliamentary party divided into its two great factions [party of order and *montagne*] and each faction divided within itself, but the party of order within parliament had fallen out with the party of order *outside* parliament. The spokesmen and writers for the bourgeoisie, their publicity and press, in short the ideologues of the bourgeoisie and the bourgeoisie itself, representatives and represented, were caught in mutual estrangement and incomprehension.

The legitimists in the provinces, with their limited horizons and unbridled enthusiasm, censured their parliamentary leaders Berryer and Falloux for deserting to Bonaparte's camp and abandoning Henri V. Their understanding, pure as their *fleur de lis*, encompassed original sin but not diplomacy.

Far more fateful and decisive was the breach between the commercial bourgeois and their politicians. They reproached them not, as the legitimists had done with theirs, for abandoning their principles, but on the contrary for clinging to principles that had become useless.

I have pointed out earlier that after Fould's accession to the cabinet a part of the commercial bourgeoisie who had taken the lion's share of power under Louis Philippe, the *financial aristocracy*, had become Bonapartist. Fould did not only represent Bonaparte's interests on the bourse, he also represented the interest of the bourse with Bonaparte. The position of the financial aristocracy is depicted most strikingly in a quotation from its European mouthpiece, the London *Economist*. In its issue of 1 February 1851 there was this dispatch from Paris: 'Now we have it stated from numerous quarters that France wishes above all things for repose. The President declares it in his message to the Legislative Assembly, it is echoed from the tribune, it is asserted in the journals, it is announced from the pulpit, *it is demonstrated by the sensitiveness of the public funds at the least prospect of disturbance, and their firmness whenever the executive power is victorious.*'

In the issue of 29 November 1851 *The Economist* itself tells us: '*The president is recognised by all Europe as the guardian of order, and on all the stock exchanges.*' The financial aristocracy thus condemned the parliamentary battle between the party of order and the executive power as a *disruption of order*, and celebrated every victory of the president over its own alleged representatives as a *victory for order*. Under financial aristocracy we must understand here not only the great merchant banks and speculators in public funds whose interests we can immediately grasp as coincident with those of the state. The whole of the modern money market, the whole banking business, is interwoven with public credit in the most intimate way. A part of their business capital is necessarily put out at interest in readily convertible government issue. Their deposits, the capital put at their disposal and divided by them amongst merchants and industrialists, derive for the most part from the dividends of government bondholders. For the whole money market and its priests in every epoch, stability of state power was all the law and the prophets; how could this not be more so today when every deluge threatens to wash away the indebtedness of existing states along with the states themselves?

Fanatical for order, the *industrial bourgeoisie* was also worked up about the quarrel between the parliamentary party of order and the executive. After voting on 18 January [1851] for Changarnier's dismissal, Thiers, Anglès, Sainte-Beuve, etc. [representatives in the 'party of order'] received a public reprimand from their constituents in just those industrial districts excoriating their coalition with the *montagne* as high treason to the cause. If, as we have seen, the open mockery, the petty intrigues that characterised the struggle between the party of order and the president, deserved no better reception, then on the other hand this bourgeois party, demanding that its representatives let military power slip, just like that, from its own parliament to a fake-on-the-make, was not worth the efforts that were wasted on intriguing for it. It demonstrated that the battle for retaining its *public* interests, its own *class interests*, its *political power*, represented only the annoyance and ill-temper of an inconvenience in private affairs.

With scarcely an exception the bourgeois dignitaries of the provincial towns, the magistrates, judges, etc. received Bonaparte in the most servile way on his tours, even when he made an unrestrained attack on the national assembly, and especially the party of order, as in Dijon [on 1 June 1851].

When trade was going well, as at the beginning of 1851, the commercial bourgeoisie objected to any parliamentary struggle lest the heart should go out of it. When trade was going badly, as it was persistently since the end of February 1851, they intoned that parliamentary struggles were the cause of the slump and shouted for them to desist so that trade could pick up. The debate on constitutional revision fell into just this period of difficulty. Since it was the existence or non-existence of the state in its present form that was at stake, here the bourgeoisie felt all the more justified in demanding that its representatives put an end to this excruciating interregnum and retain the status quo. There was no contradiction in this. By the end of the interregnum they understood its actual continuation, postponing the moment of decision to a distant future. The status quo could only be retained in two ways: by prolonging Bonaparte's authority or by retiring him as constitutionally prescribed and electing Cavaignac. One part of the bourgeoisie desired the latter solution and could give its deputies no better advice than to shut up and steer clear of the whole issue. If their representatives did not speak, so they thought, Bonaparte would not act. They wanted a parliamentary ostrich that would hide its head to make itself invisible. Another part of the bourgeoisie wanted Bonaparte to stay as president because he already occupied the position, keeping everything in the same old rut. They were worked up that their parliament had not openly breached the constitution and unceremoniously abdicated.

The councils of the *départements*, those provincial representatives of the richest bourgeoisie, meeting from 25 August [1851] onwards during the recess of the national assembly, declared almost unanimously for constitutional revision, hence against parliament and for Bonaparte.

The bourgeoisie vented its ire on its literary representatives, on its own daily press, even more unambiguously than it did when it fell out with its *parliamentary representatives*. Not only France but the whole of Europe was astounded by the judgements enforcing ruinous fines and shamefully long prison sentences that bourgeois juries brought in every time bourgeois journalists attacked Bonaparte's desire to seize power, or attempted to defend the political rights of the bourgeoisie against the executive.

I have shown how the parliamentary party of order, crying for peace, condemned itself to acquiescence, how it declared the political power of the bourgeoisie incompatible with the security and existence of the bourgeoisie by destroying with its own hand all conditions for its own regime, the parliamentary regime, in the war against other classes in society, hence the *extraparliamentary bulk of the bourgeoisie* enjoined Bonaparte to suppress, to annihilate its own pen and voice, its publicists and politicians, speakers and press, through its own servility towards the president, its vilification of parliament, its brutal mistreatment of its own press, so that it could pursue its private affairs in full confidence under the protection of a strong and unrestricted government. It declared unambiguously that it longed to be rid of its own political power in order to be rid of the burdens and dangers of ruling.

And this miserable, cowardly lot, which was scandalised by the merely parliamentary and literary battle for its own class to govern and had betrayed the leaders of this struggle, now dares to indict the proletariat for not rising up in a bloody struggle, a life and death struggle on its behalf! This lot, who every moment sacrifice their overall class interests, i.e. their political interests, to the narrowest and dirtiest private interests, and expected a similar sacrifice of their representatives, now blubbers that the proletariat has sacrificed the ideal political interests of the bourgeoisie to the material interests of the proletariat. It poses as an uncorrupted soul, misunderstood by an egotistical proletariat led astray by socialists, and abandoned at the decisive moment. And it finds an echo in the bourgeois world. Of course I am not referring here to small-time German politicians and intellectual low-life. I refer for example to *The Economist* which was still writing as late as 29 November 1851, hence four days before the *coup d'état*, that Bonaparte was the 'guardian of order', and Thiers and Berryer were 'anarchists', and then on 27 December 1851, after Bonaparte had silenced these anarchists, it was screaming about a betrayal of the 'skill, knowledge, discipline, mental influence, intellectual resources and moral weight of the middle and upper ranks of society' that had been committed by the 'masses of ignorant, untrained and stupid *prolétaires*'. The stupid, ignorant and vulgar mass was none other than the greater part of the bourgeoisie itself.

During 1851 France had in any case experienced a kind of minor economic crisis. The end of February showed a decline in exports compared with 1850; in March trade suffered and factories closed down, in April the condition of the industrial *départements* appeared to be as desperate as after the February days [of 1848], in May [1850] business had still not revived; as late as 28 June the portfolio of the bank of France revealed that production was at a standstill, as there was an immense growth in deposits and an equally great decline in cash advances on bills of exchange, and it was not till mid-October that a progressive improvement in business set in once more. The French bourgeoisie attributed this trade slump to purely political causes, the conflict between parliament and the executive, uncertainty with a merely provisional type of state, the horrifying prospect of 9 May 1852 [when Bonaparte's presidential term was to end]. I will not deny that all these circumstances depressed some branches of industry in Paris and in the *départements*. But in any case the effect of political events was only local and insignificant. Does this need any more proof than that an improvement in trade appeared about the middle of October at the time that political conditions got worse, the political horizon clouded over and a thunderbolt from the Elysée was expected at any moment? The French bourgeois, whose 'skill, knowledge, spiritual insight and intellectual resource' reach no further than his nose, could otherwise have poked it into the cause of his commercial afflictions at any time during the Great [Industrial] Exhibition [of 1851] in London. While in France factories were closed down, in England there were commercial bankruptcies. While industrial panic reached a high point in France in April and May, commercial panic peaked in England at the same time. As the French woollen industry suffered, so did the English one; as French silk manufacturing, so with English; English cotton mills continued to work, but not with the same profits as in 1849 and 1850. The difference was only that the crisis in France was industrial and in England commercial; while factories in France were idle, the ones in England expanded output but under less favourable conditions than in previous years; in France exports took the major blow, and in England imports. The common factor, which was obviously not to be found within the bounds of the French political horizon, was plain to see. The years 1849 and 1850 were a period of the greatest material prosperity, and a glut only appeared as such in 1851. At the beginning of that year it got a particular boost from the prospect of the [London] industrial exhibition. Special circumstances also contributed: first, the partial failure of the cotton crop in 1850 and 1851, then the certainty of a bigger crop than expected; first the rise, then the sudden collapse, in short, fluctuations in the price of cotton. The raw silk harvest, at least in France, turned out to be even lower than average. And finally the wool industry had expanded so much since 1848 that production could not keep up, and the price of raw wool rose out of all proportion to the price of finished cloth. Here in the raw materials for three major world industries we already have the explanation for a trade slump three times over. Abstracting from these special circumstances, the apparent crisis of 1851 was none other than the dead stop that is brought about by over-production and speculative fever as depicted in every trade cycle before they join forces for a last feverish rush through the final phase to get back to their starting point, the *general economic crisis*. During such interruptions in trade, commercial bankruptcies break out in England, while in France industry itself is made idle, partly through being forced to withdraw from markets where competition with the English was becoming unsustainable, partly because luxury goods are particularly hit by any slow down in business. So besides the general crisis, France had its own national one, which was defined and conditioned by the general situation in the world markets far more than by local influences in France. It is not without interest to contrast the prejudice of the French bourgeois with the judgement of the English. One of the great commercial houses in Liverpool wrote in its annual report for 1851 [as reported in *The Economist*]:

> Few years have more thoroughly belied the anticipations formed at their commencement than the one just closed; instead of the great prosperity which was almost unanimously looked for, it has proved one of the most discouraging that has been seen for the last quarter of a century – this, of course, refers to the mercantile, not to the manufacturing classes. And yet there certainly were grounds for anticipating the reverse at the beginning of the year – stocks of produce were moderate, money was abundant, and food

was cheap, a plentiful harvest well secured, unbroken peace on the continent, and no political or fiscal disturbances at home; indeed, the wings of commerce were never more unfettered ... To what source, then is this disastrous result to be attributed? We believe to *overtrading* both in imports and exports. Unless our merchants will put more stringent limits to their freedom of action, nothing but a *triennial* panic can keep us in check.

Now picture the French bourgeois, how in the midst of this commercial panic his trade-sick brain is tortured, addled, stunned by rumours of a *coup d'état* and of the restoration of universal manhood suffrage, by the struggle between parliament and the executive, by the guerilla warfare between Orléanists and legitimists, by communistic conspiracies in the south, by purported rural revolts in the Nièvre and Cher, by publicity from various presidential candidates, by quackish solutions from the press, by threats from the republicans to uphold the constitution and the general right to vote by force of arms, by evangelising from émigré heroes in exile who predict the end of the world on 9 May 1852, and you'll now understand why in the middle of this unspeakable, deafening chaos of fusion, revision, dissolution, constitution, conspiracy, coalition, emigration, usurpation and revolution, the crazed bourgeois snorts at his parliamentary republic: '*Better an end to terror than terror without end!*'

Bonaparte understood this cry. His powers of comprehension had been sharpened by the growing uproar amongst creditors, who, seeing settlement day 9 May 1852 draw nearer with every setting of the sun, observed a protest in the stars against their earthly bills of exchange. They had turned into veritable astrologers. The national assembly had cut off Bonaparte's hopes for a constitutional variance prolonging power, and the candidature of the prince de Joinville forbade further vacillation.

If there was ever an event that cast a shadow before it arrived it was Bonaparte's *coup d'état*. As early as 29 January 1849, scarcely a month after his election, he had put such a proposal to Changarnier. His own prime minister Odilon Barrot had secretly denounced the politics of the coup in the summer of 1849, and Thiers had done this publicly in the winter of 1850. In May 1851 Persigny had once again tried to enlist Changarnier for the coup, the paper *Messager de l'Assemblée* had published these negotiations, with every parliamentary fracas the Bonapartist journals threatened a coup, and the nearer the crisis got to them the more noise they made. In the orgies which Bonaparte celebrated every night with the men and women of the 'mob', each time midnight approached and flowing drink loosened tongues and excited imaginations, the coup would be fixed for the following morning. Swords were drawn, glasses clinked, representatives thrown out the window, the imperial mantle fell onto Bonaparte's shoulders, until the next morning the spectre vanished again and an astonished Paris learned of the danger, that it had once more escaped, from vestals of little discretion and paladins of indiscretion. During the months of September and October [1851] rumours of a *coup d'état* came thick and fast. At the same time the shades took on colour like a touched-up photographic plate. If you look up the September and October numbers of the European press you will find word-for-word intimations like the following: 'Paris seethes with rumoured coup. The capital will be entered by troops during the night, and the next morning will bring decrees to dissolve the national assembly, to place the *département* of the Seine under siege, to restore universal manhood suffrage, to appeal to the people. Bonaparte is to seek ministers for the execution of these illegal measures.' The correspondents who bring these reports always end them with the single word '*postponed*'. The *coup d'état* had always been Bonaparte's *idée fixe*. With this obsession he returned to French soil. It possessed him so thoroughly that he continually gave it away and blurted it out. He was so weak that he gave it up again just as often. The shadow of the coup had become so familiar to Parisians as a shade that they could not believe in it when it finally appeared in flesh and blood. What allowed the coup to succeed was therefore neither cautious discretion on the part of the head of the Society of 10 December nor an ambush of an unsuspecting national assembly. When it succeeded, it did so in spite of his indiscretion and with the foreknowledge of the assembly, a necessary, inevitable result of previous developments.

On 10 October [1851] Bonaparte informed his ministers of his decision to restore universal manhood suffrage once again, on the 16th they handed in their resignations, on the 26th Paris learned that a cabinet headed by [the Bonapartist] Thorigny had been formed. At the same time the prefect of police Carlier was replaced by [the Bonapartist] Maupas, the commander of the first army division. [General] Magnan concentrated the most reliable regiments in the capital. On 4 November [1851] the national assembly went back into session. It could do no more than recapitulate what it had already gone through in abbreviated form and to demonstrate that after death comes burial.

The first outpost that it lost in the battle with the executive was the cabinet. It had solemnly to acknowledge this loss by giving full credence to the Thorigny cabinet, a mere sham. The executive commission received [the minister of education] M. Giraud with laughter when he presented himself in the name of the new ministers. Such a weak cabinet for formidable measures such as the restoration of universal manhood suffrage! But that was just what it was about, to do nothing in parliament, to do everything *against* it.

On the very first day of the new session the national assembly received Bonaparte's message demanding the restoration of universal manhood suffrage and abolishing the law of 31 May 1850. The same day his ministers introduced a decree to that effect. The assembly rejected straight away the ministers' motion of urgency, and on 13 November [1851] the law itself, 355 to 348. Thus it tore up its mandate one more time; it confirmed one more time that it had transformed itself from the freely elected representative of the people into the usurping parliament of a class; it acknowledged once again that it had cut the integuments linking the parliamentary head with the body of the nation.

While the executive appealed over the national assembly to the people, through its proposal to restore universal manhood suffrage, the legislature appealed over the people to the army through its commissioners' bill. This bill was to establish a right to requisition troops directly, to form a parliamentary army. While it thus designated the army as mediator between itself and the people, between itself and Bonaparte, while it recognised the army as the superior power in the state, it had to confirm, on the other hand, that it had long ago given up its claim to command it. By debating the right of requisition, rather than requisitioning them at once, it made evident its doubts about its own power. By throwing out the commissioners' bill, it publicly confessed its impotence. This bill was 108 votes short of a majority, so the *montagne* had decided the outcome. It found itself in the position of Buridan's ass, though not between two sacks of hay and having to decide which is the more attractive, but between two thorough drubbings and having to decide which is the harder. On the one hand there was fear of Changarnier, on the other, there was fear of Bonaparte. One has to say that the situation did not allow for heroism.

On 18 November [1851] an amendment was proposed to the law on municipal elections that had been brought in by the party of order itself, changing the three-year residence requirement for municipal electors to one year. The amendment fell by a single vote, but this single vote was immediately revealed to be an error. When the party of order splintered into hostile factions, it forfeited its independent parliamentary majority. Now it demonstrated that there was no longer any parliamentary majority at all. The national assembly had become *incapable of making decisions*. Its atomistic constituent parts were no longer cohesive, it had drawn its last breath, it was dead.

Finally a few days before the catastrophe, the extra-parliamentary mass of the bourgeoisie confirmed its break with the bourgeoisie in parliament. Thiers, a parliamentary hero with an incurable case of parliamentary cretinism, had hatched a new parliamentary intrigue together with the council of state, after parliament had died; this was an accountability act to keep the president within constitutional bounds. On 15 September [1851], at the dedication of a new market hall in Paris, Bonaparte charmed the market women, the fishwives, like a second Masaniello [a fisherman who led a Neapolitan rebellion against Spanish rule in 1647] – in any case one fishwife outweighed seventeen grandees [of the 'party of order'] in terms of real power – so in the same way, after the introduction of the commissioners' bill, he inspired the lieutenants who were wined and dined at the Elysée, and again on 25 November [1851] he enthralled the industrial bourgeoisie who had gathered at the circus [in Paris] to receive their prize medals for the Great [Industrial] Exhibition in London from his very own hand. I present here the most significant part of his speech as reported in the *Journal des débats* [on the 26th]:

> With such unhoped-for results, I am justified in repeating how great the French Republic would become if she were allowed to follow her real interests, and to reform her institutions, instead of being incessantly troubled, on the one side by demagogism, and on the other by monarchical hallucinations. (Loud, stormy, repeated applause from every part of the amphitheatre.) The monarchical hallucinations impede all progress and all kinds of serious industry.

In place of advancing, there is only a struggle. Men are seen who, heretofore the most ardent supporters of the prerogatives and the authority of royalty, become partisans of a convention for the purpose of weakening that authority, which is the issue of popular suffrage. (Loud and repeated applause.) We see those who have suffered the most from, and who have deplored revolution the most, provoke a new one, simply to fetter the will of the nation ... I promise you public order in future, etc. etc. (Bravo, bravo, a storm of bravos.)

And so the industrial bourgeoisie applauded the coup of 2 December [1851], the annihilation of parliament, the downfall of its own government, the dictatorship of Bonaparte, with servile bravos. The thunderous cheers of 25 November were answered in the thunderous cannons of 3 to 6 December [1851], and it was the house of [the industrialist] M. Sallandrouze, who had clapped to the rafters, that got clapped to bits by the most bombs.

Cromwell, when he dissolved the Long Parliament, went alone into the midst of the chamber, drew out his watch so that it should not carry on a minute past the limit he had fixed for it, and then drove out every single member with jovial banter and abuse. Napoleon, smaller than his precursor, at least betook himself into the legislative body on 18 Brumaire and read out, even if in a faltering voice, its sentence of death. As it happens, the second Bonaparte found himself in possession of an executive power quite different from that of Cromwell and Napoleon, and he sought his model in the annals of the Society of 10 December, in the annals of criminality, not in the annals of world history. He robs the bank of France of 25 million francs, buys General Magnan with a million and the soldiers bit by bit with 15 francs apiece and booze, gathers his accomplices in secret like a thief in the night, has the houses of the most dangerous parliamentary leaders broken into, and Cavaignac, Lamoricière, Le Flô, Changarnier, Charras, Thiers, Baze, etc. dragged from their beds, the main squares and parliament buildings in Paris occupied by troops, propagandistic notices stuck on all the walls early in the morning proclaiming the dissolution of the national assembly and the council of state, the restoration of the general right to vote and the imposition of a state of siege in the *département* of the Seine. Shortly after that he inserted a false document in the *Moniteur* to the effect that influential parliamentarians had grouped themselves around him in a commission of state.

The rump parliament, consisting mainly of legitimists and Orléanists, assembled in the *mairie* of the 10th arrondissement and voted Bonaparte's removal amid repeated cheers of 'long live the republic', harangued the gaping crowds outside to no avail, and was finally marched off by a company of African sharpshooters first to the d'Orsay barracks, later packed into prison vans and transported to prisons at Mazas, Ham and Vincennes. Thus ended the party of order, the national assembly and the February revolution. Before we hasten to our conclusion, here is a brief summary of its history:

I *First period.* From 24 February to 4 May 1848. February period. Prologue. Sham solidarity.

II *Second period.* Period of founding the republic and of the constituent assembly.

    (1) 4 May to 25 June 1848. Struggle of all classes against the proletariat. Defeat of the proletariat in the June days.

    (2) 25 June to December 1848. Dictatorship of the pure bourgeois republicans. Drafting of the constitution. Imposition of a state of siege in Paris. The bourgeois dictatorship supplanted by Bonaparte's election to the presidency on 10 December.

    (3) 20 December 1848 to 28 May 1849. Struggle of the constituent assembly with Bonaparte and with the party of order in alliance with him. End of the constituent assembly. Fall of the republican bourgeoisie.

III *Third period.* Period of the *constitutional republic* and the *legislative national assembly.*

    (1) 28 May 1849 to 13 June 1849. Struggle of the petty-bourgeois with the bourgeoisie and with Bonaparte. Defeat of petty-bourgeois democrats.

    (2) 13 June 1849 to 31 May 1850. Parliamentary dictatorship of the party of order. Completion of its supremacy through the abolition of the general right to vote, but loss of parliamentary control over the cabinet.

    (3) 31 May 1850 to 2 December 1851. Struggle between the parliamentary bourgeoisie and Bonaparte.

        (a) 31 May 1850 to 12 January 1851. Parliament loses supreme command of the army.

(b) 12 January to 11 April 1851. It fails in its attempts to regain administrative authority. The party of order loses its independent parliamentary majority. Coalition with the republicans and the *montagne*.

(c) 11 April 1851 to 9 October 1851. Attempts at revising [the constitution], fusing [the royalist parties], suspending [presidential power]. The party of order splits into its constituent parts. The breach between bourgeois parliament and bourgeois press, and the mass of the bourgeoisie, is consolidated.

(d) 9 October 1851 to 2 December 1851. Open break between parliament and the executive. Parliament completes its death scene and fades out, left in the lurch by its own class, by the army, by all other classes. End of the parliamentary regime and of the rule of the bourgeoisie. Victory for Bonaparte. Parody of an imperial restoration.

VII

The *social republic* appeared as a phrase, as a prophecy on the threshold of the February revolution. In the June days of 1848 it was drowned in the blood of the *Paris proletariat*, but it stalked the succeeding acts of the drama as a spectre. The *democratic republic* then announced itself. It fizzled out on 13 June 1849 with its turncoat *petty-bourgeoisie*, but in fleeing it left redoubled boasts behind. The *parliamentary republic* and its bourgeoisie occupied the entire stage, living life to the full, but 2 December 1851 buried it amid anguished cries from the royalist coalition of 'long live the republic!'

The social and democratic republic took a beating but the parliamentary republic, the republic of the royalist bourgeoisie, went onto the rocks, as did the pure republic, the republic of the bourgeois republicans.

The French bourgeoisie balked at the rule of the working proletariat, so it brought the lumpenproletariat to power, making the chief of the Society of 10 December its head. The bourgeoisie kept France in breathless terror at the prospective horrors of red anarchy; Bonaparte sold it this future cheaply when on 3 and 4 December he had the distinguished citizenry of the Boulevard Montmartre and the Boulevard des Italiens shot through their own windows by the drunken army of order. It deified the sword; now the sword rules over it. It destroyed the revolutionary press; now its own press is destroyed. It put public meetings under police surveillance; now its drawing rooms are spied on by the police. It disbanded the democratic national guard; its own national guard has been disbanded. It imposed a state of siege; now a state of siege has been imposed on it. It replaced juries with military commissions; now its juries have been militarised. It put public education under the influence of the church; now the church subjects it to its own education. It transported people without trial; now it has been transported itself without trial. It suppressed every impulse in society through the use of state power; now every impulse of its society is crushed by state power. It rebelled against its own politicians and intellectuals to line its own pocket; now its politicians and intellectuals have been disposed of, but after its mouth was gagged and its presses smashed, its pocket has been picked. The bourgeoisie never tired of proclaiming to the revolution what Saint Arsenius said to the Christians: '*Fuge, Tace, Quiesce!*' 'Run away, be quiet, keep still!' Bonaparte admonishes the bourgeoisie: 'Run away, be quiet, keep still!'

The French bourgeoisie had long ago resolved the dilemma put by Napoleon: 'In fifty years Europe will either be republican or Cossack.' Their resolution was the 'Cossack republic'. That work of art, the bourgeois republic, has not been deformed by Circe's black magic. That republic has lost nothing but its rhetorical arabesques, the outward decencies, in a word, the appearance of respectability. The France of today [after the *coup d'état*] was already there within the parliamentary republic. It required only a thrust of the bayonet for the membrane to burst and the monster to spring forth.

The immediate aim of the February revolution was to overthrow the Orléans dynasty and that part of the bourgeoisie which governed under its authority. It was not until 2 December 1851 that this aim was achieved. It was then that the immense possessions of the house of Orléans, the real basis of its influence, were confiscated, and what was expected to follow the February revolution finally came to pass in December [1851]: imprisonment, exile, dispossession, banishment, disarming, humiliation of the men who had wearied France since 1830 with their pleas. But under Louis Philippe only a part of the commercial bourgeois was in power. The other factions in it formed a dynastic and republican opposition, or stood entirely outside so-called legality. Only the parliamentary republic included all factions of the commercial bourgeoisie in the realm of the state. Moreover under Louis Philippe the commercial bourgeoisie excluded the large landholders. Only the parliamentary republic put them side-by-side, joined the July monarchy to the legitimist monarchy, and merged two eras in the rule of property into one. Under Louis Philippe the privileged part of the bourgeoisie concealed its rule beneath the crown; in the parliamentary republic the rule of the bourgeoisie, after unifying its constituent parts and extending its power to power over its own class, came out into the open. So the revolution first had to create the form in which the rule of the bourgeois class gained its broadest, most general and ultimate expression, and hence could also be overthrown without being able to rise up again.

Only now was the sentence executed which was pronounced in February on the Orléanist bourgeoisie, i.e. the most viable faction of the French bourgeoisie. Now a blow was struck at its parliament, its legal chambers, its commercial courts, its provincial representatives, its notaries, its universities, its spokesmen and their platforms, its press and its literature, its administrative income and its court fees, its army salaries and its state pensions, its mind and its body. [The revolutionary communist] *Blanqui* had made the disbanding of the bourgeois guard the first demand of the [1848] revolution, and the bourgeois guard, who in the February of the revolution raised their arms to stop this, disappeared from the scene in December. The Pantheon has been transformed once again into an ordinary church. With the last version of the bourgeois regime the spell, which transformed its eighteenth-century founders into saints, has at last been broken. When Guizot learned of the successful *coup d'état* of 2 December [1851] he exclaimed: *This is the complete and final triumph of socialism!* What he meant was: this is the final and complete collapse of the rule of the bourgeoisie.

Why did the proletariat not rescue the bourgeoisie? The question boils down to this: Why did the Paris proletariat not rise up after 2 December?

The overthrow of the bourgeoisie had only been decreed, but the decree had not yet been carried out. Any genuinely revolutionary uprising of the proletariat would have put new life into the bourgeoisie, reconciled it with the army and ensured a second June [1849] defeat of the workers.

On 4 December [1851] the proletariat was goaded into a fight by grocers and traders. On the evening of that day several legions of the national guard promised to appear in the principal squares under arms and in uniform. These traders and grocers had got wind of the fact that Bonaparte had abolished their secret ballot in one of his decrees of 2 December [1851] and enjoined them to inscribe their yea or nay beneath their names in the official register. The bloody confrontation of 4 December [1851] intimidated Bonaparte. During the night he had placards posted on all the street corners of Paris announcing the restoration of the secret ballot. Traders and grocers were convinced they had achieved their aim. But it was the traders and grocers who did not turn up next morning.

During the nights of Bonaparte's *coup d'état*, 1 and 2 December [1851], the Paris proletariat had also been robbed of its leaders, the commanders of the barricades, so it was an army without officers, too enlightened by its own recollections of June 1848 and 1849 and of May 1850 to fight under the banner of the *montagnards*; it had therefore come to a correct assessment of its own power and the general situation when it left to its vanguard of secret societies the task of saving the insurrectionary honour of Paris, which the bourgeoisie had readily given up to the soldiery, so that Bonaparte could later disarm the national guard with this cynical explanation: it was not that he feared the misuse of their weapons against him but rather that anarchists would misuse these weapons against the guard itself.

'*It is the complete and final triumph of socialism!*' This was Guizot's characterisation of 2 December [1851]. Though the overthrow of the parliamentary republic contains the triumph of the proletarian revolution in embryo, the immediate tangible result was *Bonaparte's victory over parliament, the executive over the legislature, force without words over the force of words*. The unitary power of the *ancien régime* is thus freed from its limitations, becoming an unlimited absolute power. In parliament the nation elevated its general will into law, i.e. the law of the ruling class was elevated into its general will. It abdicated its own will before the executive and subjected itself to the sovereignty of an alien will, to authority. The opposition between the executive and legislative powers expresses the opposition between the heteronomy and autonomy of the nation. Hence France seems to have escaped the despotism of a class only to revert to being under the despotism of an individual, and under the authority of an individual without authority to boot. The conflict seems to have been settled so that all classes bow down equally powerless and equally voiceless before the rifle-butt.

But the revolution is thorough-going. It is still preoccupied with journeying through purgatory. It does its work methodically. By 2 December [1851] it had completed half its preparatory work, and now it is completing the other half. First it developed parliamentary power so that it could be overthrown. Now that this has been attained, it is developing the *executive power*, reducing it to its purest expression, isolating it, confronting it as sole challenger in order to concentrate all its powers of destruction against it. And when it has brought this second half of its preparatory work to completion the whole of Europe will jump up and cry: Well grubbed up, old mole!

This executive with its enormous bureaucratic and military apparatus, with its widespread and ingenious machinery of state, a complement of a half million officials alongside an army of another half million, this fearsome parasitic body, which traps French society like a net and chokes it at every pore, arose at the time of the absolute monarchy, accelerating the decline of feudalism. The political prerogatives of landowners and municipalities were transformed into so many aspects of state power, the feudal dignitaries became salaried civil servants, and the variegated pattern of conflicting medieval authorities became the disciplined layout of state power with centralised functions in a factory-like division of labour. The first French revolution had the job of centralisation, breaking down all separate local, territorial, municipal and provincial powers in order to create a civil unity in the nation as begun by absolute monarchy, but at the same time it had to develop the extent, aspects and operatives of governmental power. Napoleon perfected this machinery of state. The legitimist and July monarchies contributed only a further division of labour, growing in proportion as the division of labour created new interest groups within bourgeois society, hence new objects for the state to administer. Every *common* interest was detached from society and counterposed to it as a higher, *general* interest, torn away from the independently generated activity of individuals within society and made into an object of governmental administration, from bridges, schools and community projects in a village up to railways, national public works and the national university of France. Finally in its struggle with the revolution the parliamentary republic found itself compelled to strengthen the apparatus and centralisation of governmental power with repressive measures. All upheavals perfected this machinery instead of destroying it. The parties that grappled in turn for power regarded possession of this immense edifice of state as the chief booty of the victor.

But under the absolute monarchy, during the first revolution [1789–99], under Napoleon [1799–1815], bureaucracy was only the means of preparing the class rule of the bourgeoisie. Under the restoration [1816–30], under Louis Philippe [1830–48], under the parliamentary republic [1848–51], it was the instrument of the ruling class, however much it also strove for power in its own right.

Only under the second Bonaparte does the state seem to have achieved independence with respect to society and to have brought it into submission. The independence of the executive comes through clearly when its head no longer needs ingenuity, its army no longer needs glory, and its bureaucracy no longer needs moral authority in order to justify itself. The state machine has established itself so firmly *vis-à-vis* commercial life that the head of the Society of 10 December provides sufficient leadership, a soldier of fortune swooping down from abroad, elevated to leadership by a drunken soldiery that he bought with grub and drink and at which he has to go on chucking sausages. Hence the shamefaced despair, the feeling of terrible humiliation, degradation, which weighs down upon France and suffocates her. France feels dishonoured. Just as under Napoleon there was scarcely any pretext for freedom, so under the second Bonaparte there was no longer any pretext for servitude.

But state power is not suspended in mid-air. Bonaparte represents a class, indeed the most numerous class in French society, the *small-holding peasants*.

Just as the Bourbons were the dynasty of large landed property and the Orléans the dynasty of finance, so Bonaparte is the dynasty of peasants, i.e. of the mass of the French people. Not the Bonaparte who knuckled under to the parliament of the bourgeoisie, but the Bonaparte who disbanded it, is the chosen one of the peasantry. For three years the cities were successful in falsifying the meaning of the election of 10 December and cheating the peasantry out of the restoration of the empire. The election of 10 December 1848 has been fulfilled only through the *coup d'état* of 2 December 1851.

The small-holding peasants form an immense mass whose members live in similar conditions but without entering into complex relationships with one another. Their mode of production isolates them from one another, instead of bringing them into complex interactions. This isolation is reinforced by the terrible means of communication in France and the poverty of the peasants. Their site of production, the smallholding, does not allow any division of labour in its cultivation, no application of science and therefore no diversity in development, no diversification of talents, no wealth of social relationships. Each individual peasant family is almost self-sufficient, producing the greatest part of its consumption directly and getting its means of subsistence more in brutal exchange with nature than in relationships within society. The smallholding, the peasant and the family; alongside them another smallholding, another farmer and another family. A few score of these make a village and a few score villages make a *département*. Thus the great bulk of the French nation is formed by simple accretion, much as potatoes in a sack form a sack of potatoes. In so far as millions of families get a living under economic conditions of existence that divide their mode of life, their interests and their culture from those of other classes and counterpose them as enemies, they form a class. In so far as there is merely a local interconnection amongst peasant proprietors, the similarity of their interests produces no community, no national linkage and no political organisation, they do not form a class. They are therefore incapable of asserting their class interests in their own name, whether through a parliament or constitutional convention. They cannot represent themselves, they must be represented. Their representative must also appear as their master, as an authority over them, as an unrestricted governmental power which protects them from other classes and watches over them from on high. The political influence of peasant proprietors is ultimately expressed in the subordination of parliament to the executive, society to the state.

Through historical tradition it has come to pass that the French peasantry believed in a miracle, that a man of the name of Napoleon would bring them back their former glory. And there came an individual who presented himself as such a man because he bore the name Napoleon, in accordance with the Napoleonic Code which stipulates: 'All inquiry into paternity is forbidden.' After twenty years of bumming around and a string of grotesque adventures, the prophecy was fulfilled and the man became emperor of the French. The *idée fixe* of the nephew was realised because it coincided with the *idée fixe* of the most numerous class of the French.

But, it may be objected, what about the peasant uprisings over half of France [in late December 1851], the raids on the peasantry by the army, the mass incarceration and transportation of peasants?

Since the time of Louis XIV France has not experienced a similar persecution of the peasantry 'for intriguing with demagogues'.

But let us be clear about this. The Bonaparte dynasty does not represent the revolutionary peasants, but rather the conservative ones, not the peasant who reaches beyond his social condition of existence, the smallholding, but rather the one who wants to shore it up more firmly, not the country people who want to overthrow the old order under their own steam in conjunction with the towns, but rather the exact opposite, those who are stupidly locked up within the old order and want to see themselves saved and preferred along with their smallholdings by means of the ghost of an empire. It represents peasant superstition, not enlightenment, prejudice not judgement, the past not the future, the modern Vendée [royalist revolt of 1789–94], not the modern Cévennes [anti-feudal revolt of 1702–5].

Three years hard rule under the parliamentary republic had freed a part of the French peasantry from Napoleonic illusions and revolutionised them, albeit only superficially, but the bourgeoisie repressed them forcibly whenever they tried to do anything. Under the parliamentary republic the modern consciousness of the French peasantry fought with the traditional one. The contest advanced in the form of an incessant battle between schoolmasters and the church. The bourgeoisie defeated the schoolmasters. For the first time the peasantry made efforts to act independently against government machinations. This showed up in the persistent conflict between mayors and prefects. The bourgeoisie removed the mayors. Finally, during the parliamentary republic, peasants from different parts of France rose up against their own monstrous offspring, the army. The bourgeoisie punished them with states of siege and foreclosures on property. And this is the bourgeoisie that now whines about the stupidity of the masses, the vile multitude that has betrayed it to Bonaparte. It has greatly strengthened the fervour for empire amongst the peasant class; it conserved the conditions which are the breeding ground of this peasant religion. In any case the bourgeoisie is bound to fear the stupidity of the peasant masses so long as they remain conservative, and the insights of the peasantry as soon as they become revolutionary.

In the uprisings after the *coup d'état* a portion of the French peasantry mounted armed protests against its own vote of 10 December 1848. Since 1848 they had schooled their wits. But they had enrolled in the underworld of history, and history kept them to their word, and the majority was still so prejudiced that even in the reddest of *départements* the peasant population openly supported Bonaparte. In its view the national assembly had hindered his progress. He had now merely broken the fetters which bound the will of the countryside to the towns. Here and there they entertained the grotesque idea that a constitutional convention could co-exist with a Napoleon.

After the first revolution had transformed the semi-feudal peasantry into freeholders, Napoleon confirmed and regulated the conditions in which they could exploit their newly acquired land in France and satisfy their new found passion for property undisturbed. But what is now causing the ruin of the French peasant is his smallholding itself, the division of the land and soil, the form of property which Napoleon consolidated in France. These are the material conditions which made the French feudal peasant a smallholding peasant and Napoleon into an emperor. Two generations were sufficient to produce the inevitable result: further deterioration of agriculture, further indebtedness of agriculturists. The 'Napoleonic' form of property, which at the beginning of the nineteenth century was the condition for the liberation and enrichment of French country dwellers, has developed in the course of a century into the law of their enslavement and pauperisation. And it is just this law which is the first of the 'Napoleonic ideals' which the second Bonaparte has to uphold. If he still shares with the peasants the illusion that the cause of their ruin is to be sought, not in small-scale property, but outside it in the influence of secondary factors, then his experiments will be smashed on the relations of production like soap bubbles, cutting that illusion off from its last hiding place and at best making the disease more acute.

The economic development of small-scale landed property has fundamentally turned round the relationship of the peasantry to the other classes of society. Under Napoleon the parcelling out of land and soil complemented free competition and the beginnings of large-scale industry in the cities. Even the preferment of the peasant class was in the interest of the new bourgeois order. This newly created class was the complex expansion of the bourgeois regime beyond the gateways of the cities, its realisation on a national scale. This class was the ever present protest against the recently overthrown landed aristocracy. If it was preferred over all, it was also suited above all as a point for the restoration of feudalism to attack. The roots that small-scale property had struck in French soil deprived feudalism of all nourishment. Its boundary stones formed a natural fortification for the bourgeoisie against any reprisals from its former overlords. But in the course of the nineteenth century the place of feudal orders was taken by urban usurers, the place of feudal obligation attached to the land by the mortgage, and the place of aristocratic landed property by bourgeois capital. The smallholding of the peasant is only a means for capitalists to draw profit, interest and rent from the soil, leaving to the farmer himself how to extract his wages. The mortgage interest weighing on French soil imposes on the French peasantry an interest burden equal to the annual interest on the whole of the British national debt. In this slavery to capital, as it inevitably develops, small-scale landed property transforms the bulk of the French nation into a nation of troglodytes. Sixteen million peasants (women and children included) dwell in hovels of which the greatest number have only one opening, others only two and the best of the lot only three. Windows are to a house as five senses are to the head. The bourgeois order, which at the beginning of the century made the state a sentry over the newly emerged smallholding and manured it with laurels, has turned into a vampire which sucks out its blood and brains and throws them into the alchemist's vessel of capital. The Napoleonic Code is now but a code for foreclosures on property, public auctions and forced sales. To the four million (including children, etc.) official paupers, vagrants, criminals and prostitutes in France must be added five million people who hover on the margin of existence and either house themselves in the countryside itself or continually desert the countryside for the cities or the cities for the countryside, together with their rags and their children. The interests of the peasants are therefore no longer in accord with the bourgeoisie, as under Napoleon, but in deadliest opposition to the interests of the bourgeoisie, to capital. Hence the peasants find their natural allies and leaders in the *urban proletariat* whose task is the overthrow of the bourgeois order. But *strong and unlimited government* – and this is the second 'Napoleonic ideal' which the second Napoleon is to carry out, has the job of defending this 'material order' by force. This 'material order' also serves as a catch-phrase in all Bonaparte's proclamations against peasant unrest.

Besides the mortgage which capital imposes on it, the smallholding is burdened with *taxes*. Taxation is the source of life for the bureaucracy, the army, the church and the court, in short the whole apparatus of executive power. Strong government and heavy taxes are identical. Small-scale landed property by its very nature provides a basis for an all-pervasive and numerous bureaucracy. It uniformly levels people and relationships over the whole surface of the land. Hence it also permits uniform action from a sovereign centre to all points. It destroys the aristocratic middle levels between the mass of the people and the state power. Hence it calls forth from all sides the direct intervention by this state power and the direct use of its agents. Finally it produces an unemployed surplus population which can find a place neither in the country nor in the towns and hence seizes on state offices as a kind of respectable charity and promotes the creation of state employment. Under Napoleon these numerous government personnel were not just directly productive, since in fact they provided for the newly arisen peasantry through state coercion in the form of public works, what the bourgeoisie could not yet provide through the means of private industry. State taxation was a necessary means of coercion to maintain exchange between town and country. Otherwise the smallholder, by becoming a self-sufficient peasant, would have broken off any connection with the towns, as happened in a part of Switzerland, [and] in Norway. Napoleon repaid the forced taxation with interest when he opened new markets with the bayonet and plundered continents. This was a spur to peasant industry, though they now rob his industry of its last source of help and break down the last barriers to pauperism.

And an enormous bureaucracy, well decorated and well fed, is the 'Napoleonic ideal' which appeals the most to the second Bonaparte. How could it be otherwise since he is compelled, alongside the actual classes of society, to create an artificial caste for which the maintenance of his regime is a bread-and-butter question. Consequently one of his first financial acts was to raise official salaries once again to their old level and to create new sinecures.

Another *'Napoleonic ideal'* is the dominance of the *Church* as an instrument of state. But while the newly developed smallholding was naturally religious in its accord with society, in its dependence on the powers of nature and in its subjection to an all-high protecting authority, it becomes naturally irreligious when riddled with debt, at odds with society and authority, and driven past its own limits. Heaven was just a beautiful annex to the narrow strip of land just acquired, especially as it makes the weather; it becomes an insult as soon as it is offered as a substitute for the smallholding. The priest then appears as but the anointed bloodhound of the earthly police – another 'Napoleonic ideal' – whose duty under the second Bonaparte is not, as it was under Napoleon [I], to spy on the enemies of the peasant regime in the cities, but to spy on Bonaparte's enemies in the country. Next time the march on Rome [to put down an insurrection] will take place in France itself, but in a sense opposite to that of M. de Montalembert [who advocated a war on socialism].

The culmination of the *'Napoleonic ideals'* is the predominance of the *army*. The army was the *point d'honneur* for the smallholding peasantry; it transformed them into heroes, defended their new possessions from outside threats, glorifying their recently acquired nationality, plundering and revolutionising the world. The dazzling uniform was its own national dress, war its poetry, the smallholding, extended and rounded off in the imagination, was its fatherland, and patriotism was the ideal form of their sense of property. But the enemies against whom the French peasant now has to defend his property are not the cossacks but the bailiffs and tax collectors. The smallholding is no longer in the so-called fatherland but in the mortgage register. The army itself is no longer the flower of peasant youth, it is the fetid bloom of the peasant lumpenproletariat. It consists in the greater part of place-holders, substitutes, as the second Bonaparte is himself only a place-holder, a substitute for

Napoleon. It performs its deeds of valour in hunting down peasants like game, in police duties, and if the internal contradictions of his system drive the head of the Society of 10 December over the French border, the army will reap no laurels after skirmishing but rather take a beating.

It's plain as day: '*all Napoleonic ideals*' *are ideals of the undeveloped smallholding in its heyday*, but for the smallholding that has outlived this, they are an absurdity. They are merely hallucinations of its death struggle, words transformed into phrases, ideas into spectres, befitting dress into preposterous costumes. But the parody of the empire was necessary to liberate the bulk of the French nation from the weight of tradition and to work out in pure form the opposition between state and society. The demolition of the state machine will not endanger centralisation. Bureaucracy is only the low and brutal form of a centralisation which is still afflicted with its opposite, feudalism. When, disappointed with the Napoleonic restoration, the French peasant will cease to believe in the smallholding, the whole edifice of state erected on this smallholding will collapse, and the *proletarian revolution will obtain the chorus without which its solo becomes a swan song in all peasant countries.*

The condition of the French peasantry solves the riddle for us of *the general elections of 20 and 21 December* [1851] which led the second Bonaparte up Mount Sinai, not to receive the laws but to give and execute them. Anyway in those fateful days the French nation committed a mortal sin against democracy, which falls to its knees and prays daily: Holy Universal Suffrage, pray for us! The believers in universal manhood suffrage naturally do not want to dispense with the miraculous power which has brought great things to pass for them, which has transformed Bonaparte II into a Napoleon, a Saul into a Paul, and a Simon into Peter. The spirit of the people speaks to them through the ballot box as the God of the prophet Ezekiel [37:5] spoke to the dry bones: 'Thus saith the Lord God unto these bones: "Behold, I will cause breath to enter into you, and ye shall live."'

Evidently the bourgeoisie had no choice other than to elect Bonaparte. Despotism or anarchy. Naturally they voted for despotism. When the puritans complained at the council of Constance [1414–18] about the dissolute lives of the popes and moaned about the necessity for moral reform, Cardinal Pierre d'Ailly thundered at them: 'Only the devil himself can save the Catholic church, and you are demanding angels.' In the same way after the *coup d'état* the French bourgeoisie cried: Only the head of the Society of 10 December can save bourgeois society! Only theft can save property; only perjury, religion; bastardy, the family; disorder, order!

As an executive with independent power, Bonaparte felt that it was his vocation to safeguard 'bourgeois order'. But the strength of this bourgeois order is in the middle classes. Hence he sees himself as the representative of the middle class and issues decrees on that basis. However he is only where he is, because he has destroyed the political power of this middle class, and does it again every day. He therefore sees himself as the enemy of the political and literary power of the middle class. But because he protects its material power, he generates its public, its political power anew. The cause must therefore be kept alive, but the effect where it is revealed must be dispatched from this world. But this cannot happen without some slight confusion of cause with effect, since both lose their distinguishing characteristics when they interact. There are new decrees that muddle the boundary lines. Bonaparte sees himself opposing the bourgeoisie as the representative of the peasantry and of the people in general at the same time, wanting to please the lower classes within bourgeois society. There are new decrees that rob the 'true socialists' of their administrative brainstorms in advance. Above all Bonaparte sees himself as head of the Society of 10 December, as representative of the lumpenproletariat, to which he himself, his entourage, his government and his army belong, and for which the chief concern is how to do well oneself and to extract prizes for the California lottery from the national treasury. He vindicates himself as head of the Society of 10 December with decrees, without decrees and despite decrees.

The contradictory tasks that face this man explain the contradictions of his government, the confused poking about to try to win over and then to humiliate now this, now that class, turning them all equally against himself; and his uncertainty in practice forms a highly comic contrast to the peremptory and categorical style of governmental decrees, a style obediently copied from the uncle [Napoleon]. So the speed and recklessness of these contradictions is supposed to imitate the complicated doings and quick-wittedness of the Emperor.

Industry and commerce, the occupations of the middle class, are to flourish in this hothouse regime of strong government. They are granting an innumerable number of railway concessions. But the Bonapartist lumpenproletariat is to enrich itself. So there is insider trading with the railway concessions on the stock exchange. But this draws no capital for the railways. So the bank is obliged to make advances on railway shares. But at the same time the bank is to be exploited for a certain person and therefore must be cajoled. So it is released from the obligation to publish a weekly report. Then the government makes a heads-I-win-tails-you-lose deal with the bank. The people are to be provided with employment. So instructions are issued for public works. But the public works raise the tax burden of the people. Hence the taxes are reduced by attacking the rentiers through the conversion of 5 per cent bonds to $4\frac{1}{2}$ per cent. But the middle class must again receive a sweetener. Hence the doubling of the wine tax on the people, who buy it retail, and halving of the wine tax for the middle class, who drink it wholesale. Disbanding of real workers' association, but promises of future miracles of association. There is to be help for the peasantry. So there are mortgage banks to increase their indebtedness and promote the concentration of property. But these banks are to be used to garner money for a certain person from the confiscated estates of the house of Orléans. But no capitalist wants to agree to this condition, which is not in the decree, and the mortgage bank remains a mere decree, etc. etc.

Bonaparte would like to appear as the patriarchal benefactor of all classes. But he cannot give to one without taking from another. At the time of the Fronde [1648–53], it was said of the duc de Guise that he was the most obliging man in France, because he had transformed all his property into credits that his partisans were obliged to repay to him, and so Bonaparte would like to be the most obliging man in France and transform all his property, all the labour of France, into credits to be repaid to himself. He would like to steal the whole of France in order to be able to give it back, or rather to be able to buy France back with French money, for, as the head of the Society of 10 December, he has to buy what is to belong to him. And all the institutions of state, the senate, the council of state, the legislative chamber [under the new constitution of 14 January 1852], the legion of honour, military decorations, wash-houses, public works, railways, the general staff of the national guard excluding common ranks, and the confiscated estates of the House of Orléans become a saleroom. Every place in the army and in the governmental machine is up for sale. But the most important thing in this process of taking France in order to give it back is the percentage which goes to the head and members of the Society of 10 December during the transaction. The witty countess L[éhon], the mistress of the duc de Morny [half brother of Louis Bonaparte], characterised the confiscation of the Orléanist loot in this way: 'It's the first flight [*vol* = theft] of the [Napoleonic] eagle.' That fits every flight of this *eagle*, which is more like a *raven* [that feeds on carrion]. Every day he and his hangers-on call to each other as the Italian Carthusian called out to the miser who made a show of counting up the money on which he would be drawing for years to come: 'You are counting up your goods, but you should first be counting up your years.' So as not to get the years wrong, they count the minutes. A gang of louts are pushing their way into the court, the ministries, the chief offices in administration and the army, of whom the best to be said is that no one knows where they come from, a noisy, foul, rapacious crowd of bohemians, crawling into gold braid with the same grotesque dignity as [the emperor] Soulouque's stuffed shirts [in Haiti]. The higher stratum of the Society of 10 December can be clearly discerned by reflecting on the fact that [a philistine such as] *Véron-Crevel* preaches its morals and [the journalist] *Granier de Cassagnac* its wisdom. When Guizot made use of this Granier at the time of his cabinet [during the 1840s] for a provincial rage against the [legitimist] dynastic opposition, he was wont to boast of him with the quip: '*He's the king of the fools.*' It would be an injustice to recall the regency [of the duc d'Orléans 1715–23] or [the reign of] Louis XV [1723–74] in conjunction with Louis Bonaparte's court and clique. For 'France has often had a government of mistresses, but never before a government of kept men' [as Mme Girardin, the editor's wife, put it]. And Cato who took his own life so that he could walk in the Elysian Fields with heroes! Poor Cato!

Driven by the contradictory demands of his circumstances, and having to keep in the public eye as a substitute for Napoleon, hence executing a coup in miniature every day, Bonaparte, like a conjuror who has to come up with constant surprises, brings the whole bourgeois economy into confusion, violates everything that seemed inviolable during the revolution of 1848, makes some tolerant of revolution and others desirous of it, and produces anarchy in the name of order, while stripping the halo from the whole machinery of state, profanes it, and makes it loathsome and laughable. He replicates the cult of the holy tunic of Trier in Paris as the cult of the imperial mantle of Napoleon. But when this imperial mantle falls at last onto the shoulders of Louis Bonaparte, the bronze of Napoleon, high on the column in the Place Vendôme, will plunge to the ground.

'Introduction' to the *Grundrisse*

A. Introduction

1. Production, consumption, distribution, exchange (circulation)

(1) PRODUCTION

Autonomous individuals. Eighteenth-century ideas.

(a) The subject at hand is, to begin with, *material production.*

Individuals producing in society – hence the starting point is naturally the socially specific production [carried on] by individuals. The individual – and individuated – hunter and fisher, with which [Adam] Smith and Ricardo begin, belongs to the unimaginative conceits of eighteenth-century stories *à la Robinson Crusoe*, which in no way express, as cultural historians imagine, a simple reaction against over-refinement and a regression to a misconstrued natural life. [Those stories] no more rest on such naturalism than does Rousseau's social contract, which brings naturally independent subjects into relation and association by means of a contract. This is the pretence, and merely the aesthetic pretence, of small- and large-scale stories *à la Robinson Crusoe*. It is rather the anticipation of 'bourgeois society', which had been in preparation since the sixteenth century and had made giant strides towards its maturity in the eighteenth. In that society of free competition the individual appears detached from the natural bonds, etc., which in earlier historical epochs make him into an appendage of a specific, delimited, human conglomerate. The prophets of the eighteenth century, on whose shoulders

Smith and Ricardo are standing, conceived of that eighteenth-century individual – the product, on the one hand, of the dissolution of feudal forms of society, and on the other, of the powers of production newly developed since the sixteenth century – as an ideal [conception], which may have had an existence in the past. [They did not conceive of that individual] as a historical result, but rather as the starting point of history. Because [they conceived of him] as the individual in conformity with nature in keeping with their conception of nature, [they conceived of him] not as originating historically, but as posited by nature. That fallacy has been characteristic of each new epoch up to now. [Sir James] Steuart, who in some ways is in opposition to the eighteenth century and as an aristocrat takes a more historical point of view, has escaped that gullibility.

The further back we go into history the more the individual, hence also the producing individual, appears as dependent, [and] belonging to a larger whole: at first in a still wholly natural way in the family and in the family extended into the tribe; later in the different forms of the community, which arose from the antagonisms and mergers of tribes. In the eighteenth century, in 'bourgeois society', the different forms of the social connection first confront the individual as a mere means for his private purposes, as external necessity. However, the epoch which produces that point of view, that of the individuated individual, is precisely the epoch of the most developed social relations up to now ([the most developed social relations] are general relations from that point of view). Man is in the most literal sense a *zoön politikon*, not only a sociable animal, but an animal which can individuate itself only in society. Production by an individuated individual outside society – a rarity which can indeed happen to a civilised man (who already possesses dynamically within himself the powers of social life), driven into the wilderness by accident – is just as absurd as the development of language without individuals living *together* and talking together. This need not detain us any longer. The point would not have been touched on at all had not that inanity, which had rhyme and reason for the people of the eighteenth century, been seriously reintroduced into the very middle of the most modern [political] economy by [Frédéric] Bastiat, [H.C.] Carey, Proudhon, etc. For Proudhon (and others) it is naturally agreeable to develop historico-philosophically the source of an economic relation when he is ignorant of its historical origin, [so] that he mythologises that Adam or Prometheus fell on a ready-made idea, [and] then the idea was instituted, etc. Nothing is more tediously arid than commonplace fantasies.

Eternalisation of the historical relations of production. – Production and distribution in general. – Property

Thus if we are talking about production, we are always talking about production at a specific stage of social development – we are talking about production by social individuals. Hence it might seem that in order to speak generally about production we must either trace the historical process of development in its various phases, or declare at the outset that we are dealing with a specific historical epoch, e.g. modern bourgeois production, which is, in fact, our proper subject. However, all epochs of production have certain features in common, common definitions. *Production in general* is an abstraction, but a sensible abstraction, in so far as it actually picks out what is common, fixes it, and consequently spares us repetition. Nevertheless this *universal*, or that which is common, separated out by [a process of] comparison, is [something which is] itself many times divided, [something which] splits into different definitions. A few [of those definitions] belong to all epochs; others are common to a few epochs. The most modern epoch will have [a few] definitions in common with the oldest. One cannot conceive of production without them; however, if the most developed languages have laws and definitions in common with the least developed, then it is just what is different from this universal and common [definition] that constitutes their development, [hence] the definitions which are applicable to production generally must be precisely separated, so that the essential diversity over and above the unity – which already arises from the fact that the subject, mankind, and the object, nature, are the same – is not forgotten. For example, the whole wisdom of the modern economists who prove the eternity and harmony of the existing social relations lies in forgetting that [diversity]. For example. No production is possible without an instrument of production, even if that instrument is only the hand. No [production] is possible without past, accumulated labour, even if that labour is only the skill which is gathered and concentrated in the hand of a savage through repeated practice. Capital is, among other things, both an instrument of production and past, objectified labour. Therefore capital is a general, eternal, natural relation; that is, if I omit precisely the specific [thing] which makes 'instrument of production', [and] 'accumulated labour' into capital in the first place. Hence the whole history of the relations of production appears with Carey, for example, as a falsification maliciously perpetrated by the government.

If there is no production in general, then there is also no general production. Production is always a *particular* branch of production – e.g. agriculture, husbandry, manufacture, etc. – or it is the *totality* of production. However, political economy is not technology. The relation of the general definitions of production at a given stage of society to the particular forms of production is to be developed elsewhere (later). Finally, production is not merely a particular [form of production]. Rather it is always a certain social body, a social subject, which is active in a greater or lesser totality of branches of production. Likewise the relation of scientific presentation to real movement does not belong here yet. Production in general. Particular branches of production. Totality of production. [Three meaningful senses of 'production'.]

It is the fashion to preface the [typical work of political] economy with a general section in which the *general conditions* of all production are discussed – and it is precisely that section which figures under the title 'production' (see, for example, J.S. Mill). That general section consists or supposedly consists in: (1) the conditions without which production is not possible. This is in fact nothing but stating the essential [conceptual] moments of all production. However, this reduces itself in fact, as we shall see, to a few very simple specifications which are drawn out into superficial tautologies; (2) the conditions which more or less advance production, as for example Adam Smith's progressive and stagnant state[s] of society. In order to raise that [conception], which had its value in his work as an *aperçu*, to a more scientific meaning, inquiries would be necessary into the durations of the [different] *degrees of productivity* in the development of a single people – an inquiry which lies outside the proper limits of the subject [modern bourgeois production]; however, so far as it belongs in the subject, it is to be placed with the development of competition, accumulation, etc. In

the general understanding [of the subject] the answer [which is
given to that inquiry] amounts to the generality that an industrial
people enjoys the height of its production at the moment at which
it occupies its general historical height. In fact, a people is at its
industrial height so long as gain is yet the main thing, but [the
process of] gaining. So the Yankees are ahead of the English. Or
else [another answer]: that, for example, certain racial dispositions,
climates, natural relations like the position of the sea, the fertility
of the earth, etc., are more favourable to production than others.
[That answer] also amounts to the tautology that wealth is created
more easily to the degree that its elements are subjectively and
objectively present to a higher degree.

However, this is not all that is actually discussed by economists
in that general section. Rather, production is supposedly represented – see, for example, J.S. Mill – in distinction from distribution, etc., as framed in eternal natural laws independent of history; this is the occasion for passing off, in an underhand way,
bourgeois relations as irrevocable natural laws of society in the
abstract. This is the more or less conscious purpose of the whole
proceeding. With distribution, on the other hand, men are said to
have been allowed, in fact, all kinds of arbitrary action. Quite apart
from the crude sundering of production and distribution and their
actual relation, it must be made clear at the outset that, however
heterogeneous distribution may be at different stages of society, it
must be just as possible [with distribution] as well as with production to pick out common definitions and just as possible to con-
found or extinguish all historical differences in *general human* laws.
For example, the slave, the serf, the wage-labourer all retain a ration
of food which makes it possible for them to exist as slave, as serf,
as wage labourer. The conqueror who lives by tribute, or the official
who lives by taxes, or the landowner who lives by rents, or the
monk who lives by alms, or the Levite who lives by tithes, all retain
a share of social production, which is specified according to laws
other than that [law which specifies the ration] of the slaves, etc.
The two main points which all economists place under that rubric
are: (1) property; (2) safeguarding of property by the judiciary, the
police, etc. Those points can be answered very briefly:

On 1. All production is the appropriation of nature on the part of
the individual within and by means of a specific form of society. In
that sense it is a tautology to say that property (appropriation) is a

condition of production. However, it is ludicrous to leap from that [tautology] to a specific form of property, e.g. private property. (What is more, [private property] is an antithetical form which implies as a condition *non-property* as well as [property].) Rather history shows that common property is the more original form [of property] (e.g. in India, among the Slavs and ancient Celts, etc.), a form which still plays a significant role under the shape of communal property. We have not yet come to the question whether wealth develops better under this or that form of property. However, that there can be no talk of production, hence no talk of society, where no form of property exists, is a tautology. An appropriation which does not appropriate anything is a contradiction in the thing spoken of.

On 2. Safe-keeping of acquisitions, etc. If those trivialities are reduced to their real content, they express more than their preachers realise. Namely, that each form of production produces its own legal relations, form of government, etc. The [economists'] crudeness and the simple-minded character of their thought lie in haphazardly relating to one another things which belong together organically, [and] in bringing [them] into a simple connection based on reflection. The bourgeois economists have in mind that a modern police force lets us produce better than, for example, the law of the jungle. They simply forget that the law of the jungle is also a law, and that the law of the stronger persists under another form even in their 'Rechtsstaat'.

If the social conditions corresponding to a specific level of production are just originating, or if they are already disappearing, breakdowns of production naturally occur, although in different degrees and with different effects.

To summarise: there are definitions, common to all stages of production, which are fixed by thinking as universal; however, the so-called *general conditions* of all production are nothing [other] than those abstract [conceptual] moments, with which no actual historical stage of production is grasped.

2. The General Relation of Production to Distribution, Exchange, Consumption

Before entering into a further analysis of production, it is necessary to consider the different rubrics which the economists set alongside it.

The [economists'] conception is as plain as can be: in production, the members of society appropriate (bring forth, form) natural products to human needs; distribution specifies the proportion in which the individual shares in those products; exchange supplies him with the particular products into which he wants to translate the quota coming to him through distribution; finally, in consumption the products become objects of enjoyment, of individual appropriation. Production brings forth the objects corresponding to needs; distribution divides them according to social laws; exchange again divides, according to the individual need, that which has already been divided; finally, in consumption the product emerges from that social movement, becomes directly the object and servant of the individual need, and satisfies it in enjoyment. Thus production appears as the starting point, consumption as the endpoint, distribution and exchange as the middle term, a term which is itself twofold, since distribution is defined as the [conceptual] moment deriving from society, exchange as the [conceptual] moment deriving from individuals. In production, the person is objectified, [and] in consumption the thing is subjectified; in distribution, society in the form of general, dominating specifications takes over the mediation between production and consumption; in exchange, production and consumption are mediated through the contingent specificity of individuals.

Distribution specifies the proportion (the ration) in which products fall to individuals; exchange specifies the production in which the individual commands the share assigned to him by distribution.

Production, distribution, exchange, [and] consumption thus form a regular syllogism; production, the universality; distribution and exchange the particularity; consumption, the individuality in which the whole is contained. This is indeed a connection, but a superficial one. Production is [in that view] defined by general natural laws; distribution, by social chance, and distribution can therefore promote production more or less effectively; exchange lies between the two as a formal social movement, and the concluding act of consumption, which is understood not only as ultimate goal, but also as ultimate purpose, lies properly outside [political] economy, except in so far as it reacts back on the starting point and begins the whole operation anew.

The opponents of the political economists – whether they are opponents inside or outside their circle – who reproach the political economists with the barbarous sundering of something which belongs together, take either the same point of view as the political economists, or an inferior one. Nothing is more familiar than the objection that the political economists consider production too exclusively as an end in itself. It might just as well depend on distribution. At the basis of that objection lies the economic conception that distribution dwells next to production as an autonomous, independent sphere. Or the [conceptual] moments were not understood in their unity. As if that sundering [e.g. of production and distribution] had not sprung from real life into the textbooks, but on the contrary had sprung from the textbooks into real life, and as if it were a matter of a dialectical equation of concepts and not the apprehension of real relations!

Consumption and production
(a$_1$) Production is immediately also consumption. Consumption is twofold, subjective and objective: [First:] the individual, who develops his capabilities in producing, expends them as well; he consumes them in the act of production just as natural reproduction is a consumption of life-forces. Secondly: consumption of the means of production, which are used and worn out and decomposed into the common elements again (as for example in fuel). It is the same with the consumption of raw material, which does not remain in its natural form and condition, rather the natural form and condition are consumed. Hence the act of production is itself in all its [conceptual] moments also an act of consumption. But the [political] economists admit this. Production as directly identical with consumption, [and] consumption as directly coincident with production, they call *productive consumption*. That identity of production and consumption is tantamount to Spinoza's proposition: definition is negation.

But this definition of productive consumption is only set up in order to segregate the consumption which is identical with production from consumption proper, which is understood rather as the nullifying antithesis of production. Let us consider consumption proper.

Consumption is immediately also production, as in nature the consumption of elements and chemical materials is the production of the plant. For example, it is clear that in nourishment, a form of consumption, man produces his own body. But this is the case with any other type of consumption which in one way or another produces man in some aspect. Consumptive production. However, says [political] economy, that production which is identical with consumption is a second [form of production] arising out of the nullification of the first product. In the first [form of production] the producer materialises himself; in the second [form of production] the thing created by the producer personifies itself [i.e. becomes part of a person]. Therefore this consumptive production – although it is an immediate unity between production and consumption – differs essentially from production proper. The immediate unity, in which production coincides with consumption and consumption with production, lets their immediate duality persist.

Therefore production is immediately consumption, [and] consumption is immediately production. Each is immediately its opposite. At the same time, however, a mediating movement takes place between the two. Production mediates consumption, whose material it creates; without production, consumption lacks an object. However, consumption also mediates production, since it creates first the subject for the products, the subject for which they are products. The product only receives its last finish in consumption. A railway on which no one rides, which is therefore not worn out, which is not consumed, is only a railway virtually, not a railway in actuality. Without production there is no consumption; however, without consumption there is no production, since production [without consumption] would be purposeless. Consumption produces production in two ways, (1) since only in consumption does the product become a real product. For example, a dress actually becomes a dress only in the act of wearing [it]; a house which is not lived in, is in fact not a real house; therefore [a product], in distinction from a mere natural object, only proves itself as a product, only *becomes* a product, in consumption. Consumption, by decomposing the product, only gives it the finishing stroke, for the product is a product not as a materialised activity, but only as an object for the active subject; (2) since consumption creates the need for *new* production, [and] therefore the ideal, inner, impelling reason for production, a reason which is a presupposition of production. Consumption creates the impetus to produce; it also creates the object which is active in production as a purpose-defining object. If it is clear that production presents the object of consumption externally, then it is just as clear that consumption *posits* the object of production *ideally*, as an inner image, as a need, as an impetus, and as a purpose. It creates the objects of production in a form which is still subjective. Without need there is no production. But consumption reproduces the need.

There are corresponding points on the side of production: (1) it supplies the material, the object for consumption. Consumption without an object is not consumption; therefore production creates in this respect, [or] produces, consumption. (2) But it is not only the object which production creates for consumption. Production also gives to consumption its specificity, its character, its finish. Just as consumption gave the product its finish as a product, production gives consumption its finish. *For one thing*, the object is not an object generally but a specific object which must be consumed in a specific way, a way [to be] mediated again by production itself. Hunger is hunger, but hunger which is satisfied with cooked meat eaten with knife and fork is a hunger different from that which devours raw meat with the help of hand, nail and tooth. Hence not only the object of consumption but also the mode of consumption is produced by production, not only objectively but also subjectively. Therefore production creates the consumer. (3) Production not only supplies the need with a material, but also supplies the material with a need. If consumption has emerged from its first natural crudeness and immediacy – and lingering in that [state] would itself be the result of a [mode of] production stuck in [a state of] crudeness – then production as an impetus is itself mediated by the object. The need which consumption feels according to the object is created through the perception of the object. An *objet d'art* – just like any other product – creates a public sensitive to art and capable of enjoying beauty. Hence production produces not only an object for the subject but also a subject for the object. Hence production produces consumption, (1) since production creates the material for consumption, (2) since production specifies the mode of consumption, (3) since production produces the products which are posited by it first as an object [then] as a need in the consumer. Hence production produces the object of consumption, the mode of consumption, [and] the impetus of consumption. In the same way consumption produces the *disposition* of the producer, since consumption requires him to define a need purposefully.

Therefore the identities between consumption and production appear threefold:

(1) *Immediate identity*: production is consumption; consumption is production. Consumptive production. Productive consumption. The political economists call both productive consumption. But they still make a distinction. The first figures as reproduction; the second as productive consumption. All inquiries into the first are inquiries into productive or unproductive labour; inquiries into the second are inquiries into productive or non-productive consumption.

(2) That each appears as a means to the other; each is mediated by the other; [a mediation] which is expressed as their mutual dependence; a [mediating] movement through which they are related to one another and appear mutually indispensable, but still remain external [to each other]. Production creates the material as an external object for consumption; consumption creates the need as an inner object, as the purpose of production. Without production there is no consumption; without consumption there is no production. This figures in [political] economy in many forms.

(3) Production is not only immediately consumption and consumption immediately production; yet production is only a means for consumption and consumption a purpose for production, i.e. that each supplies the object for the other, production externally for consumption, consumption conceptually for production; but each of them is not only immediately the other, each is still only mediating the other – but each of the two creates the other as it is carried out; each is carried out as the other. Consumption only carries out the act of production, since consumption completes the product as product, since consumption decomposes the product, since consumption consumes the autonomous material form of the product, since consumption, by means of the need for repetition, raises to a skill the disposition developed in the first act of production; consumption is therefore not only the concluding act through which the product becomes a product, but also the act through which the producer becomes a producer. On the other hand, production

produces consumption, since it creates the specific mode of consumption, and further, since it creates the stimulus to consume, [and] the capacity itself to consume, as a need. That last identity, specified under (3), is illustrated many times in [political] economy in the relation of supply and demand, of objects and needs, of needs created by society and natural needs.

After this, nothing is easier for a Hegelian than to posit production and consumption [as] identical. And that has been done not only by socialist belletrists, but also by prosaic economists, e.g. [Jean-Baptiste] Say; [it has been done] in the form, that if one consider a people, [then] its production is its consumption. Or even humanity in the abstract. [H.F.] Storch has proved that Say is wrong, since a people, for example, does not purely consume its product, but also creates the means of production, etc., fixed capital, etc. Besides, to consider society as one subject is to consider it falsely, speculatively. With one subject, production and consumption appear as [conceptual] moments of one act. The important [point] to be emphasised here is that if production and consumption are considered as activities of one subject or of many individuals, they appear, in any case, as [conceptual] moments of a process in which production is the real starting point and of which it is also the transcending [conceptual] moment. Consumption as a want, as a need, is itself an inner [conceptual] moment of productive activity. But productive activity is the starting point of realisation, and hence also its transcending [conceptual] moment, the act in which the whole process is dispersed again [in its conceptual moments, as at the starting point]. The individual produces an object, and through the consumption of the object returns again as himself, but as a productive individual and a self-reproducing individual. Thus consumption appears as a [conceptual] moment of production.

In society, however, the relation of the producer to the product, as soon as the product is finished, is an external relation, and the return of the product to the subject depends on his relationships with other individuals. The product is not immediately obtainable [by the producer]. Also, the immediate appropriation of the product is not its purpose, if the product is produced in society. *Distribution,* which specifies through social laws the share of the producer in the world of products, steps between the producer and the product, [and] therefore between production and consumption.

Is distribution an autonomous sphere alongside and outside production?

Distribution and production

(b₁) If one considers the usual [works on political] economy, one must be struck above all by the fact that everything in them is posited twice over. For example, ground rent, wages, interest and profit figure in distribution while land, labour, [and] capital figure in production as agents of production. With capital it is obvious from the beginning that it is posited twice over, (1) as an agent of production; (2) as a source of income, as defining the specific forms of distribution. Hence interest and profit also figure as such in production, in so far as they are forms in which capital augments itself, increases, [and] therefore they are [conceptual] moments of the production itself of capital. Interest and profit, as forms of distribution, imply capital as an agent of production. They are modes of distribution which have, for their presupposition, capital as an agent of production. In the same way, they are modes of reproduction of capital.

In the same way, wages are wage-labour considered under another rubric: the specificity which labour has here as an agent of production appears as a specification of distribution. If labour were not specified as wage-labour, then the way in which it shares in the products would not appear as wages, as, for example, in slavery. Finally – to take the most developed form of distribution in which landed property shares in the products – ground rent implies large-scale landed property (properly large-scale agriculture) as an agent of production, not land pure and simple, any more than salary [implies] labour pure and simple. Hence the relations and modes of distribution appear only as reverse sides of the agents of production. An individual who shares in production in the form of wage-labour shares in the products (the results of production) in the form of wages. The arrangement of distribution is completely specified by the arrangement of production. Distribution is itself a product of production, not only with respect to the object, [i.e.] that only the results of production can be distributed, but also with respect to the form, [i.e.] that the specific way of sharing in production specifies the particular forms of distribution, the form in which sharing takes place in distribution. It is an out and out illusion to posit earth in production, ground rent in distribution, etc.

Economists like Ricardo, who are mostly reproached with considering only production, have defined distribution as the exclusive object of [political] economy because they instinctively understand the forms of distribution as the most specific expression in which the agents of production are fixed in a given society.

Distribution naturally appears opposed to the single individual as a social law which conditions his place within production, the place within which he produces, the place which therefore precedes production. The individual has from the start no capital, no landed property. He is assigned from birth to wage-labour through social distribution. But that assignment itself is the result [of the fact] that capital [and] landed property exist as autonomous agents of production.

If whole societies are considered, distribution appears in still another respect to precede production and to define it; distribution appears, so to speak, as a pre-economic fact. A conquering people divides the land among the conquerors and thus imposes a specific division and form of landed property; hence [it appears that] the conquering people defines production. Or the conquerors make the conquered into slaves and thus make slavery into the basis of production. Or a people, by means of revolution, breaks up large-scale landed property into parcels; therefore [a revolutionary people] gives production a new character through that new distribution. Or legislation perpetuates landed property in certain families, or divides labour [as] hereditary privilege and thus fixes labour into a caste-system. In all those cases, and they are all historical, distribution appears to be arranged and defined not by production, but, on the contrary, production appears to be arranged and defined by distribution.

Distribution, in the most superficial view, appears as the distribution of products, and thus further removed from production and quasi-autonomous against it. But before distribution is the distribution of products it is: (1) the distribution of instruments of production, and (2) (which is a further specification of the same relation) the distribution of members of society among the different types of production. (Subsumption of individuals under specific relations of production.) The distribution of products is obviously only the result of that distribution which is comprised within the production process itself, and which specifies the arrangement of production. To consider production apart from the distribution included in it is obviously empty abstraction, while on the contrary the distribution of the product is [already] given, [in and] of itself, with that distribution which originally forms a [conceptual] moment of production. Ricardo, whose object was to apprehend modern production in its specific social arrangement, and who is the economist of production *par excellence*, accordingly does *not* declare production to be the proper subject of modern [political] economy, but distribution. Another consequence of this is the absurdity of the economists who develop production as an eternal truth, while they banish history to the realm of distribution.

What relation this distribution, which defines production itself, bears to production, is obviously a question which falls within [the sphere of] production itself. If it should be said that at least distribution, in that meaning of distribution, precedes production [and] forms its presupposition, since production must proceed from a certain distribution of the instruments of production – then it can be answered that production in fact has its conditions and presuppositions which form its [conceptual] moments. Those may, in the beginning, appear as spontaneous. Through the process of production itself they are transformed from spontaneous into historical [conditions and presuppositions], and if they appear as a natural presupposition of production for one period they are, for another period, the historical result of production. They are continuously altered within production itself. For example, the employment of machinery altered the distribution of instruments of production as well as the distribution of products. Modern large-scale landed property itself is the result of modern trade and modern industry as well as the result of the employment of industry on agriculture.

The questions posed above resolve themselves in the last instance into questions [of] how general historical relations play a part in production, and questions [of] the relation of production to historical movement generally. Obviously the question belongs in the discussion and development of production itself.

Nevertheless in the trivial form in which the questions have been posed above, they can likewise be briefly dispatched. With all conquests there are three different possibilities. The conquering people subjects the conquered to its own mode of production (e.g. the English in Ireland in this century, [and] to some extent in India); or the conquering people lets the old mode of production persist and satisfies itself with tribute (e.g. the Turks and Romans); or there arises a reciprocal effect through which something new originates, a synthesis (to some extent [this was the case] in the Germanic conquests). In all cases the mode of production, whether that of the conquering people, whether that of the conquered, whether that proceeding from the merger of the two, is defining for the new distribution which arises. Although that [distribution] appears as a presupposition for the new period of production, it is itself a product of production, not only of historical production in general, but of specific historical production.

The Mongols, with their ravages in Russia, for example, acted in accordance with their [mode of] production, with pasturage, for which uninhabited stretches [of land] are a main condition. The German barbarians, for whom cultivation of the land with serfs was the traditional [mode of] production and [for whom there was an] isolated life on the land, could subject the Roman provinces more easily to those conditions, since the concentration of landed property which had taken place there had already completely overthrown the older agricultural relations.

It is a well-established conception that in certain periods people lived only by stealing. But in order to be able to steal, there must be something there to be stolen; therefore there was production. And the type of stealing is itself defined by the type of production. A stock-jobbing nation, for example, cannot be robbed [in the same way] as a nation of cowherds.

In the slave the instrument of production is stolen directly. But then production in the country for which the slave is stolen must be so arranged as to permit slave-labour, or (as in South America, etc.) a mode of production corresponding to the slave must be created.

Laws can perpetuate an instrument of production, e.g. land, in certain families. Those laws only receive an economic meaning if large-scale landed property is in harmony with social production, as for example in England. In France small-scale agriculture was carried on in spite of large-scale landed property, hence large-scale landed property was broken up by the revolution. But the perpetuation of the parcelling out [of land] by laws, for example? In spite of those laws, property again concentrates itself. The influence of laws towards retention of the relations of distribution, and thereby their effect on production, is to be specified in particular cases.

(c₁) Exchange, finally, and circulation
Exchange and production

Circulation itself is only a specific [conceptual] moment of exchange or of exchange considered in its totality.

Thus far *exchange* is only a mediating [conceptual] moment between production and the distribution (with consumption) which is defined by production; however, in so far as consumption itself appears as a [conceptual] moment of production, exchange is obviously also comprised in production as a [conceptual] moment.

First, it is clear that the exchange of activities and capabilities, which takes place in production itself, belongs directly to production and constitutes it essentially. Secondly, the same applies to the exchange of products as far as exchange is a means for the preparation of the finished product, for the immediate consumption of a specific product. Thus far exchange itself is an act comprised in production. Thirdly, the so-called exchange between dealers and dealers, both with respect to its organisation and as a producing activity itself, is wholly defined by production. Only in its last stage does exchange appear independent alongside, indifferent towards production, the stage where the product is immediately exchanged for consumption. However, (1) there is no exchange without division of labour, whether the division of labour is spontaneous or is itself already a historical result; (2) private exchange presupposes private production; (3) the intensiveness of exchange, like its extension, like its type, is defined by the development and arrangement of production. For example, exchange between town and country, exchange in the country, in the town, etc. Thus exchange appears in all its [conceptual] moments either directly comprised in production or defined by it.

The result which we have reached is not that production, distribution, exchange, [and] consumption are identical, but that they all form members of a totality, differences within a unity. Production transcends not only over [*sic*] itself in the antithetical definition of production [i.e. consumptive production] but also over [*sic*] the other [conceptual] moments [i.e. distribution, exchange and consumption]. The process always begins anew from production. It is clear [in and] of itself that exchange and consumption cannot be the transcending [conceptual moment]. In the same way [this is true] of distribution as the distribution of products. As distribution of the agents of production, however, distribution is itself a [conceptual] moment of production. Therefore a specific [form of] production defines a specific [form of] consumption, distribution, exchange, and the *specific relations of those different [conceptual] moments to one another*. Of course, production *in its one-sided form* is also defined for its part by the other [conceptual] moments. For example, if the market, i.e. the sphere of exchange, expands, [then] production grows in extent and is more thoroughly compartmentalised. Production varies with variations in distribution; for example, with the concentration of capital, with a different distribution of population in town and country, etc. Finally, the needs of consumption define production. A reciprocal effect takes place between the different [conceptual] moments. This is the case with any organic whole.

3. The method of political economy

If we consider a given country in the manner of political economy, then we begin with its population, division of the population into classes, town, country, sea, different branches of production, export and import, yearly production and consumption, commodity prices, etc.

It appears to be correct to begin with the real and concrete, the actual presupposition, therefore, e.g. in [political] economy, with the population, which is the basis and the subject of the whole social act of production. Nevertheless this is shown, upon closer consideration, to be false. Population is an abstraction, if I omit the classes, for example, of which it consists. Those classes are once again an empty word if I do not know the elements on which they are based. For example, wage-labour, capital, etc. These imply exchange, division of labour, prices, etc. Capital, for example, is nothing without wage-labour, without value, money, price, etc. Therefore if I began with population, then that would be a chaotic conception of the whole, and through closer definition I would come analytically to increasingly simpler concepts; from the conceptualised concrete to more and more tenuous abstractions, until I arrived at the simplest definitions. From there the journey would be taken up again in reverse until I finally arrived again at population, this time, however, not [with population] as a chaotic conception of a whole, but as a rich totality of many definitions and relationships. The first way [of proceeding] is one which [political] economy has taken up historically in its formation. The economists of the seventeenth century, for example, always begin with the living whole, the population, the nation, the state, more states, etc.; they always end, however, in such a way that they discover a few defining, abstract, universal relationships, like division of labour, money, value, etc., through analysis. As soon as those individual [conceptual] moments were more or less fixed and abstracted, the economic systems which ascend from the simple [conceptual moment], such as labour, division of labour, need, [and] exchange-value, up to the state, exchange among nations and the world market, began [to be formulated]. The latter is obviously the scientifically correct method. The concrete is concrete, because it is the sum of many definitions, [and] therefore a unity of diversity. Hence the concrete appears in thinking as a process of summarisation, as a result rather than a starting point, although the concrete is the actual starting point and hence also the starting point of perception and conceptualisation. In the first way [of proceeding] the full conception was broken down to the abstract definition; in the second, the abstract definitions lead to the reproduction of the concrete by means of thinking. Hence Hegel falls into the illusion of understanding the real as the result of self-summarising, self-engrossing, self-motivating thinking, whereas the method of ascending from the abstract to the concrete is merely the way for thinking to appropriate the concrete, to reproduce it as a mental concrete. However, this is in no way the process of origination of the concrete itself. For example, the simplest economic category, say for example exchange-value, implies population, population producing in specific relations; also, exchange-value implies certain sorts of familial or communal or political existence etc. Exchange-value can never exist as an abstract, one-sided relationship outside a given, concrete, living whole. On the other hand, exchange-value as a category leads an antediluvian existence. Hence for consciousness –

and philosophical consciousness is defined in this [following] way –
for philosophical consciousness conceptual thinking is the actual
man and hence the conceived world as such is the only actuality –
hence the movement of categories appears as the actual act of production (which alas keeps merely an initial impulse from outside),
the result of which is the world; and this – however, this is again
a tautology – is correct so far as the concrete totality as a thought-
totality, as a concrete thought-object, is in fact a product of thinking, of conceiving; however, the concrete totality is in no way a
product of the self-delivering concept, of the concept thinking outside or above perception and conception, but of the working up of
perception and conception into concepts. The whole, as it appears
in the head as a thought-whole, is a product of the thinking head
which appropriates the world in the only mode possible for it, a
mode which is different from the artistic, religious, [and] practical-
mental appropriation of that world. The real subject, after as before,
remains outside the head in autonomous existence; so long, that is,
as the head acts, only speculatively, only theoretically. Hence with
the theoretical method the subject, society, must always be borne
in mind as the presupposition of [any] conception.

However, do these simple categories not have an independent
historical or natural existence before the more concrete categories?
That depends. For example, Hegel begins the *Philosophy of Right*
correctly with possession as the subject's simplest relationship to
do with rights. However, possession does not exist before the family
or before relations of domination and servitude, which are much
more concrete relations. On the other hand, it would be correct to
say that families, [and] whole tribes exist which only just *possess*
[but] do not have *property*. The simpler category [possession]
appears, therefore as a relation of simple familial or tribal association
in regard to property. In the higher [forms of] society the simpler
category [possession] appears as the simpler relation of a developed
organisation. The concrete substratum, whose relationship [to man]
is possession, is however always presupposed. One can conceive of
an individual savage possessing [things]. However, possession is
then not a relation of right. It is not correct [to say] that possession
develops historically into the family. Rather possession always
implies that 'more concrete category of right' [the family]. Yet
this much always remained the case, that the simple categories

[e.g. possession] are expressions of relations in which the less developed concrete [i.e. familial or tribal association] may have been realised, without the many-sided relationship or relation [property rights] which is mentally expressed in the more concrete category [property] having been posited; while the more developed concrete [e.g. bourgeois society] retains that same category [property] as a subordinate relation. Money can exist, and it has existed historically, before capital existed, before banks existed, before wage-labour existed, etc. In that respect it can be said that the simpler category [money] can express the dominating relations of a less developed whole [e.g. a pre-bourgeois society] or the subordinate relations of a more developed whole [e.g. bourgeois society], relations which already had a historical existence before the whole [i.e. society] was developed with respect to an aspect of a more concrete category [e.g. capital, wage-labour, etc.]. Thus far the path of abstract thinking, which ascends from that which is simplest towards that which has been combined, corresponds to the actual historical process.

In another respect it can be said that there are very developed but still historically less mature forms of society in which the highest forms of economy, e.g. cooperation, developed division of labour, etc., have a place, without the existence of any kind of money, e.g. Peru. As in the Slavic commune, money (and the exchange conditioning it) does not emerge, or does so [very] little, inside the individual commune, but does emerge at its boundaries in commerce with others, so it is then generally false to posit exchange in the midst of the commune as the original constituting element. Rather exchange, to begin with, emerges earlier in the relationship of different communes to one another than for members within one and the same commune. Further: although money plays a role very early and all-round, it is assigned in antiquity as a dominating element only one-sidedly to specific nations, trading nations. And in the most advanced [period of] antiquity itself, with the Greeks and Romans, the complete development of money, which is presupposed in modern bourgeois society, appears only in the period of their dissolution. Therefore that wholly simple category does not appear historically in its intensiveness as it appears in the most developed states of society. By no means [is that simple category] wading through all economic relations. For example, in the Roman empire at its greatest development the [economic] basis stayed taxes and payments in kind. The existence of money [in the] proper [sense of the term] was only completely developed there in the army. Also, money never got a grip on the whole of labour. Thus, although the simpler category [money] may have existed historically before the more concrete category [e.g. capital], it [money] can belong in its complete intensive and extensive development to a combined form of society [e.g. bourgeois society], while [on the other hand] the more concrete category [cooperation] was more completely developed in a less developed form of society [e.g. Peru, the Slavic commune].

Labour appears to be a quite simple category. Also, the conception of it in that universality – as labour generally – is very old. Nevertheless, understood economically in that simple way 'labour' is a modern category in the same way as the relations which produce that simple abstraction. The monetary system, for example, still posits wealth quite objectively as a thing outside itself in money. It was a great advance against that standpoint [i.e. the doctrines of the monetary system] when the manufacturing or commercial system put the source of wealth out of the object into the subjective activity – commercial and manufacturing labour – but that activity itself was always simply viewed in a limited way as money-making. Opposed to that system is the physiocratic system, which posits a specific form of labour – agriculture – as that which creates wealth, and posits the object itself no longer in the guise of money, but as the product generally, as the universal result of labour. That product is still [posited], in conformity with the limitation on the activity, as a naturally defined product – an agricultural product, an earth-product *par excellence.*

It was a prodigious advance of Adam Smith to throw away any specificity in wealth-producing activity – labour pure and simple, neither manufacturing nor commercial nor agricultural labour, but the one as much as the other. With the abstract generality of wealth-creating activity [there is] also the generality of the object defined as wealth, as the product generally or, again, labour generally, but as past, objectified labour. How immense and difficult that transition was, emerges from the fact that Adam Smith himself still lapses from time to time into the physiocratic system. It might appear thereby as if only the abstract expression for the simplest and oldest relationship has been discovered, the relationship in which men – in whatever form of society – emerge as producing. This is correct in one way, [but] not in another. The indifference towards a specific form of labour presupposes a very developed totality of actual types of labour, of which one is no longer dominating [over] the others. Thus the most general abstractions generally develop only with the richest concrete development, where one [abstraction] appears common to many, common to all. Then one ceases to be able to think only [in terms] of a particular form. On the other hand, this abstraction of labour generally is not merely the mental result of [abstracting from] a concrete totality of labours. The indifference towards the specific type of labour corresponds to a form of society in which individuals transfer with ease from one type of labour into another and the specific type of labour is contingent to them, hence indifferent. Here labour has become not only in the category but in actuality a means to the creation of wealth generally and has ceased being attached to individuals as a specification in a particular situation. Such a condition is at its highest development in the most modern form of existence of bourgeois society – the United States. Therefore the abstraction [consisting] of the category 'labour', 'labour generally', labour *sans phrase*, the starting point of modern [political] economy, only here becomes truly practical. Therefore the simplest abstraction, which modern [political] economy puts at its head and which expresses a very old relationship, a relationship valid for all forms of society, appears truly practical in that [degree of] abstraction only as a category of the most modern society. One could say [that] that which appears in the United States as a historical product – that indifference towards the specific [form of] labour – appears, for example, with the Russians, as a spontaneous disposition. Only it makes a fiendish difference whether barbarians have the disposition to be applied to anything, or whether civilised men apply themselves to everything. And then with the Russians the traditional doggedness in an utterly specific [form of] labour – from which they can be shaken only by an outside influence – corresponds practically to that indifference towards the specificity of labour.

That example of labour shows strikingly how the most abstract categories themselves are, in the specificity of that abstraction itself – in spite of their validity for all epochs – their validity just on account of being abstractions, just as much the product of historical relations, and how they possess their full validity only for and within those relations.

Bourgeois society is the most developed and most diverse historical organisation of production. The categories which express its relations [and] the essence of its arrangement, allow at the same time an insight into the arrangement of production and the relations of production of all extinct forms of society with whose fragments and elements bourgeois society is constructed, whose remains, still not yet entirely obsolete, persist in bourgeois society, [and what were] mere indications [in extinct forms of society] have been developed to a specialised significance. In the anatomy of man there is a key to the anatomy of the ape. The indications of the higher types in the subordinate types of animal life can only be understood, on the other hand, if the higher type itself is already well known. Thus bourgeois economy offers the key to [the economy of] antiquity. However, by no means [is this revealed] by the approach of economists who obliterate all historical differences and see in all forms of society the bourgeois forms. One can understand tribute, tithes, etc., if one is acquainted with ground rent. However, one must not identify them [with each other]. Furthermore, since bourgeois society itself is only an antithetical form of development, relations of earlier forms will often be found in it only in a completely stunted form, or quite travestied. For example, communal property. Hence, if it is true that the categories of bourgeois economy possess a truth for all other forms of society, then it is to be taken with a grain of salt. They could contain them [in a] developed, stunted, caricatured [form], etc., always different in [an] essential respect. So-called historical development is generally based on [the fact] that the last form considers the past as stages [in the development] of itself, and, since the last form is seldom capable of criticising itself, and [then] only under wholly specific conditions, it always views itself one-sidedly – we are here naturally not discussing those historical periods which present themselves as a time of decay. The Christian religion was only capable of starting on the objective understanding of earlier mythologies as soon as its self-criticism was at a certain stage of completion, [as soon as it was there] virtually, so to speak. Thus bourgeois [political] economy only came to an understanding of feudal, ancient, [and] oriental society as soon as the self-criticism of bourgeois society had begun. To the extent that bourgeois [political] economy does not purely identify itself with the past in a mythologising way, its critique resembles earlier critiques, namely the feudal critique [of bourgeois society] with which it had to battle directly, [or] the critique which Christianity practised on paganism, or the critique by Protestantism of Catholicism.

As with any historical social science generally, one must always bear in mind with the progress of economic categories that, as in actuality, so in the head, the subject, here modern bourgeois society, is given, and that the categories express forms of being, specifications of existence, often only single sides of that specific society, of that subject, and hence that it [social science] does not *really* begin *scientifically* where it is first talked about *as such*. This is to be borne in mind because there is something that is immediately to hand that is decisive for the classification [of categories]. For example, nothing appears more in accord with nature than to begin with ground rent, with landed property, since it is bound up with the earth, the source of all production and all existence, and with the first form of production of all societies which are established to some extent – agriculture. However, nothing would be more false. In all forms of society there is a specific [form of] production which directs all the others, and whose relations therefore direct all the other relations, [and their] position and influence. There is a general illumination in which all other colours are submerged and [which] modifies them in their particularity. There is a particular ether which defines the specific gravity of everything in it. For example, with herdsmen (peoples who merely hunt and fish lie outside the point where actual development begins). With them a certain form of cultivation of the earth comes to the fore, a sporadic form. Landed property is thereby defined. It is common [property] and that form is retained more or less as those people more or less cling to their tradition, e.g. the communal property of the Slavs. With peoples [who have reached the stage] of settled cultivation of the land – that settling is already an important step – where that form predominates, as in antiquity and the feudal [epoch], industry itself (and its organisation and the forms of property which correspond to it) has more or less the character of landed property; industry is either wholly dependent on landed property, as with the ancient Romans, or, as in the middle ages, industry, in the town and according to its relations, imitates the country. So far as it is not pure money-capital, capital itself in the middle ages, as the traditional tool, etc., has the character of landed property. In bourgeois society this is reversed. Agriculture becomes more and more a simple branch of industry and is wholly dominated by capital. It is the same with ground rent. In all forms in which ground rent dominates, the natural relationship is still predominating. In those [forms] where capital dominates, the socially, historically created element [predominates]. Ground rent cannot be understood without capital. However, capital [can] indeed [be understood] without ground rent. Capital is the economic power of bourgeois society, the power ruling over everything. It must form the starting point as [well as] the terminal point and must be developed before landed property. After both are considered particularly, their reciprocal relationship must be considered.

Therefore it would be impracticable and false to let the economic categories succeed one another in the sequence in which they were the defining categories historically. Rather, their order of succession is specified by the relationship which they have to one another in modern bourgeois society, and that relationship is exactly the reverse of that which appears as their succession in accordance with nature or that which corresponds to the order of their historical development. We are not dealing with the relation [to each other] which the economic relations take up historically in the sequence of different forms of society. Still less [are we dealing with] their order of succession 'in the idea' (*Proudhon*) (a hallucinatory conception of historical movement). Rather [we are dealing] with their arrangement within modern bourgeois society.

The purity (abstract specificity) in which the trading peoples – Phoenicians, Carthaginians – appear in the ancient world is given through the predominance of the agricultural peoples themselves. Where capital is not yet the ruling element of society, capital as trading or money capital appears in that very abstraction. Lombards [and] Jews take the same place in opposition to the agricultural societies of the middle ages.

As a further example of the different place which the same categories take in different stages of society: one of the latest forms of bourgeois society: *joint-stock companies*. However, they also appear in the beginning of bourgeois society in the great privileged trading companies, which were provided with monopolies.

The concept of national wealth itself creeps in with the economists of the seventeenth century – a conception which continues to some extent in the economists of the eighteenth century – that wealth is created merely for the state, but [at the same time] the power of the state stands in proportion to that wealth. It was this still unconsciously hypocritical form in which wealth itself, and the production of it, was proclaimed as the purpose of the modern state, and the modern state is considered [in this view] only as a means to the production of wealth.

Thus the classification to be made is obviously, (1) the general abstract definitions which more or less belong to all forms of society, but in the sense elucidated above. (2) The categories which constitute the inner arrangement of bourgeois society and on which the fundamental classes are based. Capital, wage-labour, landed property. Their relationship to one another. Town and country. The three great social classes. Exchange between them. Circulation. Credit in general (private). (3) Summary of bourgeois society in the form of the state. [The state] considered in relationship to itself. The 'unproductive' classes. Taxes. National debt. Public credit. Population. Colonies. Emigration. (4) International relation of production. International division of labour. International exchange. Export and import. Rate of exchange. (5) The world market and crises.

4. Production, means of production and relations of production, relations of production and relations of commerce. Forms of the state and forms of consciousness in relation to the relations of production and commerce. Legal relations. Family relations.

NB in regard to points which are to be mentioned here and must not be forgotten:

(1) In the past *war* has developed, like peace; [that is the] way, as through war and in the army, etc., [that] certain economic relations, like wage labour, machinery, etc., are developed earlier than in the interior of bourgeois society. Also the relation of productive force and the relations of commerce are particularly clear in the army.

(2) *Relation of historiography, hitherto ideal, to real historiography, namely* [the relation] *of so-called cultural history*, which [includes] all history of religion and political history, [to real historiography]. (On this occasion something can also be said about the different

types of historiography up to now. The so-called objective [type]. The subjective [type]. (The moral [type], among others.) The philosophical [type].)

(3) *Secondary* [relation] *and tertiary* [relation], generally *derivative, transmitted*, relations of production, which are not original. Here relations play a role internationally.

(4) *Objections concerning the materialism of this view. Relation to naturalistic materialism.*

(5) *Dialectic of the concept productive force (means of production) and relations of production*, a dialectic whose limits are to be specified and which does not abolish the real difference.

(6) *The unequal relation of the development of material production, for example, to artistic production.* Generally the concept of progress is not to be understood in its familiar abstraction. Modern art, etc. That disproportion is still not so important and difficult to understand as a disproportion within practical-social relations themselves. For example, education. The relation of the *United States* to Europe. But the really difficult point to be examined here is how the relations of production enter as legal relations into unequal development. Therefore, for example, the relation of Roman civil law (in criminal law and public law it is less the case) to modern production.

(7) *This view appears as* [a view of] *necessary development.* However, justification of the contingent [as opposed to the necessary]. How [to do this?]. (Freedom, among other [subjects], also.) (Operation of the means of communication. World history did not always exist; history as world history is a result.)

(8) *The starting point is naturally that of natural specificity*; subjectively and objectively. Tribes, races, etc.

(1) It is known in the case of art that specific times of artistic flowering by no means stand in a proportional relation to the general development of society, therefore [they do not stand in a proportional relation] to the general development of the material basis, to the general development, as it were, of the bone-structure of its organisation. For example, the Greeks compared with the moderns or Shakespeare. It is recognised of certain forms of art, e.g. the epic, that they can never be produced in their epoch-making classical form as soon as there arises the production of art as such; therefore [it is the case] that within the compass of art itself certain

meaningful forms of it are only possible at an undeveloped stage of artistic development. If this is the case in the relation of the different types of art within the realm of art itself, [then] it is already less striking that it is the case in the relation of the whole realm of art to the general development of society. The difficulty consists only in the general understanding of those contradictions. As soon as they have been specified, they are already clarified.

Let us take, for example, the relation of Greek art and then Shakespeare's art to the present. It is known that Greek mythology is not only the arsenal of Greek art but [also] its ground. Is the perception of nature and of social relations which lies at the basis of the Greek imagination, and hence of Greek [mythology], possible with self-actors [in spinning factories] and trains and locomotives and electrical telegraphs? What has become of Vulcan against Roberts and Co. [manufacturers of 'self-actors'], Jupiter against the lightning conductor, and Hermes against the [financial practices of the] *crédit mobilier?* All mythology controls and rules and forms the powers of nature in the imagination and through the imagination; therefore mythology disappears with actual domination over natural powers. What has become of Fama beside [*The Times* newspaper in] Printing House Square? Greek art presupposes Greek mythology, that is, nature and social forms themselves are already worked up in an unconsciously artistic mode by the folk imagination. That is its material. Not just any mythology, that is, not just any unconsciously artistic working-up of nature (here under nature everything has the character of an object [for mythology], hence society is included [among the objects for mythology]). Egyptian mythology could never be the seed bed or the womb of Greek art. However, in any case there must be a mythology. Therefore in no case is there a development of society which excludes all mythological relation to it; [it] demands of the artist an imagination independent of mythology.

From another side: is Achilles possible with powder and shot? Or, generally, the *Iliad* with the printing press, and, specifically, with the printing machine? Do not singing and recitation and the muse cease being necessary with the press-bar [in mechanical printing], therefore do not the necessary conditions of epic poetry disappear?

However, the difficulty does not lie in understanding that Greek art and epic are tied up with a certain social form of development. The difficulty is that they still give us artistic enjoyment and serve in a certain relationship as the norm and unreachable standard.

A man cannot become a child again, or he becomes childish. But does not the *naïveté* of a child delight him, and must he not himself strive to reproduce its truth again at a higher level? Does not the character of every epoch revive true to its nature in the nature of the child? Why should not the historical childhood of mankind, where mankind is displayed at its most beautiful, exercise an eternal charm as a never-recurring stage? There are naughty children and precocious children. Many of the ancient peoples belong in that category. The Greeks were normal children. The charm of their art for us is not in contradiction with the undeveloped stage of society on which it grew. Rather, [the charm] is the result of the art and is inseparably connected with the fact that the immature social conditions under which it originated, and alone could originate, can never recur.

A Contribution to the Critique of Political Economy

Preface

I am surveying the bourgeois economic system in this sequence: *capital, landed property, wage-labour; the state, foreign trade, world market*. Under the first three headings I investigate the economic circumstances of the three great classes into which modern bourgeois society is divided; the relevance of the other three headings is obvious at a glance. The first instalment of the first book, which deals with capital, consists of the following chapters: (1) The Commodity; (2) Money or Simple Circulation; (3) Capital in General. The first two chapters form the content of the present volume. All the material lies before me in the form of monographs written at widely different times for my own self-clarification, not for publication, and their coherent exposition according to the plan above depends on the vagaries of circumstance.

I am omitting a general introduction [of 1857 to the *Grundrisse*] which I had dashed off, because on further reflection any anticipation of results yet to be proved seems disruptive, and the reader who wants to follow me at all must resolve to progress from the individual instance to the general case. At this point, however, a few remarks concerning the course of my own politico-economic studies would appear to be in order.

At university my major subject was jurisprudence, which I pursued as a subordinate course alongside philosophy and history. It was during the years 1842–3 as editor of the *Rheinische Zeitung* that I first encountered the embarrassment of having to discuss so-called material interests. The debates of the Rhineland Assembly concerning wood-gathering rights in forests and land sales on country estates, the official polemic, which Herr [Edgar] von Schaper, then lord lieutenant of the Rhine Province, initiated with the *Rheinische Zeitung* concerning the circumstances of the Mosel peasantry, and finally the controversy concerning free trade and protective tariffs, provided the first occasions to pursue economic questions. On the other hand, as the desire 'to make progress' often outweighed factual knowledge at that time, an echo of French socialism and communism, faintly tinged with philosophy, made itself audible in the *Rheinische Zeitung*. I made clear my opposition to this botching, but at the same time frankly admitted in a controversy with the *Allgemeine Augsburger Zeitung* that my previous studies did not permit me to venture any kind of judgement on the content of the French movements themselves. So I eagerly made use of the illusion held by the backers of the *Rheinische Zeitung* – that it was possible to reverse the sentence of death passed on the paper by taking a weaker editorial line – to draw back from the public stage into the private study.

The first work undertaken to dispel the doubts which disturbed me was a critical examination of the Hegelian legal philosophy, the introduction to which appeared in the *Deutsch-Französische Jahrbücher* published in Paris in 1844. The upshot of my investigation was that legal relationships as well as types of state are to be understood neither on their own terms nor in terms of the so-called general development of the human intellect, but are rather rooted in the material relations of life, the totality of which Hegel termed 'bourgeois society', following English and French practice of the eighteenth century, but that the anatomy of bourgeois society is to be sought in political economy. The investigation of the latter, which I began in Paris, I continued in Brussels, where I had migrated following an expulsion order issued by M. Guizot. The general conclusion that I reached and which, once attained, served as a guide for my studies, can be formulated briefly as follows: In the social production of their lives men enter into relations that are specific, necessary and independent of their will, relations of production which correspond to a specific stage of development of their material productive forces. The totality of these relations of production forms the economic structure of society, the real basis from which rises a legal and political superstructure, and to which correspond specific forms of social consciousness. The mode of production of material life conditions the social, political and intellectual life-process generally. It is not the consciousness of men that specifies their being, but on the contrary their social being that specifies their consciousness. At a certain level of their development the material productive forces of society come into contradiction with the already existing relations of production, or in what is merely a legal expression for this, with the property relations within which they had previously functioned. From forms of development of the productive forces these relations turn into their fetters. Then an epoch of social revolution commences. With the alteration of the economic foundation the whole colossal superstructure is more or less rapidly transformed. In examining such transformations one must always distinguish between the transformation in the economic conditions of production, to be established with the accuracy of physical science, and the legal, political, religious, artistic or philosophical, in short ideological forms in which men become conscious of this conflict and fight it out. Just as one does not assess an individual by what he thinks of himself, so one does not assess such an epoch of transformation from its own consciousness, rather one must instead explain this consciousness from the contradictions of material life, from the already existing conflict between the forces of production and relations of production in society. A social formation never comes to an end before all the forces of production which it can accommodate are developed, and new, higher relations of production never come into place before the material conditions of their existence have gestated in the womb of the old society. Hence humanity only sets itself such problems as it can solve, for on careful consideration one always finds that the problems themselves only arise where the material conditions of their solution are known to be on hand or at least in the process of development. In broad outline Asiatic, ancient, feudal and modern bourgeois modes of production can be designated as progressive epochs in the economic development of society. Bourgeois relations of production are the last antagonistic form of the social process of production, antagonistic not in the sense of individual antagonism, rather of an antagonism growing out of the conditions of life in society for individuals, but at the same time the productive forces developing in the womb of bourgeois society create the material conditions for the resolution of this antagonism. With that social formation the pre-history of human society draws to a close.

Friedrich Engels, with whom, since the appearance of his inspired sketch of a critique of the economic categories (in the *Deutsch-Französische Jahrbücher*), I maintained a constant exchange of ideas by correspondence, had arrived at the same conclusion as I by another road (compare his *Condition of the Working Class in England*), and as he also settled in Brussels in the spring of 1845, we made up our minds to develop our viewpoint together in opposition to the ideological one of German philosophy, in fact to settle up with our former philosophical conscience. The intention was carried out in the form of a critique of post-Hegelian philosophy [*The German Ideology: Critique of the New German Philosophy . . . and Socialism*]. The manuscript, two stout octavo volumes, had long arrived at its place of publication in Westphalia when we received the news that changed circumstances did not permit printing it. We abandoned the manuscript to the gnawing criticism of the mice all the more willingly as we had accomplished our main purpose – self-clarification. Of the disparate works through which we laid our views before the public at one time or another, I mention only the Manifesto of the Communist Party composed by Engels and myself, and a 'Discourse on Free Trade' published by me. The distinguishing features of our view were first scientifically, though only polemically indicated in my *Poverty of Philosophy*, published in 1847 and directed against Proudhon. An excerpt on 'Wage-labour' written in German, in which I pieced together my lectures on the subject as delivered to the German Workers Association of Brussels, was discontinued in press by the February revolution and my consequent forced departure from Belgium.

Editing the *Neue Rheinische Zeitung* in 1848 and 1849 and ensuing circumstances interrupted my economic studies, which could only be resumed in 1850 in London. The immense collections on the history of political economy in the British Museum, the convenience of London for observing bourgeois society, and finally the new stage of development which bourgeois society appears to have attained through the discovery of gold in California and Australia, made me resolved to begin again from the beginning and to work critically through the new material. In themselves these studies led to seemingly remote subjects on which I had to work for shorter or longer periods. But the time available to me was really diminished through the harsh necessity of grubwork. My eight-year-long association with the first Anglo-American newspaper, the *New-York Tribune*, forced an extraordinary fragmentation of my studies, since only rarely was I engaged in journalism in the proper sense. Because articles on current economic conditions in England and on the Continent formed such a significant part of my output, it became necessary for me to make myself conversant with practical details which lie outside the scope of political economy proper.

This sketch of the course of my studies in the realm of political economy is intended merely to demonstrate that my views, however one may judge them, and however little they coincide with the interests and prejudices of the ruling classes, are the result of conscientious and lengthy research. But over the entrance to science, as over the entrance to hell, this demand must be registered:

Here you must leave all wariness behind;
All trace of cowardice must be extinguished. (Dante, *The Divine Comedy*, III.14–15)

KARL MARX
London, January 1859

The Civil War in France[1]
Address of the General Council of the International Working-Men's Association To All the Members of the Association in Europe and the United States

I

On the 4th of September 1870, when the working men of Paris proclaimed the republic, which was almost instantaneously acclaimed throughout France, without a single voice of dissent, a cabal of place-hunting barristers, with Thiers for the statesman and Trochu for their general, took hold of the Hôtel de Ville. At that time they were imbued with so fanatical a faith in the mission of Paris to represent France in all epochs of historical crises, that, to legitimise their usurped titles as governors of France, they thought it quite sufficient to produce their lapsed mandates as representatives of Paris. In our second address on the late [Franco-Prussian] War [of 1870–1], five days after the rise of these men, we told you who they were. Yet, in the turmoil of surprise, with the real leaders of the working class still shut up in Bonapartist prisons and the Prussians already marching upon Paris, Paris bore with their assumption of power, on the express condition that it was to be wielded for the single purpose of national defence. Paris, however, was not to be defended without arming its working class, organising them into an effective force, and training their ranks by the war itself. But Paris armed was the revolution armed. A victory of Paris over the Prussian aggressor would have been a victory of the French

---

[1] Marx's insertions into quoted or paraphrased material are indicated by double square brackets [[ ]]; editorial insertions are in square brackets [ ], as usual. I have largely modernised the spelling, capitalisation and other conventions of the English editions of 1871.

workman over the French capitalist and his state parasites. In this conflict between national duty and class interest, the government of national defence did not hesitate one moment to turn into a government of national defection.

The first step they took was to send Thiers on a roving tour to all the courts of Europe, there to beg mediation by offering the barter of the republic for a king. Four months after the commencement of the siege [on 19 September 1870], when they thought the opportune moment come for breaking the first word of capitulation, Trochu, in the presence of Jules Favre and others of his colleagues, addressed the assembled mayors of Paris in these terms:-

> The first question put to me by my colleagues on the very evening of the 4th of September was this: Paris, can it, with any chance of success stand a siege by the Prussian army? I did not hesitate to answer in the negative. Some of my colleagues here present will warrant the truth of my words and the persistence of my opinion. I told them, in these very terms, that, under the existing state of things, the attempt of Paris to hold out a siege by the Prussian army, would be a folly. Without doubt, I added, it would be an heroic folly; but that would be all ... The events [[managed by himself]] have not given the lie to my provision.

This nice little speech of Trochu was afterwards published by M. Corbon, one of the mayors present.

Thus, on the very evening of the proclamation of the republic, Trochu's 'plan' was known to his colleagues to be the capitulation of Paris. If national defence had been more than a pretext for the personal government of Thiers, Favre, & Co., the upstarts of the 4th of September would have abdicated on the 5th – would have initiated the Paris people into Trochu's 'plan', and called upon them to surrender at once, or to take their own fate into their own hands. Instead of this, the infamous impostors resolved upon curing the heroic folly of Paris by a regimen of famine and broken heads, and to dupe her in the meanwhile by ranting manifestos, holding forth that Trochu, 'the Governor of Paris, will never capitulate', and Jules Favre, the Foreign minister, will 'not cede an inch of our territory, nor a stone of our fortresses.' In a letter to Gambetta, that very same Jules Favre avows that what they were 'defending' against were not the Prussian soldiers, but the working men of Paris.

During the whole continuance of the siege [19 September 1870 to 28 January 1871] the Bonapartist cutthroats, whom Trochu had wisely intrusted with the command of the Paris army, exchanged, in their intimate correspondence, ribald jokes at the well-understood mockery of defence (see, for instance, the correspondence of Alphonse Simon Guiod, supreme commander of the artillery of the Army of Defence of Paris and Grand Cross of the Legion of Honour, to Susane, general of division of artillery, a correspondence published by the *Journal Officiel* of the Commune). The mask of imposture was at last dropped on the 28th of January, 1871. With the true heroism of utter self-debasement, the government of national defence, in their *capitulation*, came out as the government of France by Bismarck's prisoners – a part so base that Louis Bonaparte himself had, at Sedan, shrunk from accepting it. After the events of the 18th of March [1871], on their wild flight to Versailles, the capitulards left in the hands of Paris the documentary evidence of their treason, to destroy which, as the Commune says in its manifesto to the provinces, 'those men would not recoil from battering Paris into a heap of ruins washed by a sea of blood.'

To be eagerly bent upon such a consummation, some of the leading members of the government of Defence had, besides, most peculiar reasons of their own.

Shortly after the conclusion of the armistice [on 28 January 1871], M. Milière, one of the representatives of Paris to the national assembly, now shot by express order of Jules Favre, published a series of authentic legal documents in proof that Jules Favre, living in concubinage with the wife of a drunkard resident at Algiers, had, by a most daring concoction of forgeries, spread over many years, contrived to grasp, in the name of the children of his adultery, a large succession, which made him a rich man, and that, in a lawsuit undertaken by the legitimate heirs, he only escaped exposure by the connivance of the Bonapartist tribunals. As these dry legal documents were not to be got rid of by any amount of rhetorical horsepower, Jules Favre, for the first time in his life, held his tongue, quietly awaiting the outbreak of the civil war, in order, then, frantically to denounce the people of Paris as a band of escaped convicts in utter revolt against family, religion, order, and property. This same forger had hardly got into power, after the 4th of September, when he sympathetically let loose upon society [the editor] Pic and [the Bonapartist] Taillefer, convicted, even under the Empire, of forgery, in the scandalous affair of the [fraudulent newspaper] *Etendard*. One of these men, Taillefer, having dared to return to Paris under the Commune, was at once reinstated in prison; and then Jules Favre exclaimed, from the tribune of the national assembly, that Paris was setting free all her jailbirds!

Ernest Picard, the [comedian] Joe Miller of the government of national defence, who appointed himself home minister of the republic after having in vain striven to become the home minister of the Empire, is the brother of one Arthur Picard, an individual expelled from the Paris Bourse as a blackleg (see report of the prefecture of Police, dated 13th July, 1867), and convicted, on his own confession, of a theft of 300,000 francs, while manager of one of the branches of the Société Générale [du Crédit Mobilier], rue Palestro, No. 5 (see report of the Prefecture of Police, 11th December, 1868). This Arthur Picard was made by Ernest Picard the editor of his paper, *l'Electeur Libre*. While the common run of stockjobbers were led astray by the official lies of this home office paper, Arthur was running backwards and forwards between the home office and the Bourse, there to discount the disasters of the French army. The whole financial correspondence of that worthy pair of brothers fell into the hands of the Commune.

Jules Ferry, a penniless barrister before the 4th of September, contrived, as mayor of Paris during the siege, to job a fortune out of famine. The day on which he would have to give an account of his maladministration would be the day of his conviction.

These men, then, could find, in the ruins of Paris only, their tickets-of-leave [as on parole from prison]: they were the very men Bismarck wanted. With the help of some shuffling of cards, Thiers, hitherto the secret prompter of the government, now appeared at its head, with the ticket-of-leave men for his ministers.

Thiers, that monstrous gnome, has charmed the French bourgeoisie for almost half a century, because he is the most consummate intellectual expression of their own class-corruption. Before he became a statesman he had already proved his lying powers as an historian. The chronicle of his public life is the record of the misfortunates of France. Banded, before 1830, with the republicans, he slipped into office under [King] Louis Philippe by betraying his protector [the prime minister] Lafitte, ingratiating himself with the king by exciting mob-riots against the clergy, during which the church of Saint Germain l'Auxerrois and the Archbishop's palace were plundered, and by acting the minister-spy upon, and the jail-accoucheur of, the duchess de Berry [who led the legitimist rebellion of 1831]. The massacre of the republicans in the Rue Transnonain [in 1834], and the subsequent infamous laws of September [1835] against the press and the right of association, were his work. Reappearing as the chief of the cabinet in March 1840, he astonished France with his plan of fortifying Paris. To the republicans, who denounced this plan as a sinister plot against the liberty of Paris, he replied from the tribune of the chamber of deputies:– 'What! to fancy that any works of fortification could ever endanger liberty! And first of all you calumniate any possible government in supposing that it could some day attempt to maintain itself by bombarding the capital; . . . but that government would be a hundred times more impossible after its victory than before.' Indeed, no government would ever have dared to bombard Paris from the forts, but that government which had previously surrendered these forts to the Prussians.

When King 'Bomba' [Ferdinand II of Naples] tried his hand at Palermo, in January, 1848, Thiers, then long since out of office, again rose in the chamber of deputies:

> You know, gentlemen, what is happening at Palermo. You, all of you, shake with horror [[in the parliamentary sense]] on hearing that during forty-eight hours a large town has been bombarded – by whom? Was it by a foreign enemy exercising the rights of war? No, gentlemen, it was by its own government. And why? Because that unfortunate town demanded its rights. Well, then, for the demand of its rights it has got forty-eight hours of bombardment . . . Allow me to appeal to the opinion of Europe. It is doing a service to mankind to arise, and to make reverberate, from what is perhaps the greatest tribune in Europe, some words [[indeed words]] of indignation against such acts . . . When the regent Espartero, who had rendered services to his country, [[which M. Thiers never did]] intended bombarding Barcelona, in order to suppress its insurrection, there arose from all parts of the world a general outcry of indignation.

Eighteen months afterwards, M. Thiers was amongst the fiercest defenders of the bombardment of Rome [in May 1849] by a French army. In fact, the fault of King Bomba seems to have consisted in this only, that he limited his bombardment to forty-eight hours.

A few days before the revolution of February [1848], fretting at the long exile from place and pelf to which Guizot had condemned him, and sniffling in the air the scent of an approaching popular commotion, Thiers, in that pseudo-heroic style which won him the nickname of *Mirabeau-mouche*, declared to the chamber of deputies: 'I am of the party of revolution, not only in France, but in Europe. I wish the government of the revolution to remain in the hands of moderate men ... but if that government should fall into the hands of ardent minds, even into those of radicals, I shall, for all that, not desert my cause. I shall always be of the party of the revolution.' The revolution of February [1848] came. Instead of displacing the Guizot cabinet by the Thiers cabinet, as the little man had dreamt, it superseded [King] Louis Philippe by the republic. On the first day of the popular victory he carefully hid himself, forgetting that the contempt of the working men screened him from their hatred. Still, with his legendary courage, he continued to shy the public stage, until the June [1848] massacres had cleared it for his sort of action. Then he became the leading mind of the 'party of order' and its parliamentary republic, that anonymous interregnum, in which all the rival factions of the ruling class conspired together to crush the people, and conspired against each other to restore each of them its own monarchy. Then, as now, Thiers denounced the republicans as the only obstacle to the consolidation of the republic; then, as now, he spoke to the republic as the hangman spoke to Don Carlos [in Schiller's play] – 'I shall assassinate thee, but for thy own good.' Now, as then, he will have to explain on the day after his victory: *L'Empire est fait* – the Empire is consummated. Despite his hypocritical homilies about necessary liberties and his personal grudge against Louis Bonaparte, who had made a dupe of him, and kicked out parliamentarism – and outside of its factitious atmosphere the little man is conscious of withering into nothingness – he had a hand in all the infamies of the Second Empire, from the occupation of Rome by French troops to the war with Prussia, which he incited by his fierce invective against German unity – not as a cloak of Prussian despotism, but as an encroachment upon the vested right of France in German disunion. Fond of brandishing, with his dwarfish arms, in the face of Europe the sword of the first Napoleon, whose historical shoe-black he had become, his foreign policy always culminated in the utter humiliation of France, from the London convention of 1840 to the Paris capitulation of [March] 1871, and the present civil war, where he hounds on the prisoners of Sedan and Metz [where the French were defeated in September and October 1870] against Paris by special permission of Bismarck. Despite his versatility of talent and shiftiness of purpose, this man has his whole lifetime been wedded to the most fossil routine. It is self-evident that to him the deeper under-currents of modern society remained for ever hidden; but even the most palpable changes on its surface were abhorrent to a brain all the vitality of which had fled to the tongue. That he never tired of denouncing as a sacrilege any deviation from the old French protective system. When a minister of Louis Philippe, he railed at railways as a wild chimera; and when in opposition under Louis Bonaparte, he branded as a profanation every attempt to reform the rotten French army system. Never in his long political career has he been guilty of a single – even the smallest – measure of any practical use. Thiers was consistent only in his greed for wealth and his hatred of the men that produce it. Having entered his first ministry under Louis Philippe poor as Job, he left it a millionaire. His last ministry under the same king (of the 1st of March, 1840) exposed him to public taunts of peculation in the chamber of deputies, to which he was content to reply by tears – a commodity he deals in as freely as Jules Favre, or any other crocodile. At [the] Bordeaux [meeting of the national assembly after the armistice of January 1871] his first measure for saving France from impending financial ruin was to endow himself with three millions a year, the first and the last word of the 'economical republic', the vista of which he had opened to his Paris electors in 1869. One of his former colleagues of the chamber of deputies of 1830, himself a capitalist [and follower of Proudhon] and, nevertheless, a devoted member of the Paris Commune, M. Beslay, lately addressed Thiers thus in a public placard: – 'The enslavement of labour by capital has always been the cornerstone of your policy, and from the very day you saw the republic of labour installed at the Hôtel de Ville, you have never ceased to cry out to France: "These are criminals!"' A master in small state roguery, a virtuoso in perjury and treason, a craftsman in all the petty stratagems, cunning devices, and base perfidies of parliamentary party-warfare; never scrupling, when out of office, to fan a revolution, and to stifle it in blood when at the helm of the state; with class prejudices standing him in the place of ideas, and vanity in the place of a heart; his private life as infamous as his public life is odious – even now, when playing the part of a French Sulla, he cannot help setting off the abomination of his deeds by the ridicule of his ostentation.

The capitulation of Paris, by surrendering to Prussia not only Paris, but all France, closed the long-continued intrigues of treason with the enemy, which the usurpers of the 4th September [1870] had begun, as Trochu himself said, on the very same day. On the other hand, it initiated the civil war [in January 1871] they were now to wage, with the assistance of Prussia, against the republic and Paris. The trap was laid in the very terms of the capitulation. At that time above one-third of the territory was in the hands of the enemy, the capital was cut off from the provinces, all communications were disorganised. To elect under such circumstances a real representation of France was impossible, unless ample time were given for preparation. In view of this, the capitulation stipulated that a national assembly must be elected within eight days; so that in many parts of France the news of the impending election arrived on its eve only. This assembly, moreover, was, by an express clause of the capitulation, to be elected for the sole purpose of deciding on peace or war, and, eventually, to conclude a treaty of peace. The population could not but feel that the terms of the armistice [of 28 January 1871] rendered the continuation of the war impossible, and that for sanctioning the peace imposed by Bismarck, the worst men in France were the best. But not content with these precautions, Thiers, even before the secret of the armistice had been broached to Paris, set out for an electioneering tour through the provinces, there to galvanise back into life the legitimist party, which now, along with the Orléanists, had to take the place of the then imposs-ible Bonapartists. He was not afraid of them. Impossible as a government of modern France, and, therefore, contemptible as rivals, what party were more eligible as tools of counter-revolution than the party whose action, in the words of Thiers himself (chamber of deputies, 5th January, 1833), 'had always been confined to the three resources of foreign invasion, civil war, and anarchy'? They verily believed in the advent of their long-expected retrospective millenium. There were the heels of foreign invasion trampling upon France; there was the downfall of an empire, and the captivity of a Bonaparte [after the Battle of Sedan on 2 September 1870]; and there they were themselves. The wheel of history had evidently rolled back to stop at the [reactionary] 'chambre introuvable' of 1816 [in the restoration parliament]. In the Assemblies of the republic, 1848 to '51, they had been represented by their educated and trained parliamentary champions; it was the rank-and-file of the party which now rushed in – all the [philistine] Pourceaugnacs of France.

As soon as this assembly of 'rurals' had met at Bordeaux, Thiers made it clear to them that the peace preliminaries must be assented to at once, without even the honours of a parliamentary debate, as the only condition on which Prussia would permit them to open the war against the republic and Paris, its stronghold. The counter-revolution had, in fact, no time to lose. The Second Empire had more than doubled the national debt, and plunged all the large towns into heavy municipal debts. The war had fearfully swelled the liabilities, and mercilessly ravaged the resources of the nation. To complete the ruin, the Prussian Shylock was there with his bond [in the preliminary peace treaty of February 1871] for the keep of half a million of his soldiers on French soil, his indemnity of five milliards, and interest at 5 per cent, on the unpaid instalments thereof. Who was to pay the bill? It was only by the violent overthrow of the republic that the appropriators of wealth could hope to shift on to the shoulders of its producers the cost of a war which they, the appropriators, had themselves originated. Thus, the immense ruin of France spurred on these patriotic representatives of land and capital, under the very eyes and patronage of the invader, to graft upon the foreign war a civil war – a slaveholders' rebellion.

There stood in the way of this conspiracy one great obstacle – Paris. To disarm Paris was the first condition of success. Paris was therefore summoned by Thiers to surrender its arms. Then Paris was exasperated by the frantic anti-republican demonstrations of the 'rural' assembly and by Thiers's own equivocations about the legal status of the republic; by the threat to decapitate and decapitalise Paris; the appointment of Orléanist ambassadors; Dufaure's laws on over-due commercial bills and house-rents, inflicting ruin on the commerce and industry of Paris; Pouyer-Quertier's tax of two centimes upon every copy of every imaginable publication; the sentences of death against Blanqui and Flourens; the suppression of the republican journals; the transfer of the national assembly to Versailles; the renewal of the state of siege declared by [General] Palikao, and expired on the 4th of September [1870]; the appointment of [General] Vinoy, the *Décembriseur* [supporter of Louis Bonapart's coup of 2 December 1851], as governor of Paris – of [General] Valentin, the imperialist *gendarme*, as its prefect of police – and of [the legitimist] D'Aurelles de Paladine, the Jesuit general, as the commander-in-chief of its national guard.

And now we have to address a question to M. Thiers and the man of national defence, his understrappers. It is known that, through the agency of M. Pouyer-Quertier, his finance minister, Thiers had contracted a loan of two milliards, to be paid down at once. Now, is it true, or not, –

1. That the business was so managed that a consideration of several hundred millions was secured for the private benefit of Thiers, Jules Favre, Ernest Picard, Pouyer-Quertier, and Jules Simon? and –

2. That no money was to be paid down until after the 'pacification' of Paris?

At all events, there must have been something very pressing in the matter, for Thiers and Jules Favre, in the name of the majority of the Bordeaux assembly, unblushingly solicited the immediate occupation of Paris by Prussian troops. Such, however, was not the game of Bismarck, as he sneeringly, and in public, told the admiring Frankfurt philistines [in the German federal diet] on his return to Germany.

II

Armed Paris was the only serious obstacle in the way of the counter-revolutionary conspiracy. Paris was, therefore, to be disarmed. On this point the Bordeaux assembly was sincerity itself. If the roaring rant of its rurals had not been audible enough, the surrender of Paris by Thiers to the tender mercies of the triumvirate of Vinoy the *Décembriseur*, Valentin the Bonapartist *gendarme*, and Aurelles de Paladine the Jesuit general, would have cut off even the last

subterfuge of doubt. But while insultingly exhibiting the true purpose of the disarmament of Paris, the conspirators asked her to lay
down her arms on a pretext which was the most glaring, the most
barefaced of lies. The artillery of the Paris national guard, said
Thiers, belonged to the state, and to the state it must be returned.
The fact was this: – From the very day of the capitulation, by
which Bismarck's prisoners had signed the surrender of France,
but reserved to themselves a numerous body-guard for the express
purpose of cowing Paris, Paris stood on the watch. The national
guard reorganised themselves [as a republican federation] and
intrusted their supreme control to a central committee elected by
their whole body, save some fragments of the old Bonapartist for-
mations. On the eve of the entrance of the Prussians into Paris, the
central committee took measures for the removal to Montmartre,
Belleville, and La Villette of the cannon and *mitrailleuses* [machine
guns] treacherously abandoned by the *capitulards* in and about the
very quarters the Prussians were to occupy. That artillery had been
furnished by the subscriptions of the national guard. As their private property, it was officially recognised in the capitulation of the
28th of January [1871], and on that very title exempted from the
general surrender, into the hands of the conqueror, of arms belonging to the government. And Thiers was so utterly destitute of even
the flimsiest pretext for initiating the war against Paris, that he had
to resort to the flagrant lie of the artillery of the national guard
being state property!

The seizure of her artillery was evidently but to serve as the
preliminary to the general disarmament of Paris, and, therefore, of
the revolution of the 4th of September [1870]. But that revolution
had become the legal status of France. The republic, its work, was
recognised by the conqueror in the terms of the capitulation. After
the capitulation, it was acknowledged by all the foreign powers, and
in its name the national assembly had been summoned [in late January 1871]. The Paris working men's revolution of the 4th of September was the only legal title of the national assembly seated at
Bordeaux, and of its executive. Without it, the national assembly
would at once have to give way to the *corps législatif* [of the Second
Empire], elected in 1869 by universal [manhood] suffrage under
French, not under Prussian, rule, and forcibly dispersed by the arm
of the revolution. Thiers and his ticket-of-leave men would have

had to capitulate for safe-conducts signed by Louis Bonaparte [then a Prussian prisoner in exile], to save them from a voyage to [the penal colony in] Cayenne [in South America]. The national assembly, with its power of attorney to settle the terms of peace with Prussia, was but an incident of that revolution, the true embodiment of which was still armed Paris, which had initiated it [in September], undergone for it a five months' siege [from 19 September 1870 to 28 January 1871], with its horrors of famine, and made her prolonged resistance, despite Trochu's plan, the basis of an obstinate war of defence in the provinces. And Paris was now either to lay down her arms at the insulting behest of the rebellious slaveholders of Bordeaux, and acknowledge that her revolution of the 4th of September [1870] meant nothing but a simple transfer of power from Louis Bonaparte to his royal rivals; or she had to stand forward as the self-sacrificing champion of France, whose salvation from ruin, and whose regeneration were impossible, without the revolutionary overthrow of the political and social conditions that had engendered the Second Empire, and, under its fostering care, matured into utter rottenness. Paris, emaciated by a five months' famine, did not hesitate one moment. She heroically resolved to run all the hazards of a resistance against the French conspirators, even with Prussian cannon frowning upon her from her own forts. Still, in its abhorrence of the civil war into which Paris was to be goaded, the central committee continued to persist in a merely defensive attitude, despite the provocations of the assembly, the usurpations of the Executive, and the menacing concentration of troops in and around Paris.

Thiers opened the civil war [in earnest in March 1871] by sending Vinoy, at the head of a multitude of [police] *sergents-de-ville* and some regiments of the line, upon a nocturnal expedition against Montmartre, there to seize, by surprise, the artillery of the national guard. It is well known how this attempt broke down before the resistance of the national guard and the fraternisation of the line with the people. Aurelles de Paladine had printed beforehand his bulletin of victory, and Thiers held ready the placards announcing his measures of *coup d'état*. Now these had to be replaced by Thiers' appeals, imparting his magnanimous resolve to leave the national guard in the possession of their arms, with which, he said, he felt sure they would rally round the government against the rebels. Out of 300,000 national guards only 300 responded to the summons to rally round little Thiers against themselves. The glorious working men's revolution of the 18th March [1871] took undisputed sway of Paris. The central committee was its provisional government. Europe seemed, for a moment, to doubt whether its recent sensational performances of state and war had any reality in them, or whether they were the dreams of a long bygone past.

From the 18th of March [1871] to the entrance of the Versailles troops into Paris [in May], the proletarian revolution remained so free from the acts of violence in which the revolutions, and still more the counter-revolutions, of the 'better classes' abound, that no facts were left to its opponents to cry out about, but the execution of generals Lecomte and Clément Thomas, and the affair of the Place Vendôme.

One of the Bonapartist officers engaged in the nocturnal attempt against Montmartre, General Lecomte, had four times ordered the 81st line regiment to fire at an unarmed gathering in the Place Pigale, and on their refusal fiercely insulted them. Instead of shooting women and children, his own men shot him. The inveterate habits acquired by the soldiery under the training of the enemies of the working class are, of course, not likely to change the very moment these soldiers change sides. The same men executed Clément Thomas.

'General' Clément Thomas, a malcontent ex-quartermaster-sergeant, had, in the latter times of Louis Philippe's reign [1830–48], enlisted at the office of the republican newspaper *Le National*, there to serve in the double capacity of responsible man-of-straw (*gérant responsable*) and of duelling bully to that very combative journal. After the revolution of February [1848], the men of the *National* having got into power, they metamorphosed this old quartermaster-sergeant into a general on the eve of the butchery of June [1848], of which he, like Jules Favre, was one of the sinister plotters, and became one of the most dastardly executioners. Then he and his generalship disappeared for a long time, to again rise to the surface on the 1st November 1870. The day before, the government of Defence, caught at the Hôtel de Ville, had solemnly pledged their parole to Blanqui, Flourens, and other representatives of the working class, to abdicate their usurped power into the hands of a commune to be freely elected by Paris. Instead of keeping their word, they let loose on Paris the Bretons of Trochu, who now replaced the Corsicans of Bonaparte. General Tamisier alone, refusing to sully his name by such a breach of faith, resigned the commandership-in-chief of the national guard, and in his place Clément Thomas for once became again a general. During the whole of his tenure of command, he made war, not upon the Prussians, but upon the Paris national guard. He prevented their general armament, pitted the bourgeois battalions against the working men's battalions, weeded out the officers hostile to Trochu's 'plan', and disbanded, under the stigma of cowardice, the very same proletarian battalions whose heroism has now astonished their most inveterate enemies. Clément Thomas felt quite proud of having reconquered his June [1848] pre-eminence as the personal enemy of the working class of Paris. Only a few days before the 18th of March [1871], he laid before the War minister, Le Flô, a plan of his own for 'finishing off *la fine flue* [the cream] of the Paris *canaille*.' After Vinoy's rout, he must needs appear upon the scene of action in the quality of an amateur spy. The central committee and the Paris working men were as much responsible for the killing of Clément Thomas and Lecomte as the Princess of Wales was for the fate of the people crushed to death on the day of her entrance into London.

The massacre of unarmed citizens in the Place Vendôme is a myth which M. Thiers and the rurals persistently ignored in the assembly, intrusting its propagation exclusively to the servants' hall of European journalism. 'The men of order', the reactionists of Paris, trembled at the victory of the 18th of March [1871]. To them it was the signal of popular retribution at last arriving. The ghosts of the victims assassinated at their hands from the days of June 1848, down to the [second Blanquist insurrection on] 22nd of January, 1871, arose before their faces. Their panic was their only punishment. Even the *sergents-de-ville*, instead of being disarmed and locked up, as ought to have been done, had the gates of Paris flung wide open for their safe retreat to Versailles. The men of order were left not only unharmed, but allowed to rally and quietly to seize more than one stronghold in the very centre of Paris. This indulgence of the central committee – this magnanimity of the armed working men – so strangely at variance with the habits of the 'party of order', the latter misinterpreted as mere symptoms of conscious weakness. Hence their silly plan to try, under the cloak of an unarmed demonstration, what Vinoy had failed to perform with his cannon and *mitrailleuses*. On the 22nd of March [1871] a riotous mob of swells started from the quarters of luxury, all the [foppish] *petits crevés* in their ranks, and at their head the notorious familiars of the Empire – the Heeckeren, Coëtlogon, Henri de Pène, etc. Under the cowardly pretence of a pacific demonstration, this rabble, secretly armed with the weapons of the bravo, fell into marching order, ill-treated and disarmed the detached patrols and sentries of the national guards they met with on their progress, and, on debouching from the Rue de la Paix, with the cry of 'Down with the central committee! Down with the assassins! The national assembly for ever!' attempted to break through the line drawn up there, and thus to carry by a surprise the head-quarters of the national guard in the Place Vendôme. In reply to their pistol-shots, the regular *sommations* (the French equivalent of the English Riot Act) were made, and, proving ineffective, fire was commanded by the general of the national guard. One volley dispersed into wild flight the silly cox-combs, who expected that the mere exhibition of their 'respectability' would have the same effect upon the revolution of Paris as Joshua's trumpets upon the walls of Jericho. The runaways left behind them two national guards killed, nine severely wounded (among them a member of the central committee), and the whole scene of their exploit strewn with revolvers, daggers, and sword-canes, in evidence of the 'unarmed' character of their 'pacific' demonstration. When, on the 13th of June 1849, the national guard made a really pacific demonstration in protest against the felonious assault of French troops upon Rome, Changarnier, then general of the party of order, was acclaimed by the national assembly, and especially by M. Thiers, as the saviour of society, for having launched his troops from all sides upon these unarmed men, to shoot and sabre them down, and to trample them under their horses' feet. Paris, then, was placed under a state of siege. Dufaure hurried through the assembly new laws of repression. New arrests, new proscriptions – a new reign of terror set in. But the lower orders manage these things otherwise. The central committee of 1871 simply ignored the heroes of the 'pacific demonstration'; so much so, that only two days later they were enabled to muster, under Admiral Saisset, for the armed demonstration, crowned by the famous stampede to Versailles. In their reluctance to continue the civil war opened by Thiers' burglarious attempt on Montmartre, the central committee made themselves, this time, guilty of a decisive mistake in not at once marching upon Versailles, then completely helpless, and thus putting an end to the conspiracies of Thiers and his rurals. Instead of this, the party of order was again allowed to try its strength at the ballot-box, on the 26th of March [1871], the day of the election of the Commune. Then, in the *mairies* of Paris, they exchanged bland words of conciliation with their too generous conquerors, muttering in their hearts solemn vows to exterminate them in due time.

Now, look at the reverse of the medal. Thiers opened his second campaign against Paris in the beginning of April [1871]. The first batch of Parisian prisoners brought into Versailles was subjected to revolting atrocities, while Ernest Picard, with his hands in his trousers' pockets, strolled about jeering them, and while Mesdames Thiers and Favre, in the midst of their ladies of honour (?) applauded, from the balcony, the outrages of the Versailles mob. The captured soldiers of the line were massacred in cold blood; our brave friend, General Duval, the ironfounder, was shot without any form of trial. [General] Gallifet, the kept man of his wife, so notorious for her shameless exhibitions at the orgies of the Second Empire, boasted in a proclamation of having commanded the murder of a small troop of national guards, with their captain and lieutenant, surprised and disarmed by his *chasseurs*. [General] Vinoy, the runaway, was appointed by Thiers Grand Cross of the Legion of Honour, for his general order to shoot down every soldier of the line taken in the ranks of the federals [of the national guard]. Desmarêt, the gendarme, was decorated for the treacherous butcher-like chopping in pieces of the high-souled and chivalrous Flourens, who had saved the heads of the government of [national] defence [from the first Blanquist insurrection] on the 31st of October, 1870. 'The encouraging particulars' of his assassination were triumphantly expatiated upon by Thiers in the national assembly. With the elated vanity of a parliamentary Tom Thumb, permitted to play the part of a Tamerlane, he denied the rebels against his littleness every right of civilised warfare, up to the right of neutrality for ambulances. Nothing more horrid than that monkey allowed for a time to give full fling to his tigerish instincts, so foreseen by Voltaire [in *Candide*].[2]

After the decree of the Commune of the 5th April [1871], ordering reprisals and declaring it to be its duty 'to protect Paris against the cannibal exploits of the Versailles banditti, and to demand an eye for an eye, a tooth for a tooth', Thiers did not stop the barbarous treatment of prisoners, moreover insulting them in his bulletins as follows: – 'Never have more degraded countenances of a degraded democracy met the afflicted gazes of

---

[2] 'The column of prisoners halted in the Avenue Uhrich, and was drawn up, four or five deep, on the footway facing to the road. General Marquis de Gallifet and his staff dismounted and commenced an inspection from the left of the line. Walking down slowly and eyeing the ranks, the General stopped here and there, tapping a man on the shoulder or beckoning him out of the rear ranks. In most cases, without further parley, the individual thus selected was marched out into the centre of the road, where a small supplementary column was, thus, soon formed . . . It was evident that there was considerable room for error. A mounted officer pointed out to General Gallifet a man and woman for some particular offence. The woman, rushing out of the ranks, threw herself on her knees, and, with outstretched arms, protested her innocence in passionate terms. The general waited for a pause, and then with most impassible face and unmoved demeanour, said, "Madame, I have visited every theatre in Paris, your acting will have no effect on me" ("*ce n'est pas la peine de jouer la comédie*") . . . It was not a good thing on that day to be noticeably taller, dirtier, cleaner, older, or uglier than one's neighbours. One individual in particular struck me as probably owing his speedy release from the ills of this world to his having a broken nose . . . Over a hundred being thus chosen, a firing party told off, and the column resumed its march, leaving them behind. A few minutes afterwards a dropping fire in our rear commenced, and continued for over a quarter of an hour. It was the execution of these summarily-convicted wretches.' – Paris Correspondent *Daily News*, June 8th [1871].[[– This Gallifet, 'the kept man of his wife, so notorious for her shameless exhibitions at the orgies of the Second Empire', went, during the war, by the name of the French 'Ensign Pistol'.]]

'The *Temps*, which is a careful journal, and not given to sensation, tells a dreadful story of people imperfectly shot and buried before life was extinct. A great number were buried in the square round St. Jacques-la-Bouchière; some of them very superficially. In the daytime the roar of the busy streets prevented any notice being taken; but in the stillness of the night the inhabitants of the houses in the neighbourhood were roused by distant moans, and in the morning a clenched hand was seen protruding through the soil. In consequence of this, exhumations were ordered to take place . . . That many wounded have been buried alive I have not the slightest doubt. One case I can vouch for. When Brunel was shot with his mistress on the 24th ult. in the courtyard of a house in the Place Vendôme, the bodies lay there until the afternoon of the 27th. When the burial party came to remove the corpses, they found the woman living still, and took her to an ambulance. Though she had received four bullets she is now out of danger.' – Paris Correspondent *Evening Standard*, June 8th [1871].

honest men', – honest like Thiers himself and his ministerial ticket-of-leave men. Still the shooting of prisoners was suspended for a time. Hardly, however, had Thiers and his Decembrist generals become aware that the Communal decree of reprisals was but an empty threat, that even their gendarme spies caught in Paris under the disguise of national guards, that even *sergents-de-ville* taken with incendiary shells upon them, were spared – when the wholesale shooting of prisoners was resumed and carried on uninterruptedly to the end. Houses to which national guards had fled were surrounded by gendarmes, inundated with petroleum (which here occurs for the first time in this war), and then set fire to, the charred corpses being afterwards brought out by the ambulance of the press at the Ternes. Four national guards having surrendered to a troop of mounted *chasseurs* at Belle Epine, on the 25th of April [1871], were afterwards shot down, one after another, by the captain, a worthy man of Gallifet's. One of his four victims, left for dead, Scheffer, crawled back to the Parisian outposts, and deposed to this fact before a commission of the Commune. When [the Proudhonist deputy] Tolain interpellated the war minister upon the report of this commission, the rurals drowned his voice and forbade Le Flô to answer. It would be an insult to their 'glorious' army to speak of its deeds. The flippant tone in which Thiers' bulletins announced the bayoneting of the federals [of the national guard] surprised asleep at Moulin Saquet, and the wholesale fusillades at Clamart shocked the nerves even of the not over-sensitive London Times. But it would be ludicrous today to attempt recounting the merely preliminary atrocities committed by the bombarders of Paris and the fomenters of a slaveholders' rebellion protected by foreign invasion. Amidst all these horrors, Thiers, forgetful of his parliamentary laments on the terrible responsibility weighing down his dwarfish shoulders, boasts in his bulletins that *l'Assemblée siège paisiblement* (the assembly continues meeting in peace), and proves by his constant carousals, now with Decembrist generals, now with German princes, that his digestion is not troubled in the least, not even by the ghosts of Lecomte and Clément Thomas.

III

On the dawn of the 18th of March [1871], Paris arose to the thunderburst of 'Vive la Commune!' What is the Commune, that sphinx so tantalising to the bourgeois mind?

'The proletarians of Paris', said the central committee in its manifesto of the 18th March [1871], 'amidst the failures and treasons of the ruling classes, have understood that the hour has struck for them to save the situation by taking into their own hands the direction of public affairs. ... They have understood that it is their imperious duty and their absolute right to render themselves masters of their own destinies, by seizing upon the governmental power.' But the working class cannot simply lay hold of the ready-made state machinery, and wield it for its own purposes.

The centralised state power, with its ubiquitous organs of standing army, police, bureaucracy, clergy, and judicature – organs wrought after the plan of a systematic and hierarchic division of labour – originates from the days of absolute monarchy, serving nascent middle-class society as a mighty weapon in its struggles against feudalism. Still, its development remained clogged by all manner of medieval rubbish, seignorial rights, local privileges, municipal and guild monopolies and provincial constitutions. The gigantic broom of the French revolution of the eighteenth century swept away all these relics of bygone times, thus clearing simultaneously the social soil of its last hindrances to the superstructure of the modern state edifice raised under the First Empire, itself the offspring of the coalition wars of old semi-feudal Europe against modern France. During the subsequent regimes the government, placed under parliamentary control – that is, under the direct control of the propertied classes – became not only a hotbed of huge national debts and crushing taxes; with its irresistible allurements of place, pelf, and patronage, it became not only the bone of contention between the rival factions and adventurers of the ruling classes; but its political character changed simultaneously with the economic changes of society. At the same pace at which the progress of modern industry developed, widened, intensified the class-antagonism between capital and labour, the state power assumed more and more the character of the national power of capital over labour, of a public force organised for social enslavement, of an engine of class despotism. After every revolution marking a progressive phase in the class struggle, the purely repressive character of the state power stands out in bolder and bolder relief. The revolution of 1830, resulting in the transfer of government from the landlords to the capitalists, transferred it from the more remote to the more direct antagonisms of the working men. The bourgeois republicans, who, in the name of the revolution of February [1848], took the state power, used it for the June [1848] massacres, in order to convince the working class that 'social' republic meant the republic ensuring their social subjection, and in order to convince the royalist bulk of the bourgeois and landlord class that they might safely leave the cares and emoluments of government to the bourgeois 'republicans'. However, after their one heroic exploit of June [1848], the bourgeois republicans had, from the front, to fall back to the rear of the 'party of order' – a combination formed by all the rival fractions and factions of the appropriating class in their new openly declared antagonism to the producing classes. The proper form of their joint-stock government was the *parliamentary republic*, with Louis Bonaparte for its President. Theirs was a *regime* of avowed class terrorism and deliberate insult towards the 'vile multitude'. If the parliamentary republic, as M. Thiers said, 'divided them [[the different fractions of the ruling class]] least', it opened an abyss between that class and the whole body of society outside their spare ranks. The restraints by which their own divisions had under former regimes still checked the state power, were removed by their union; and in view of the threatening upheaval of the proletariat, they now used that state power mercilessly and ostentatiously as the national war-engine of capital against labour. In their uninterrupted crusade against the producing masses they were, however, bound not only to invest the executive with continually increased powers of repression, but at the same time to divest their own parliamentary stronghold – the national assembly – one by one, of all its own means of defence against the executive. The executive, in the person of Louis Bonaparte, turned them out. The natural offspring of the 'party-of-order' republic was the Second Empire.

The Empire, with the *coup d'état* [of 2 December 1851] for its certificate of birth, universal [manhood] suffrage for its sanction, and the sword for its sceptre, professed to rest upon the peasantry, the large mass of producers not directly involved in the struggle of capital and labour. It professed to save the working class by breaking down parliamentarism, and, with it, the undisguised subserviency of government to the propertied classes. It professed to save the propertied classes by upholding their economic supremacy over the working class; and, finally, it professed to unite all classes by reviving for all the chimera of national glory. In reality, it was the only form of government possible at a time when the bourgeoisie had already lost, and the working class had not yet acquired, the faculty of ruling the nation. It was acclaimed throughout the world as the saviour of society. Under its sway, bourgeois society, freed from political cares, attained a development unexpected even by itself. Its industry and commerce expanded to colossal dimensions; financial swindling celebrated cosmopolitan orgies; the misery of the masses was set off by a shameless display of gorgeous, meretricious, and debased luxury. The state power, apparently soaring high above society, was at the same time itself the greatest scandal of that society and the very hot-bed of all its corruptions. Its own rottenness, and the rottenness of the society it had saved, were laid bare by the bayonet of Prussia, herself eagerly bent upon transferring the supreme seat of the regime from Paris to Berlin. Imperialism is, at the same time, the most prostitute and the ultimate form of the state power which nascent middle-class society had commenced to elaborate as a means of its own emancipation from feudalism, and which full-grown bourgeois society had finally transformed into a means for the enslavement of labour by capital.

The direct antithesis to the [Second] Empire was the Commune. The cry of 'social republic', with which the revolution of February [1848] was ushered in by the Paris proletariat, did but express a vague aspiration after a republic that was not only to supersede the monarchical form of class-rule, but class-rule itself. The Commune was the positive form of that republic.

Paris, the central seat of the old governmental power, and, at the same time, the social stronghold of the French working class, had risen in arms against the attempt of Thiers and the rurals to restore and perpetuate that old governmental power bequeathed to them by the [Second] Empire. Paris could resist only because, in consequence of the siege, it had got rid of the army, and replaced it by a national guard, the bulk of which consisted of working men. This fact was now to be transformed into an institution. The first decree of the Commune, therefore, was the suppression of the standing army, and the substitution for it of the armed people.

The Commune was formed of the municipal councillors, chosen by universal [manhood] suffrage in the various wards of the town, responsible and revocable at short terms. The majority of its members were naturally working men, or acknowledged representatives of the working class. The Commune was to be a working, not a parliamentary, body, executive and legislative at the same time. Instead of continuing to be the agent of the Central government, the police was at once stripped of its political attributes, and turned into the responsible and at all times revocable agent of the Commune. So were the officials of all other branches of the administration. From the members of the Commune downwards, the public service had to be done at *workmen's wages*. The vested interests and the representation allowances of the high dignitaries of state disappeared along with the high dignitaries themselves. Public functions ceased to be the private property of the tools of the Central government. Not only municipal administration, but the whole initiative hitherto exercised by the state was laid into the hands of the Commune.

Having once got rid of the standing army and the police, the physical force elements of the old government, the Commune was anxious to break the spiritual force of repression, the 'parson-power', by the disestablishment of and disendowment of all churches as proprietary bodies. The priests were sent back to the recesses of private life, there to feed upon the alms of the faithful in imitation of their predecessors, the Apostles. The whole of the educational institutions were opened to the people gratuitously, and at the same time cleared of all interference of church and state. Thus, not only was education made accessible to all, but science itself freed from the fetters which class prejudice and governmental force had imposed upon it.

The judicial functionaries were to be divested of that sham independence which had but served to mask their abject subserviency to all succeeding governments to which, in turn, they had taken, and broken, the oaths of allegiance. Like the rest of public servants, magistrates and judges were to be elective, responsible, and revocable.

The Paris Commune was, of course, to serve as a model to all the great industrial centres of France. The communal *regime* once established in Paris and the secondary centres, the old centralised government would in the provinces, too, have to give way to the self-government of the producers. In a rough sketch of national organisation which the Commune had no time to develop, it states clearly that the Commune was to be the political form of even the smallest country hamlet, and that in the rural districts the standing army was to be replaced by a national militia, with an extremely short term of service. The rural communes of every district were to administer their common affairs by an assembly of delegates in the central town, and these district assemblies were again to send deputies to the national delegation in Paris, each delegate to be at any time revocable and bound by the *mandat impératif* (formal instructions) of his constituents. The few but important functions which still would remain for a central government were not to be suppressed, as has been intentionally mis-stated, but were to be discharged by Communal, and therefore strictly responsible agents. The unity of the nation was not to be broken, but, on the contrary, to be organised by the Communal constitution, and to become a reality by the destruction of the state power which claimed to be the embodiment of that unity independent of, and superior to, the nation itself, from which it was but a parasitic excrescence. While the merely repressive organs of the old governmental power were to be amputated, its legitimate functions were to be wrested from an authority usurping pre-eminence over society itself, and restored to the responsible agents of society. Instead of deciding once in three or six years which member of the ruling class was to misrepresent the people in Parliament, universal suffrage was to serve the people, constituted in Communes, as individual suffrage serves every other employer in the search for the workmen and managers in his business. And it is well known that companies, like individuals, in matters of real business generally know how to put the right man in the right place, and, if they for once make a mistake, to redress it promptly. On the other hand, nothing could be more foreign to the spirit of the Commune than to supersede universal suffrage by hierarchic investiture.

It is generally the fate of completely new historical creations to be mistaken for the counterpart of older and even defunct forms of social life, to which they may bear a certain likeness. Thus, this new Commune, which breaks the modern state power, has been mistaken for a reproduction of the medieval Communes, which first preceded, and afterwards became the substratum of, that very state power. – The communal constitution has been mistaken for an attempt to break up into a federation of small states, as dreamt of by Montesquieu and the Girondins [bourgeoisie of the French revolution of 1789], that unity of great nations which, if originally brought about by political force, has now become a powerful coefficient of social production. – The antagonism of the Commune against the state power has been mistaken for an exaggerated form of the ancient struggle against over-centralisation. Peculiar historical circumstances may have prevented the classical development, as in France, of the bourgeois form of government, and may have allowed [it], as in England, to complete the great central state organs by corrupt vestries, jobbing councillors, and ferocious poor-law guardians in the towns, and virtually hereditary magistrates in the counties. The Communal constitution would have restored to the social body all the forces hitherto absorbed by the state parasite feeding upon, and clogging the free movement of, society. By this one act it would have initiated the regeneration of France. – The provincial French middle-class saw in the Commune an attempt to restore the sway their order had held over the country under [King] Louis Philippe, and which, under [President, then Emperor] Louis Napoleon, was supplanted by the pretended rule of the country over the towns. In reality, the Communal constitution brought the rural producers under the intellectual lead of the central towns of their districts, and there secured to them, in the working men, the natural trustees of their interests. – The very existence of the Commune involved, as a matter of course, local municipal liberty, but no longer as a check upon the, now superseded, state power. It could only enter into the head of a Bismarck, who, when not engaged on his intrigues of blood and iron, always likes to resume his old trade, so befitting his mental calibre, of contributor to *Kladderadatsch* (the Berlin *Punch*), it could only enter into such a head,

to ascribe to the Paris Commune aspirations after that caricature of
the old French municipal organisation of 1791, the Prussian municipal constitution which degrades the town governments to mere secondary wheels in the police-machinery of the Prussian state. – The
Commune made that catchword of bourgeois revolutions, cheap
government, a reality, by destroying the two greatest sources of
expenditure – the standing army and state functionarism. Its very
existence pre-supposed the non-existence of monarchy, which, in
Europe at least, is the normal incumbrance and indispensable cloak
of class-rule. It supplied the republic with the basis of really democratic institutions. But neither cheap government nor the 'true
republic' was its ultimate aim; they were its mere concomitants.

The multiplicity of interpretations to which the Commune has
been subjected, and the multiplicity of interests which construed it
in their favour, show that it was a thoroughly expansive political
form, while all previous forms of government had been emphatically
repressive. Its true secret was this. It was essentially a working-class
government, the produce of the struggle of the producing against
the appropriating class, the political form at last discovered under
which to work out the economical emancipation of labour.

Except on this last condition, the Communal constitution would
have been an impossibility and a delusion. The political rule of the
producer cannot coexist with the perpetuation of his social slavery.
The Commune was therefore to serve as a lever for uprooting the
economical foundations upon which rests the existence of classes,
and therefore of class rule. With labour emancipated, every man
becomes a working man, and productive labour ceases to be a class
attribute.

It is a strange fact. In spite of all the tall talk and all the immense
literature, for the last sixty years, about Emancipation of Labour,
no sooner do the working men anywhere take the subject into their
own hands with a will, than uprises at once all the apologetic phras-
eology of the mouthpieces of present society with its two poles of
capital and wages-slavery (the landlord now is but the sleeping part-
ner of the capitalist), as if capitalist society was still in its purest
state of virgin innocence, with its antagonisms still undeveloped,
with its delusions still unexploded, with its prostitute realities not
yet laid bare. The Commune, they exclaim, intends to abolish property, the basis of all civilisation! Yes, gentlemen, the Commune

intended to abolish that class-property which makes the labour of the many the wealth of the few. It aimed at the expropriation of the expropriators. It wanted to make individual property a truth by transforming the means of production, land and capital, now chiefly the means of enslaving and exploiting labour, into mere instruments of free and associated labour. But this is communism, 'impossible' communism! Why, those members of the ruling classes who are intelligent enough to perceive the impossibility of continuing the present system – and they are many – have become the obtrusive and full-mouthed apostles of co-operative production. If co-operative production is not to remain a sham and a snare; if it is to supersede the capitalist system; if united co-operative societies are to regulate national production upon a common plan, thus taking it under their own control, and putting an end to the constant anarchy and periodical convulsions which are the fatality of Capitalist production – what else, gentlemen, would it be but communism, 'possible' communism?

The working class did not expect miracles from the Commune. They have no ready-made utopias to introduce *par décret du peuple*. They know that in order to work out their own emancipation, and along with it that higher form to which present society is irresistibly tending, by its own economical agencies, they will have to pass through long struggles, through a series of historic processes, transforming circumstances and men. They have no ideas to realise, but to set free the elements of the new society with which old collapsing bourgeois society itself is pregnant. In the full consciousness of their historic mission, and with the heroic resolve to act up to it, the working class can afford to smile at the coarse invective of the gentlemen's gentlemen with the pen and inkhorn, and at the didactic patronage of well-wishing bourgeois-doctrinaires, pouring forth their ignorant platitudes and sectarian crotchets in the oracular tone of scientific infallibility.

When the Paris Commune took the management of the revolution in its own hands; when plain working men for the first time dared to infringe upon the governmental privilege of their 'natural superiors', and, under circumstances of unexampled difficulty, performed their work modestly, conscientiously, and efficiently – performed it at salaries the highest of which barely amounted to one-fifth of what, according to high scientific authority, is the minimum

required for a secretary to a certain metropolitan school-board –
the old world writhed in convulsions of rage at the sight of the red
flag, the symbol of the republic of labour, floating over the Hôtel
de Ville.

And yet, this was the first revolution in which the working class
was openly acknowledged as the only class capable of social initiative, even by the great bulk of the Paris middle class – shopkeepers,
tradesmen, merchants – the wealthy capitalists alone excepted. The
Commune had saved them by a sagacious settlement [on 16 April
1871] of that ever-recurring cause of dispute among the middle
classes themselves – the debtor and creditor accounts [which were
put under moratorium]. The same portion of the middle class, after
they had assisted in putting down the working men's insurrection
of June, 1848, had been at once unceremoniously sacrificed to their
creditors by the then constituent assembly. But this was not their
only motive for now rallying round the working class. They felt
that there was but one alternative – the Commune, or the empire –
under whatever name it might reappear. The [Second] Empire had
ruined them economically by the havoc it made of public wealth,
by the wholesale financial swindling it fostered, by the props it
lent to the artificially accelerated centralisation of capital, and the
concomitant expropriation of their own ranks. It had suppressed
them politically, it had shocked them morally by its orgies, it had
insulted their Voltairianism by handing over the education of their
children to the *frères Ignorantins* [of conservative Catholicism], it
had revolted their national feeling as Frenchmen by precipitating
them headlong into a war which left only one equivalent for the
ruins it made – the disappearance of the [Second] Empire. In fact,
after the exodus from Paris of the high Bonapartist and capitalist
bohème, the true middle-class party of order came out in the shape
of the 'union republicaine' [of provincial representatives in Paris],
enrolling themselves under the colours of the Commune and
defending it against the wilful misconstruction of Thiers. Whether
the gratitude of this great body of the middle class will stand the
present severe trial, time must show.

The Commune was perfectly right in telling the peasants [in
April 1871] that 'its victory was their only hope.' Of all the lies
hatched at [the national assembly at] Versailles and re-echoed by
the glorious European penny-a-liner, one of the most tremendous

was that the rurals [elected in January 1871] represented the French peasantry. Think only of the love of the French peasant for the men to whom, after 1815, he had to pay the milliard of indemnity [when the restored monarchy granted compensation to landowners expropriated by the revolution]! In the eyes of the French peasant, the very existence of a great landed proprietor is in itself an encroachment of his conquests of 1789. The bourgeois, in 1848, had burthened his plot of land with the additional tax of forty-five cent[ime]s in the franc; but then he did so in the name of the revolution; while now he had fomented a civil war against the revolution, to shift on the peasant's shoulders the chief load of the five milliards of indemnity to be paid to the Prussian. The Commune, on the other hand, in one of its first proclamations, declared that the true orginators of the war would be made to pay its cost. The Commune would have delivered the peasant of the blood tax [of conscription] – would have given him a cheap government – transformed his present blood-suckers, the notary, advocate, executor, and other judicial vampires, into salaried communal agents, elected by, and responsible to, himself. It would have freed him of the [village] tyranny of the *garde champêtre*, the gendarme, and the prefect; would have put enlightenment by the schoolmaster in the place of stultification by the priest. And the French peasant is, above all, a man of reckoning. He would find it extremely reasonable that the pay of the priest, instead of being extorted by the tax-gatherer, would only depend upon the spontaneous action of the parishioners' religious instincts. Such were the great immediate boons which the rule of the Commune – and that rule alone – held out to the French peasantry. It is, therefore, quite superfluous here to expatiate upon the more complicated but vital problems which the Commune alone was able, and at the same time compelled, to solve in favour of the peasant, viz., the hypothecary debt, lying like an incubus upon his parcel of soil, the *prolétariat foncier* (the rural proletariat), daily growing upon it, and his expropriation from it enforced, at a more and more rapid rate, by the very development of modern agriculture and the competition of capitalist farming.

The French peasant had elected Louis Bonaparte president of the republic; but the party of order created the [Second] Empire. What the French peasant really wants he commenced to show in 1849 and 1850, by opposing his maire to the government's prefect, his schoolmaster to the government's priest, and himself to the government's gendarme. All the laws made by the party of order in January and February 1850 were avowed measures of repression against the peasant. The peasant was a Bonapartist, because the great revolution, with all its benefits to him, was, in his eyes, personified in Napoleon. This delusion, rapidly breaking down under the Second Empire (and its very nature hostile to the rurals), this prejudice of the past, how could it have withstood the appeal of the Commune to the living interests and urgent wants of the peasantry?

The rurals – this was, in fact, their chief apprehension – knew that three months' free communication of Communal Paris with the provinces would bring about a general rising of the peasants, and hence their anxiety to establish a police blockade around Paris, so as to stop the spread of the rinderpest.

If the Commune was thus the true representative of all the healthy elements of French society, and therefore the truly national government, it was, at the same time, as a working men's government, as the bold champion of the emancipation of labour, emphatically international. Within sight of the Prussian army, that had annexed to Germany two French provinces [Alsace and Lorraine], the Commune annexed to France the working people all over the world.

The Second Empire had been the jubilee of cosmopolitan blackleggism, the rakes of all countries rushing in at its call for a share in its orgies and in the plunder of the French people. Even at this moment the right hand of Thiers is Ganesco, the foul Wallachian, and his left hand is Markowski, the Russian spy. The Commune admitted all foreigners to the honour of dying for an immortal cause. Between the foreign war lost by their treason, and the civil war fomented by their conspiracy with the foreign invader, the bourgeoisie had found the time to display their patriotism by organising police-hunts upon the Germans in France. The Commune made a German working-man [Leo Frankel] its minister of labour. Thiers, the bourgeoisie, the Second Empire, had continually deluded Poland by loud professions of sympathy, while in reality betraying her to, and doing the dirty work of, Russia. The Commune honoured the heroic sons of Poland [Jaroslaw Dombrowski and Walery Wroblewski] by placing them at the head of the defenders of Paris. And, to broadly mark the new era of history it was conscious of initiating, under the eyes of the conquering Prussians on the one side, and of the Bonapartist army, led by Bonapartist generals, on the other, the Commune pulled down that colossal symbol of martial glory, the Vendôme column [on 16 May 1871].

The great social measure of the Commune was its own working existence. Its special measures could but betoken the tendency of a government of the people by the people. Such were the abolition of the nightwork of journeymen bakers; the prohibition, under penalty, of the employers' practice to reduce wages by levying upon their workpeople fines under manifold pretexts – a process in which the employer combines in his own person the parts of legislator, judge, and executor, and filches the money to boot. Another measure of this class was the surrender, to associations of workmen, under reserve of compensation, of all closed workshops and factories, no matter whether the respective capitalists had absconded or preferred to strike work.

The financial measures of the Commune, remarkable for their sagacity and moderation, could only be such as were compatible with the state of a besieged town. Considering the colossal robberies committed upon the city of Paris by the great financial companies and contractors, under the protection of Haussmann [prefect of the *département* of the Seine], the Commune would have had an incomparably better title to confiscate their property than Louis Napoleon had against the Orléans family. The Hohenzollern [royal family in Prussia] and the English oligarchs who both have derived a good deal of their estates from church plunder, were, of course, greatly shocked at the Commune clearing but 8,000 f[rancs] out of secularisation.

While the Versailles government, as soon as it had recovered some spirit and strength, used the most violent means against the Commune; while it put down the free expression of opinion all over France, even to the forbidding of meetings of delegates from the large towns; while it subjected Versailles and the rest of France to an espionage far surpassing that of the Second Empire; while it burned by its gendarme inquisitors all papers printed at Paris, and sifted all correspondence from and to Paris; while in the national assembly the most timid attempts to put in a word for Paris were howled down in a manner unknown even to the *chambre introuvable* of 1816; with the savage warfare of Versailles outside, and its attempts at corruption and conspiracy inside Paris – would the Commune not have shamefully betrayed its trust by affecting to keep up all the decencies and appearances of liberalism as in a time of profound peace? Had the government of the Commune been akin to that of M. Thiers, there would have been no more occasion to suppress party-of-order [news]papers at Paris than there was to suppress Communal [news]papers at Versailles.

It was irritating indeed to the rurals that at the very same time they declared the return to the church to be the only means of salvation for France, the infidel Commune unearthed the peculiar mysteries of the Picpus nunnery, and of the Church of Saint Laurent [where there was illegal incarceration, torture, and secret burial]. It was a satire upon M. Thiers that, while he showered grand crosses upon the Bonapartist generals in acknowledgment of their mastery in losing battles, signing capitulations, and turning cigarettes at Wilhelmshöhe [with the exiled ex-emperor and his generals], the Commune dismissed and arrested its generals whenever they were suspected of neglecting their duties. The expulsion from, and arrest by, the Commune of one of its members [the police informer Stanislas Blanchet], who had slipped in under a false name, and had undergone at Lyons six days' imprisonment for simple bankruptcy, was it not a deliberate insult hurled at the forger, Jules Favre, then still the foreign minister of France, still selling France to Bismarck, and still dictating his orders to the paragon government of Belgium? But indeed the Commune did not pretend to infallibility, the invariable attribute of all governments of the old stamp. It published its doings and sayings, it initiated the public into all its shortcomings.

In every revolution there intrude, at the side of its true agents, men of a different stamp; some of them survivors of and devotees to past revolutions, without insight into the present movement, but preserving popular influence by their known honesty and courage, or by the sheer force of tradition; others mere bawlers, who, by dint of repeating year after year the same set of stereotyped declamations against the government of the day, have sneaked into the reputation of revolutionists of the first water. After the 18th of March [1871], some such men did also turn up, and in some cases contrived to play pre-eminent parts. As far as their power went, they hampered the real action of the working class, exactly as men of that sort have hampered the full development of every previous revolution. They are an unavoidable evil: with time they are shaken off; but time was not allowed to the Commune.

Wonderful, indeed, was the change the Commune had wrought in Paris! No longer any trace of the meretricious Paris of the Second Empire. No longer was Paris the rendezvous of British landlords, Irish absentees, American ex-slaveholders and shoddy men, Russian ex-serfowners, and Wallachian boyards. No more corpses at the morgue, no nocturnal burglaries, scarcely any robberies; in fact, for the first time since the days of February 1848, the streets of Paris were safe, and that without any police of any kind. 'We', said a member of the Commune, 'hear no longer of assassination, theft, and personal assault; it seems indeed as if the police had dragged along with it to Versailles all its Conservative friends.' The *cocottes* had refound the scent of their protectors – the absconding men of family, religion, and, above all, of property. In their stead, the real women of Paris showed again at the surface – heroic, noble, and devoted, like the women of antiquity. Working, thinking, fighting, bleeding Paris – almost forgetful, in its incubation of a new society, of the cannibals at its gates – radiant in the enthusiasm of its historic initiative!

Opposed to this new world at Paris, behold the old world at Versailles – that assembly of the ghouls of all defunct regimes, legitimists and Orléanists, eager to feed upon the carcass of the nation – with a tail of antediluvian republicans, sanctioning, by their presence in the assembly, the slaveholders' rebellion, relying for the maintenance of the parliamentary republic upon the vanity of the senile mountebank at its head, and caricaturing 1789 by holding their ghastly meetings in the *Jeu de Paume* [where the representatives of the Third Estate declared for a constitution]. There it was, this assembly, the representative of everything dead in France, propped up to the semblance of life by nothing but the swords of the generals of Louis Bonaparte. Paris all truth, Versailles all lie; and that lie vented through the mouth of Thiers.

Thiers tells a deputation of the mayors of the Seine-et-Oise, – 'You may rely upon my word, which I have never broken!' He tells the assembly itself that 'it was the most freely elected and most liberal assembly France ever possessed'; he tells his motley soldiery that it was 'the admiration of the world, and the finest army France ever possessed'; he tells the provinces that the bombardment of Paris by him was a myth: 'If some cannon-shots have been fired, it is not the deed of the army of Versailles, but of some insurgents trying to make believe that they are fighting, while they dare not show their faces.' He again tells the provinces that 'the artillery of Versailles does not bombard Paris, but only cannonades it.' He tells the Archbishop of Paris that the pretended executions and reprisals [[!]] attributed to the Versailles troops were all moonshine. He tells Paris that he was only anxious 'to free it from the hideous tyrants who oppress it', and that, in fact, the Paris of the Commune was 'but a handful of criminals'.

The Paris of M. Thiers was not the real Paris of the 'vile multitude', but a phantom Paris, the Paris of the [renegade] *francs-fileurs*, the Paris of the Boulevards, male and female – the rich, the capitalist, the gilded, the idle Paris, now thronging with its lackeys, its blacklegs, its literary *bohème*, and its *cocottes* at Versailles, Saint-Denis, Rueil, and Saint-Germain; considering the civil war but an agreeable diversion, eyeing the battle going on through telescopes, counting the rounds of cannon, and swearing by their own honour and that of their prostitutes, that the performance was far better got up than it used to be at the Porte Saint-Martin. The men who fell were really dead; the cries of the wounded were cries in good earnest; and, besides, the whole thing was so intensely historical.

This is the Paris of M. Thiers, as the [royalist] emigration of Coblenz [during the revolution of 1789] was the France of M. de Calonne [and his government in exile].

IV

The first attempt [at the armistice of 28 January 1871] of the slaveholders' conspiracy to put down Paris by getting the Prussians to occupy it, was frustrated by Bismarck's refusal. The second attempt, that of the 18th of March [1871], ended in the rout of the army and the flight to Versailles of the government, which ordered the whole administration to break up and follow in its track. By the semblance of peace-negotiations with Paris, Thiers found the time to prepare for war against it. But where to find an army? The remnants of the line regiments were weak in number and unsafe in character. His urgent appeal to the provinces to succour Versailles, by their National guards and volunteers, met with a flat refusal. Brittany alone furnished a handful of *chouans* fighting under a white flag [of the royalists], every one of them wearing on his breast the heart of Jesus in white cloth, and shouting 'Vive le Roi!' (Long live the King!) Thiers was, therefore, compelled to collect, in hot haste, a motley crew, composed of sailors, marines, Pontifical Zouaves [from the aristocracy], [the police prefect] Valentin's gendarmes, and [the former police prefect] Pietri's *sergents de ville* and *mouchards* [informers]. This army, however, would have been ridiculously ineffective without the instalments of imperialist war-prisoners, which Bismarck granted in numbers just sufficient to keep the civil war a-going and keep the Versailles government in abject dependence on Prussia. During the war itself, the Versailles police had to look after the Versailles army, while the gendarmes had to drag it on by exposing themselves at all posts of danger. The forts which fell were not taken, but bought. The heroism of the federals [of the republican national guard] convinced Thiers that the resistance of Paris was not to be broken by his own strategic genius and the bayonets at his disposal.

Meanwhile, his relations with the provinces became more and more difficult. Not one single address of approval came in to gladden Thiers and his rurals. Quite the contrary. Deputations and addresses demanding, in a tone anything but respectful, conciliation with Paris on the basis of the unequivocal recognition of the republic, the acknowledgment of the Communal liberties, and the dissolution of the national assembly, whose mandate was extinct, poured in from all sides, and in such numbers that Dufaure, Thiers's minister of justice, in his circular of April 23rd [1871] to the public prosecutors, commanded them to treat 'the cry of conciliation' as a crime. In regard, however, of the hopeless prospect held out by his campaign, Thiers resolved to shift his tactics by ordering, all over the country, municipal elections to take place on the 30th of April [1871], on the basis of the new municipal law dictated by himself to the national assembly. What with the intrigues of his prefects, what with police intimidation, he felt quite sanguine of imparting, by the verdict of the provinces, to the national assembly that moral power it had never possessed, and of getting at last from the provinces the physical force required for the conquest of Paris.

His banditti-warfare against Paris, exalted in his own bulletins, and the attempts of his ministers at the establishment, throughout France, of a reign of terror, Thiers was from the beginning anxious to accompany with a little byplay of conciliation, which had to serve more than one purpose. It was to dupe the provinces, to inveigle the middle-class element in Paris, and, above all, to afford the professed republicans in the national assembly the opportunity of hiding their treason against Paris behind their faith in Thiers. On the 21st of March [1871], when still without an army, he had declared to the assembly: 'Come what may, I will not send an army to Paris.' On the 27th March he rose again: 'I have found the republic an accomplished fact, and I am firmly resolved to maintain it.' In reality, he put down the [communard] revolution at Lyons and Marseilles in the name of the republic, while the roars of his rurals drowned the very mention of its name at Versailles. After this exploit, he toned down the 'accomplished fact' into an hypothetical fact. The Orléans princes, whom he had cautiously warned off Bordeaux, were now, in flagrant breach of the law, permitted to intrigue at Dreux. The concessions held out by Thiers in his interminable interviews with the delegates from Paris and the provinces, although constantly varied in tone and colour, according to time and circumstances, did in fact never come to more than the prospective restriction of revenge to the 'handful of criminals implicated in the murder of Lecomte and Clément Thomas', on the well-understood premiss that Paris and France were unreservedly to accept M. Thiers himself as the best of possible republics, as he, in 1830, had done with Louis Philippe [as 'king of the French']. Even these concessions he not only took care to render doubtful by the official comments put upon them in the assembly through his ministers. He had his Dufaure to act. Dufaure, this old Orléanist lawyer, had always been the justiciary of the state of siege, as now in 1871, under Thiers, so in 1839 under Louis Philippe, and in 1849 under Louis Bonaparte's presidency. While out of office he made a fortune by pleading for the Paris capitalists, and made political capital by pleading against the laws he had himself originated. He now hurried through the national assembly not only a set of repressive laws which were, after the fall of Paris, to extirpate the last remnants of republican liberty in France; he foreshadowed the fate of Paris by abridging the, for him, too slow procedure of courts-martial, and by a new-fangled, Draconic code of deportation. The revolution of 1848, abolishing the penalty of death for political crimes, had replaced it by deportation. Louis Bonaparte did not dare, at least not in theory, to re-establish the regime of the guillotine. The rural assembly, not yet bold enough even to hint that the Parisians were not rebels, but assassins, had therefore to confine its prospective vengeance against Paris to Dufaure's new code of deportation. Under all these circumstances Thiers himself could not have gone on with his comedy of conciliation, had it not, as he intended it to do, drawn forth shrieks of rage from the rurals, whose ruminating mind understood neither the play, nor its necessities of hypocrisy, tergiversation, and procrastination.

In sight of the impending municipal elections of the 30th April [1871], Thiers enacted one of his great conciliation scenes on the 27th April. Amidst a flood of sentimental rhetoric, he exclaimed from the tribune of the assembly: 'There exists no conspiracy against the republic but that of Paris, which compels us to shed French blood. I repeat it again and again. Let those impious arms fall from the hands which hold them, and chastisement will be arrested at once by an act of peace excluding only the small number of criminals.' To the violent interruption of the rurals he replied. 'Gentlemen, tell me, I implore you, am I wrong? Do you really regret that I could have stated the truth that the criminals are only a handful? Is it not fortunate in the midst of our misfortunes that those who have been capable of shedding the blood of Clément Thomas and General Lecomte are but rare exceptions?'

France, however, turned a deaf ear to what Thiers flattered himself to be a parliamentary siren's song. Out of 700,000 municipal councillors returned by the 35,000 communes still left to France, the united legitimists, Orléanists, and Bonapartists did not carry 8,000. The supplementary elections which followed were still more decidedly hostile. Thus, instead of getting from the provinces the badly-needed physical force, the national assembly lost even its last claim of moral force, that of being the expression of the universal [manhood] suffrage of the country. To complete the discomfiture, the newly-chosen municipal councils of all the cities of France openly threatened the usurping assembly at Versailles with a counter-assembly at Bordeaux.

Then the long-expected moment of decisive action had at last come for Bismarck. He peremptorily summoned Thiers to send to Frankfurt plenipotentiaries for the definitive settlement of peace. In humble obedience to the call of his master, Thiers hastened to despatch his trusty Jules Favre, backed by Pouyer-Quertier. Pouyer-Quertier, an 'eminent' Rouen cotton-spinner, a fervent and even servile partisan of the Second Empire, had never found any fault with it save its commercial treaty [reducing tariffs in 1860] with England, prejudicial to his own shop-interest. Hardly installed at Bordeaux as Thiers's minister of finance, he denounced that 'unholy' treaty, hinted at its near abrogation, and had even the effrontery to try, although in vain (having counted without Bismarck), the immediate enforcement of the old protective duties against Alsace, where, he said, no previous international treaties stood in the way. This man, who considered counter-revolution as a means to put down wages at Rouen, and the surrender of French provinces as a means to bring up the price of his wares in France, was he not *the one* predestined to be picked out by Thiers as the helpmate of Jules Favre in his last and crowning treason?

On the arrival at Frankfurt of this exquisite pair of plenipotentiaries, bully Bismarck at once met them with the imperious alternative: either the restoration of the empire, or the unconditional acceptance of my own peace terms! These terms included a shortening of the intervals in which the war indemnity was to be paid, and the continued occupation of the Paris forts by Prussian troops until Bismarck should feel satisfied with the state of things in France; Prussia thus being recognised as the supreme arbiter in internal French politics! In return for this he offered to let loose, for the extermination of Paris, the captive Bonapartist army, and to lend them the direct assistance of [German] Emperor William's troops. He pledged his good faith by making payment of the first instalment of the indemnity dependent on the 'pacification' of Paris. Such a bait was, of course, eagerly swallowed by Thiers and his plenipotentiaries. They signed the treaty of peace on the 10th of May [1871], and had it endorsed by the Versailles assembly on the 18th.

In the interval between the conclusion of peace and the arrival of the Bonapartist prisoners, Thiers felt the more bound to resume his comedy of conciliation, as his republican tools stood in sore need of a pretext for blinking their eyes at the preparations for the carnage of Paris. As late as the 8th May [1871] he replied to a deputation of middle-class conciliators – 'Whenever the insurgents will make up their minds for capitulation, the gates of Paris shall be flung wide open during a week for all except the murderers of Generals Clément Thomas and Lecomte.'

A few days afterwards, when violently interpellated on these premises by the rurals, he refused to enter into any explanations; not, however, without giving them this significant hint: – 'I tell you there are impatient men amongst you, men who are in too great a hurry. They must have another eight days; at the end of these eight days there will be no more danger, and the task will be proportionate to their courage and to their capacities.' As soon as [General] MacMahon was able to assure him that he could shortly enter Paris, Thiers declared to the assembly that 'he would enter Paris with the *laws* in his hands, and demand a full expiation from the wretches who had sacrificed the lives of soldiers and destroyed public monuments.' As the moment of decision drew near he said – to the assembly, 'I shall be pitiless!' – to Paris, that it was doomed; and to his Bonapartist banditti, that they had state licence to wreak vengeance upon Paris to their hearts' content. At last, when treachery had opened the gates of Paris to General Douay, on the 21st May [1871], Thiers, on the 22nd, revealed to the rurals the 'goal' of his conciliation comedy, which they had so obstinately persisted in not understanding. 'I told you a few days ago that we were approaching *our goal*; to-day I come to tell you *the goal* is reached. The victory of order, justice, and civilisation is at last won!'

So it was. The civilisation and justice of bourgeois order comes out in its lurid light whenever the slaves and drudges of that order rise against their masters. Then this civilisation and justice stand forth as undisguised savagery and lawless revenge. Each new crisis in the class struggle between the appropriator and the producer brings out this fact more glaringly. Even the atrocities of the bourgeois in June 1848, vanish before the ineffable infamy of 1871. The self-sacrificing heroism with which the population of Paris – men, women, and children – fought for eight days after the entrance of the Versaillese, reflects as much the grandeur of their cause, as the infernal deeds of the soldiery reflect the innate spirit of that civilisation of which they are the mercenary vindicators. A glorious civilisation, indeed, the great problem of which is how to get rid of the heaps of corpses it made after the battle was over!

To find a parallel for the conduct of Thiers and his blood-hounds we must go back to the [brutal] times of [the dictator] Sulla and the two triumvirates [60–53 BC, and 46–43 BC] of Rome. The same wholesale slaughter in cold blood; the same disregard, in massacre, of age and sex; the same system of torturing prisoners; the same proscriptions, but this time of a whole class; the same savage hunt after concealed leaders, lest one might escape; the same denunciations of political and private enemies; the same indifference for the butchery of entire strangers to the feud. There is but this difference, that the Romans had no *mitrailleuses* [machine guns] for the despatch, in the lump, of the proscribed, and that they had not 'the law in their hands', nor on their lips the cry of 'civilisation'.

And after those horrors, look upon the other, still more hideous, face of that bourgeois civilisation as described by its own press!

'With stray shots', writes the Paris correspondent of a London Tory paper, 'still ringing in the distance, and untended wounded wretches dying amid the tombstones of Père la Chaise – with 6,000 terror-stricken insurgents wandering in an agony of despair in the labyrinth of the catacombs, and wretches hurried through the streets to be shot down in scores by the *mitrailleuse* – it is revolting to see the cafés filled with the votaries of absinthe, billiards, and dominoes; female profligacy perambulating the boulevards, and the sound of revelry disturbing the night from the *cabinets particuliers* of fashionable restaurants.' M. Edouard Hervé writes in the *Journal de Paris*, a Versaillist journal suppressed by the Commune: – 'The way in which the population of Paris [[!]] manifested its satisfaction yesterday was rather more than frivolous, and we fear it will grow worse as time progresses. Paris has now a *fête* day appearance, which is sadly out of place; and, unless we are to be called the *Parisiens de la décadence*, this sort of thing must come to an end.' And then he quotes the passage from Tacitus: – 'Yet, on the morrow of that horrible struggle, even before it was completely over, Rome – degraded and corrupt – began once more to wallow in the voluptuous slough which was destroying its body and polluting its soul – *alibi praelia et vulnera, alibi balnea popinaeque* [[– here fits and wounds, there baths and restaurants]]'. M. Hervé only forgets to say the 'population of Paris' he speaks of is but the population of the Paris of M. Thiers – the [renegade] *francs fileurs* returning in throngs from Versailles, Saint-Denis, Rueil, and Saint-Germain – the Paris of the 'Decline'.

In all its bloody triumphs over the self-sacrificing champions of a new and better society, that nefarious civilisation, based upon the enslavement of labour, drowns the moans of its victims in a hue-and-cry of calumny, reverberated by a world-wide echo. The serene working men's Paris of the Commune is suddenly changed into a pandemonium by the blood-hounds of 'order'. And what does this tremendous change prove to the bourgeois mind of all countries? Why, that the Commune has conspired against civilisation! The Paris people die enthusiastically for the Commune in numbers unequalled in any battle known to history. What does that prove? Why, that the Commune was not the people's own government, but the usurpation of a handful of criminals! The women of Paris joyfully give up their lives at the barricades and on the places of execution. What does this prove? Why, that the demon of the Commune has changed them into Megaeras and Hecates! The moderation of the Commune during two months of undisputed sway is equalled only by the heroism of its defence. What does that prove? Why, that for months the Commune carefully hid, under a mask of moderation and humanity, the blood-thirstiness of its fiendish instincts, to be let loose in the hour of its agony!

The working men's Paris, in the act of its heroic self-holocaust, involved in its flames buildings and monuments. While tearing to pieces the living body of the proletariat, its rulers must no longer expect to return triumphantly into the intact architecture of their abodes. The government of Versailles cries, 'Incendiarism!' and whispers this one to all its agents, down to the remotest hamlet, to hunt up its enemies everywhere as suspect of professional incendiarism. The bourgeoisie of the whole world, which looks complacently upon the wholesale massacre after the battle, is convulsed by horror at the desecration of brick and mortar!

When governments give state-licenses to their navies to 'kill, *burn*, and destroy', is that a license for incendiarism? When the British troops wantonly set fire to the Capitol at Washington [in 1814] and to the summer palace of the Chinese Emperor [in 1860], was that incendiarism? When the Prussians, not for military reasons, but out of the mere spite of revenge, burnt down, by the help of petroleum, towns like Châteaudun and innumerable villages, was that incendiarism? When Thiers, during six weeks, bombarded Paris, under the pretext that he wanted to set fire to those houses only in which there were people, was that incendiarism? In war, fire is an arm as legitimate as any. Buildings held by the enemy are shelled to set them on fire. If their defenders have to retire, they themselves light the flames to prevent the attack from making use of the buildings. To be burnt down has always been the inevitable fate of all buildings situated in the front of battle of all the regular armies of the world. But in the war of the enslaved against their enslavers, the only justifiable war in history, this is by no means to hold good! The Commune used fire strictly as a means of defence. They used it to stop up to the Versailles troops those long straight avenues which Haussmann had expressly opened to artillery fire; they used it to cover their retreat, in the same way as the Versaillese, in their advance, used their shells which destroyed at least as many buildings as the fire of the Commune. It is a matter of dispute, even now, which buildings were set fire to by the defence, and which by the attack. And the defence resorted to fire only then, when the Versaillese troops had already commenced their wholesale murdering of prisoners. Besides, the Commune had, long before, given full public notice that, if driven to extremities, they would bury themselves under the ruins of Paris, and make Paris a second Moscow [burnt down in self-defence in 1812], as the government of [national] defence, but only as a cloak for its treason, had promised to do. For this purpose Trochu had found them the petroleum. The Commune knew that its opponents cared nothing for the lives of the Paris people, but cared much for their own Paris buildings. And Thiers, on the other hand, had given them notice that he would be implacable in his vengeance. No sooner had he got his army ready on one side, and the Prussians shutting up the trap on the other, than he proclaimed: 'I shall be pitiless! The expiation will be complete, and justice will be stern!' If the acts of the Paris working men were vandalism, it was the vandalism of defence in despair, not the vandalism of triumph, like that which the Christians perpetrated upon the really priceless art treasures of heathen antiquity; and even that vandalism has been justified by the historian as an unavoidable and comparatively trifling concomitant to the Titanic struggle between a new society arising and an old one breaking down. It was still less the vandalism of Haussmann, razing historic Paris to make place for the Paris of the sightseer!

But the execution by the Commune of the sixty-four hostages, with the Archbishop of Paris at their head! The bourgeoisie and its army in June 1848 re-established a custom which had long disappeared from the practice of war – the shooting of their defenceless prisoners. This brutal custom has since been more or less strictly adhered to by the suppressors of all popular commotions in Europe and India; thus proving that it constitutes a real 'progress of civilisation'! On the other hand, the Prussians, in France, had re-established the practice of taking hostages – innocent men, who, with their lives, were to answer to them for the acts of others. When Thiers, as we have seen, from the very beginning of the conflict, enforced the humane practice of shooting down the Communal prisoners, the Commune, to protect their lives, was obliged to resort to the Prussian practice of securing hostages. The lives of the hostages had been forfeited over and over again by the continued shooting of prisoners on the part of the Versaillese. How could they be spared any longer after the carnage with which [General] Mac-Mahon's praetorians celebrated their entrance into Paris? Was even the last check upon the unscrupulous ferocity of bourgeois governments – the taking of hostages – to be made a mere sham of? The real murderer of Archbishop Darboy is Thiers. The Commune again and again had offered to exchange the archbishop, and ever so many priests in the bargain, against the single Blanqui, then in the hands of Thiers. Thiers obstinately refused. He knew that with Blanqui he would give to the Commune a head; while the archbishop would serve his purpose best in the shape of a corpse. Thiers acted upon the precedent of [General] Cavaignac. How, in June, 1848, did not Cavaignac and his men of order raise shouts of horror by stigmatising the insurgents as the assassins of Archbishop Affre! They knew perfectly well that the archbishop had been shot by the soldiers of order. M. Jacquemot, the archbishop's vicar-general, present on the spot, had immediately afterwards handed them in his evidence to that effect.

All this chorus of calumny, which the party of order never fail, in their orgies of blood, to raise against their victims, only proves that the bourgeois of our days considers himself the legitimate successor to the baron of old, who thought every weapon in his own hand fair against the plebeian, while in the hands of the plebeian a weapon of any kind constituted in itself a crime.

The conspiracy of the ruling class to break down the revolution by a civil war carried on under the patronage of a foreign invader – a conspiracy which we have traced from the very 4th of September [1870] down to the entrance of [General] MacMahon's praetorians through the gate of Saint-Cloud – culminated in the carnage of Paris. Bismarck gloats over the ruins of Paris, in which he saw perhaps the first instalment of that general destruction of great cities he had prayed for when still a simple rural in the [reactionary] Prussian *chambre introuvable* of 1849. He gloats over the cadavers of the Paris proletariat. For him this is not only the extermination of revolution, but the extinction of France, now decapitated in reality, and by the French government itself. With the shallowness characteristic of all successful statesmen, he sees but the surface of this tremendous historic event. Whenever before has history exhibited the spectacle of a conqueror crowning his victory by turning into, not only the gendarme, but the hired bravo of the conquered government? There existed no war between Prussia and the Commune of Paris. On the contrary, the Commune had accepted the peace preliminaries, and Prussia had announced her neutrality. Prussia was, therefore, no belligerent. She acted the part of a bravo, a cowardly bravo, because incurring no danger; a hired bravo, because stipulating beforehand the payment of her blood-money of 500 millions on the fall of Paris. And thus, at last, came out the true character of the war, ordained by Providence as a chastisement of godless and debauched France by pious and moral Germany! And this unparalleled breach of the law of nations, even as understood by the old world lawyers, instead of arousing the 'civilised' governments of Europe to declare the felonious Prussian government, the mere tool of the St. Petersburg cabinet, an outlaw amongst nations, only incites them to consider whether the few victims who escape the double cordon around Paris are not to be given up to the hangman at Versailles!

That after the most tremendous war of modern times, the conquering and the conquered hosts should fraternise the common massacre of the proletariat – this unparalleled event does indicate, not, as Bismarck thinks, the final repression of a new society upheaving, but the crumbling into dust of bourgeois society. The highest heroic effort of which old society is still capable is national war; and this is now proved to be a mere governmental humbug, intended to defer the struggle of classes, and to be thrown aside as soon as that class struggle bursts out in civil war. Class rule is no longer able to disguise itself in a national uniform; the national governments are *one* as against the proletariat!

After Whit Sunday 1871, there can be neither peace nor truce possible between the working men of France and the appropriators of their produce. The iron hand of a mercenary soldiery may keep for a time both classes tied down in common oppression. But the battle must break out again and again in ever-growing dimensions, and there can be no doubt as to who will be the victor in the end – the appropriating few, or the immense working majority. And the French working class is only the advanced guard of the modern proletariat.

While the European governments thus testify, before Paris, to the international character of class rule, they cry down the International Working Men's Association – the international counter-organisation of labour against the cosmopolitan conspiracy of capital – as the head fountain of all these disasters. Thiers denounced it as the despot of labour, pretending to be its liberator. [Ernest] Picard ordered that all communications between the French Internationals and those abroad should be cut off; Count Jaubert, Thiers' mummified accomplice of 1835, declares it the great problem of all civilised governments to weed it out. The rurals roar against it, and the whole European press joins the chorus. An honourable French writer [Jean Robinet], completely foreign to our Association, speaks as follows: – 'The members of the central committee of the national guard, as well as the greater part of the members of the Commune, are the most active intelligent, and energetic minds of the International Working Men's Association ... men who are thoroughly honest, sincere, intelligent, devoted, pure, and fanatical in the *good* sense of the word.' The police-tinged bourgeois mind naturally figures to itself the International Working-Men's Association as acting in the manner of a secret conspiracy, its central body ordering, from time to time, explosions in different countries. Our association is, in fact, nothing but the international bond between the most advanced working men in the various countries of the civilised world. Wherever, in whatever shape, and under whatever conditions the class struggle obtains any consistency, it is but natural that members of our association should stand in the foreground. The soil out of which it grows is modern society itself. It cannot be stamped out by any amount of carnage. To stamp it out, the governments would have to stamp out the despotism of capital over labour – the condition of their own parasitical existence.

Working men's Paris, with its Commune, will be for ever celebrated as the glorious harbinger of a new society. Its martyrs are enshrined in the great heart of the working class. Its exterminators history has already nailed to that eternal pillory from which all the prayers of their priests will not avail to redeem them.

Critique of the Gotha Programme[1]
Marginal Notes on the Programme of the German Workers' Party

I

(1) 'Labour is the source of all wealth and culture, *and since* it is only possible to have useful labour in and through society, all members of society have an equal right to the undiminished return from labour.' *First part of the paragraph:* 'Labour is the source of all wealth and all culture.'

Labour is *not the source* of all wealth. *Nature* is just as much the source of use-values (and what else is material wealth?) as labour, which is itself only the expression of a natural power, human labour power.

This line can be found in any children's primer and is correct in so far as the *implication* is that labour requires certain means and materials. However a socialist programme cannot allow a bourgeois phrase like this to conceal the very *circumstances* that give it some sense. Only in so far as man acts as the proprietor of nature, the primary source of all the means and materials of labour, and treats nature as his own from the outset, does his labour become the source of use-values, and hence of wealth. The bourgeoisie have

[1] In these manuscript notes Marx quotes from the draft programme for the proposed Socialist Workers' Party of Germany. Quotations from this programme, as transcribed by Marx, appear in **boldface** type, with his own emphasis in ***boldface italic***. The congress at Gotha united the Social Democratic Workers' party ('Eisenachers', after their founding congress at Eisenach in 1869, also known as 'honest' social-democrats) with the General German Workers' Union ('Lassalleans', after their founder Ferdinand Lassalle, who led it from 1863 to his death in 1864). Marx refers generically to the Workers' Party in anticipation of the union.

very good reason to credit labour with *a supernatural generative power*, for it follows directly from the fact that nature is a precondition for labour, that a man who has no property other than his labour power must in all cultural and social circumstances be a slave to those who have become the owners of labour's material prerequisites. He can only work by permission, and hence live by permission.

Let us leave the sentence as it runs, or rather limps. What sort of conclusion is supposed to follow? Obviously this:

> 'Since labour is the source of all wealth, no one in society can appropriate wealth except as the product of labour. Therefore anyone who does not work lives off the labour of others and also acquires his culture at the expense of those who work.'

Instead of this, the words *and since* link up a second proposition, in order to draw a conclusion from it, not from the first one.

Second part of the paragraph.

'It is only possible to have useful labour in and through society.'

According to the first proposition, labour was the source of all wealth and culture, hence no society at all was possible without labour. Now we hear the opposite, that no 'useful' labour is possible without society.

One could just as well have said that only in society can useless labour or even socially destructive labour become a regular occupation, that only in society can people live in idleness, etc. etc., in short one could have copied down the whole of Rousseau.

And what is 'useful' labour? Surely only the labour which produces the intended useful effect. A savage – and man was a savage after he had ceased being an ape – who kills an animal with a stone, gathers fruit, etc., is performing 'useful' labour.

Thirdly: the conclusion: 'And since it is only possible to have useful labour in and through society – all members of society have an equal right to the undiminished return from labour.'

A fine conclusion! If useful labour is only possible in society and by means of society, then the return from labour belongs to society – and the individual worker only gets what is left over after preserving society, [which is] the 'prerequisite' for labour.

In fact, this proposition has been useful to *apologists for the prevailing conditions in society* at any given time. First come the claims of the government and everything that goes along with it, since it is the agency in society maintaining social order; then come the claims of property owners of different types, because the different types of private property are the foundation of society, etc. We see how hollow phrases such as these can be turned and twisted at will.

The first and second parts of the paragraph have some kind of intelligible connection only in this sense:

'Only as social labour', or what is the same thing, 'in and by means of society', 'does labour become the source of wealth and cultural advantages'.

This proposition is indisputably correct, for although isolated labour (given the material conditions) can create use values, it can create neither wealth nor cultural advantages.

But this proposition is also equally indisputable:

'To the degree that labour develops in society, and in that way becomes the source of wealth and cultural advantages, poverty and destitution also develop amongst the workers, but wealth and cultural advantages [develop] amongst the non-workers.'

This has been the rule in all history up to now. Instead of generalising about '*labour*' and '*society*', this was the place to demonstrate how in present-day capitalist society the material etc. conditions have finally been created that will render workers capable of lifting this historical curse, and compel them to do it.

In fact, the whole paragraph, defective in both style and content, is only there to inscribe Lassalle's catch-phrase 'undiminished return from labour' as a motto on the party banner. Later I shall come back to the 'return from labour', 'equal right' etc., since the same subjects recur in somewhat different form.

(2) '**In modern society the means of labour are a monopoly of the capitalist class; the resulting dependency of the working class is the cause of poverty and servitude in whatever form.**'

This sentence, borrowed from the rules of the International [Working-Men's Association], is falsified in the 'improved' version here.

In modern society, the means of labour are a monopoly of landowners (the monopoly of landed property is the very basis of the monopoly of capital) *and* of the capitalists. In the relevant passage the rule of the International mentions neither the one nor the other class of monopolists. It speaks of a '*monopoly of the means of labour, i.e. of the sources of life*'; the addition of 'sources of life' is sufficient indication that land is included in the means of labour.

The amendment was made because Lassalle, for reasons now generally known, tackled *only* the capitalist class, not the owners of landed property. In England the capitalist is usually not the owner of the land on which his factory stands.

(3) '**The emancipation of labour requires the elevation of the means of labour to the common stock of society, the co-operative management of all labour, with a just distribution of the return.**'

'Elevation of the means of labour to the common stock!' This is better rendered as their 'transformation into common stock'. But this is only in passing.

What is the '*return from labour*'? The product of labour or its value? And in the latter case, is it the total value of the product, or only the value newly added by labour to the value of the means of production as they are consumed?

'Return from labour' is a loose notion used by Lassalle instead of precise economic concepts.

What is a 'just' distribution?

Don't the bourgeoisie claim that the present distribution is 'just'? And on the basis of the present mode of production, isn't it in fact the only 'just' distribution? Are economic relations regulated by legal concepts, or on the contrary, don't legal relations arise from economic ones? Don't sectarian socialists have the most varied ideas about 'just' distribution?

To find out what the phrase 'just distribution' was supposed to mean in this context, we must take the first paragraph together with this one. The latter presupposes a society in which 'the means of labour are common property and all labour is co-operatively managed', and from the first paragraph we gather that 'all members of society have an equal right to the undiminished return from labour'.

'All members of society'? Even the non-workers? Then where's 'the undiminished return from labour'? Only the working members of society? Then where's 'the equal right' of all members of society?

'All members of society' and 'equal right' are obviously just figures of speech. The nub of the matter is that in this communist society every worker has to get his 'undiminished return from labour', as Lassalle would have it.

Let's start by taking the term 'return from labour' to mean 'product of labour', so the co-operative return from labour is the *total social product*.

Now to be deducted from this:

First: funds to replace the means of production [as it is] used up;

Secondly: additional resources to expand production;

Thirdly: a reserve or insurance against accidents, disruptions due to natural catastrophe etc.

These deductions against the 'undiminished return from labour' are an economic necessity, and the amounts will be determined by the materials and resources available, and in part by actuarial reckoning, but they are in no way calculable through principles of justice.

Then there's the remaining part of the total product, destined to serve as the means of consumption.

But before this gets down to individual portions, there are further outgoings:

First: the general administrative costs not directly linked to production.

In comparison with present-day society, this part will be very significantly restricted from the outset, and it will diminish proportionately as the new society develops.

Secondly: whatever is dedicated to the collective satisfaction of needs, like schools, health services etc.

In comparison with present-day society this part will expand significantly from the outset, and will grow proportionately as the new society develops.

Thirdly: resources for those incapable of work etc., shorthand for what today comprises so-called official poor relief.

Only now do we come to 'distribution', which is the only thing considered in this narrow-minded programme, influenced as it is by Lassalleans, to wit, the part of the means of consumption which is distributed amongst the individual producers in the co-operative.

The 'undiminished return from labour' has already been secretly converted into the 'diminished [return from labour]', although what is extracted from the producer in his role as private individual comes back to him directly or indirectly in his role as member of society.

The general term 'return from labour' now vanishes, just the way the term 'undiminished return from labour' disappeared.

Within a co-operatively organised society based on common ownership in the means of production, the producers do not exchange their products; nor does the labour expended on the products appear any more *as the value* of these products, one of the material properties that they possess, because now in contrast to capitalist society, the labour of individuals will no longer be a constituent part of the total labour in a roundabout way, but will be part of it directly. The term 'return from labour', which is useless even today on account of its ambiguity, thus loses all semblance of meaning.

Here we are dealing with a communist society, not as it *has developed* from first principles, but on the contrary, just as it *emerges* from capitalist society, hence in every respect – economically, morally, intellectually – as it comes forth from the womb, it is stamped with the birthmarks of the old society.

The individual producer retains proportionately, after deductions, exactly what he put into it. What he has put into it is a quantity of his individual labour. E.g. the working day for society comprises the sum of individual hours of work. The individual labour time of the individual producer is the part of the working day in society contributed by him, his share of it. He gets from society a receipt that he has contributed such and such an amount of labour (after a deduction of labour for common reserves) and withdraws from society's stores of the means of consumption an equal amount costed in labour terms. The same quantity of labour he puts into society in one form comes back to him in another.

Obviously the principle here is the same as the one that applies in the exchange of commodities, so far as the exchange is one of equal values. The content and form have changed, because under the altered conditions no one can contribute anything except his own labour, and nothing can become a person's property except the individual means of consumption. But as far as the distribution of the means of consumption amongst individual producers is concerned, the operative principle is the same as under the exchange of equivalent values: a given amount of labour in one form is exchanged for an equal amount in another form.

Thus *equal right* is still – at least in principle – a *bourgeois right*, although principle and practice are no longer at loggerheads, and anyway in commodity exchange the exchange of equivalents exists only *on average*, not in each individual case.

In spite of this advance, this *equal right* is continually beset with bourgeois limitations. The right of the producers is *proportional* to the labour they contribute; the equality consists in measurement in terms of a common standard, labour. But one person is physically or mentally superior to another, and hence contributes more work in the same time or can work longer; and labour, in order to serve as a measure, must be defined by its duration or intensity; otherwise it would cease to be standard. This equal right is an unequal right for unequal labour. It acknowledges no distinctions of class, because everyone is a worker just like everyone else, but it tacitly recognises unequal individual talent and hence productivity in labour as natural privileges. *Therefore in content this is a right to inequality, like all rights.* By its nature a right can only consist in the application of a common standard; but unequal individuals (and they would not be different individuals if they were not unequal) are only commensurable in terms of a common standard, if they are brought within a common purview, grasped only in terms of a *specific* aspect, e.g. considered in a given case *only as workers*, and nothing else about them is taken into account, all else being disregarded.

Furthermore: one worker is married, another not; one has more children than another, etc. etc. Given equal productivity and hence an equal share in the socialised resources for consumption, one worker will in fact receive more than another, be richer than another. To avoid all these faults, rights would have to be unequal, instead of equal.

But these faults are unavoidable in the first phase of communist society when it has just emerged from capitalist society after a long and painful birth. Rights can never be higher than the economic form of society and the cultural development which is conditioned by it.

In a higher phase of communist society, after the subjection of individuals to the division of labour, and thereby the antithesis between mental and physical labour, has disappeared; after labour has become not merely a means to live but the foremost need in life; after the multifarious development of individuals has grown along with their productive powers, and all the springs of co-operative wealth flow more abundantly – only then can the limited horizon of bourgeois right be wholly transcended, and society can inscribe on its banner: from each according to his abilities, to each according to his needs!

I have engaged at length with the 'undiminished return' from labour on the one hand, and with 'equal right' [and] 'just distribution' on the other, in order to show how outrageous it is that, on the one hand, people want to make party dogma out of conceptions which made sense at a certain point, but are now a junkheap of phrases, [and] on the other hand, people twist the realistic outlook, adopted by the party with much effort and now well rooted there, into an ideology of rights-and-so-forth, just the arrant nonsense common amongst democrats and French socialists.

Quite apart from the analysis so far, it was an overall mistake to make an issue of so-called *distribution* and to make it the focus of attention.

At any given time the distribution of the means of consumption is only a characteristic feature of the very distribution of the conditions for production; the latter distribution is a consequence of the mode of production itself. The capitalist mode of production, for instance, is founded on the fact that the material conditions for production are assigned to non-workers in the form of property in capital and land, whilst most people own only the condition of production that is personal, labour power. If the elements of production are distributed in this way, then the present distribution of the means of consumption arises by itself. If the material conditions for production are the co-operative property of the workers themselves, then a distribution of the means of consumption arises that is different from today's. Vulgar socialism has taken from bourgeois economists the analysis and theorisation of distribution as independent of the mode of production (and some of the democrats got this in turn from the socialists), hence they represent socialism as turning mainly on questions of distribution. Given that the real relationship was clarified long ago, why are we going backwards again?

(4) 'The emancipation of labour must be the work of the labouring class, against which all other classes are *only a reactionary mass.*'

The first clause is from the introduction to the rules of the International, only 'improved'. Originally it read: 'The emancipation of the labouring class must be the work of the labourers themselves'; here by contrast 'the labouring class' is to emancipate – what? – 'labour'. Make sense of that, if you can.

In compensation, the contrasting clause is a quote from Lassalle in purest form.

'against which (the labouring class) all other classes are *only a reactionary mass.*'

The Communist Manifesto says:

'Of all the classes which today oppose the bourgeoisie, the only *truly revolutionary class* is the proletariat. The other classes come to the fore and then decline to extinction with large-scale industry, whereas the proletariat is its particular product.'

The bourgeoisie is understood here to be a revolutionary class – the bringer of large-scale industry – contrasting with the feudal estates and lower middle classes, which want to retain the whole social hierarchy, the product of outdated modes of production. Hence they do not form merely a reactionary mass *together with the bourgeoisie.*

In contrast to the bourgeoisie, the proletariat is indeed revolutionary, because having arisen from large-scale industry, it is striving to strip production of its capitalist character, which the bourgeoisie seeks to perpetuate. But the [Communist] Manifesto adds: that the 'lower middle classes ... (become) revolutionary ... because they recognise that they face a descent into the proletariat'.

From this point of view it is therefore nonsense once again [to say] that they [the lower middle classes], 'together with the bourgeoisie' and the feudal estates to boot, form 'only a reactionary mass', in contrast to the labouring class.

At the last elections, did we say to the artisans, small manufacturers, etc. and *peasants:* are you, along with the bourgeoisie and feudal estates, just a reactionary mass, compared to us?

Lassalle knew the Communist Manifesto off by heart, just as his converts know his sacred writings. Therefore if he has falsified it so crudely, it can only be to gloss over his alliance with absolutist and feudal opponents of the bourgeoisie.

In the above paragraph, this pearl of wisdom is dredged up

without any connection to the bastardised quote from the rules of the International. Thus it is simply an impertinence here, and anyway sure to please Herr Bismarck, one of those cheap jibes in which the Marat of Berlin [Wilhelm Hasselmann, editor of the Lassallean newspaper] specialises.

(5) 'At first the working class struggles for its emancipation within *the bounds of the present-day national state*, well aware that the necessary result of its efforts will be the international brotherhood of all nations, which is common to the workers of civilised countries.'

Contrary to the Communist Manifesto and to all earlier forms of socialism, Lassalle approached the workers' movement from the narrowest national perspective. Here they toe his line – and this after the work of the International!

It is self-evident that to be capable of struggle at all, the working class must organise itself at home *as a class*, and that its own country must be the immediate arena for struggle. To that extent, the class struggle is national, not in content, but as the Communist Manifesto says, 'in form'.

But the 'bounds of the present-day national state', e.g. the German empire, is itself 'within the bounds of the world market' economically, and 'within the bounds of the state-system' politically. Any good businessman knows that German trade is at the same time foreign trade, and that the great strength of Herr Bismarck is in just this kind of *international* politics.

And what does the internationalism of the German Workers' Party come down to? To the knowledge that the result of their efforts 'will be the *international brotherhood of all nations*' – a phrase borrowed from the bourgeois League of Peace and Freedom, intended to pass as an equivalent to the international brotherhood of the working classes in their united struggle against the ruling classes and their governments. *About the international activities* of the German working class there is not one word! And this is how it is supposed to challenge its own bourgeoisie, and the international intrigues of Herr Bismarck, when the bourgeoisie of all other countries is already in league against it!

In fact the commitment to internationalism in the programme *is infinitely* less than that of even the free-traders. They also claim that the result of their efforts will be 'the international brotherhood of all nations'. But they are also *doing* something to internationalise trade, and are in no way satisfied in the knowledge – that all nations are engaged in commerce at home.

The international activity of the working classes does not depend in any way on the existence of the '*International Working-Men's Association*'. This was only the first attempt at creating a central agency for that activity; an attempt that was an abiding success owing to the impetus it gave, but which could no longer be continued in *its initial historical form* after the fall of the Paris Commune [in 1871].

Bismarck's [newspaper] *Norddeutsche* [*Allgemeine Zeitung*] was absolutely right when it declared to its master's satisfaction that the German Workers' Party had forsworn internationalism in its new programme.

II

'Starting from these fundamental principles, the German Workers' Party will strive, using all legal means, for a free state – *and* – a socialist society: the abolition of the wage system *along with* the *iron law of wages* – and – of exploitation in every form; the elimination of all social and political inequality.'

The 'free' state will be dealt with later.

So in future the German Workers' Party will have to believe in Lassalle's 'iron law of wages'! So as not to lose this [phrase], they talk nonsense about 'abolition of the wage system (this should read: system of wage-labour) *along with* the iron law of wages'. If I abolish wage-labour, then I naturally abolish its laws as well, whether they are 'iron' or jelly. Lassalle's attack on wage-labour turns entirely on this so-called law. In order to prove that Lassalle's sect has conquered, the 'wage system' must be abolished '*along with* the iron law of wages', and not without it.

It is well known that nothing in the 'iron law of wages' is Lassalle's except the word 'iron', pinched from Goethe's 'great, eternal, iron laws'. The word *iron* is a sign by which true believers recognise each other. But if I take the law with Lassalle's stamp on it, and hence in his sense, then I must also take it with his justification. And what is that? As demonstrated by [Friedrich] Lange [the neo-Kantian philosopher] shortly after Lassalle's death: the Malthusian theory of population growth (professed by Lange himself). But if this theory is right, then I can *not* abolish the law, even if I abolish wage-labour a hundred times over, because the law governs not only the system of wage labour, but *every* social system. Basing themselves on this, the economists have been proving for fifty years and more that socialism cannot abolish *naturally occurring* poverty, but only *generalise* it, distributing it equally across the whole range of society!

But all this is not the main thing. *Quite apart* from the *false* Lassallean formulation of the law, the really outrageous backsliding consists in the following:

Since Lassalle's death [in 1864], the scientific view has made headway in *our* party:

that *wage-labour* is not what it *appears* to be, namely *the price of labour* in relation to its *value*, but only a disguised form for the *price of labour power in relation to its value*. With that, the whole preceding bourgeois conception of wage-labour was thrown onto the rubbish heap once and for all, including all the criticisms previously directed against it, and it has been made clear that the wage-labourer is only allowed to work for his own livelihood, i.e. *to live*, by working for a certain amount of time for free for the capitalist (and thus for his fellow consumers of surplus value as well); that the whole capitalist system of production turns on prolonging this free labour by extending the working day or by developing productivity, increasing the intensity of labour power, etc.; that the system of wage-labour is therefore a system of slavery, and indeed a kind of slavery that becomes proportionately harder as the social productive powers of labour are developed, whether the worker is now well paid or badly off. And after this insight had gained more and more ground in our party, they turn back to Lassalle's dogma, although they must surely know that Lassalle *knew nothing* about what wages really are, but rather mistook appearance for reality, following in the wake of the bourgeois economists.

It is as if there were some slaves who finally got out from under the mystery of slavery and started up a rebellion, but one slave, a prisoner to old-fashioned ideas, wrote in their manifesto: slavery must be abolished because board and lodging for slaves in a system of slavery can never go over a certain minimal ceiling!

This insight was spreading throughout the membership, and the mere fact that the representatives of our party were capable of perpetrating such a monstrous attack on it, just goes to show how they set to work composing this compromise programme with real criminal levity and total lack of conscience!

In place of the ill-defined concluding phrase of the paragraph, 'the elimination of all social and political inequality', they should have said that when class divisions are abolished, then all the corresponding social and political inequality will disappear.

III

'To facilitate the resolution of the social question, the German Workers' Party demands *state aid* for setting up producers' co-operatives *under the democratic control of the working people.* Producers' co-operatives in industry and agriculture *will be brought to life* to such an extent that *from them will develop the socialistic organisation of the whole of labour.'*

After Lassalle's 'iron law of wages', we have faith healing! This is 'facilitated' in the worthiest way! In place of the existing class struggle, we get journalistic phrases – *'the* social *question',* the *'resolution'* of which is 'facilitated'. Instead of arising from the revolutionary transformation of society, 'the socialistic organisation of the whole of labour' 'will develop' from 'state aid' given to producers' co-operatives, which it, not the workers, 'brings to life'. The idea that one can build a new society with state loans just as easily as a new railway is a fantasy worthy of Lassalle!

The last remnant of shame made them put the 'state aid' 'under the democratic control of the working people'.

First, the majority of 'the working people' in Germany are peasants and not proletarians.

Secondly, 'democratic' means 'ruled by the people'. But what is 'control by the working people that is ruled by the people' supposed to mean? And particularly in the case of the working people who put these demands to the state in full knowledge that they neither rule nor are ready to!

It would be superfluous here to go into the criticisms of [Philippe] Buchez's [Christian socialist] plan, which was concocted under [King] Louis Philippe in *opposition* to the French socialists and then taken up by the reactionary workers of the [magazine] *Atelier*. The worst offence lies not in writing this particular miracle cure into their programme, but retreating generally from the standpoint of a class movement to mere sectarianism.

That the workers want to create the conditions for co-operative production in all society, and hence first of all on a national scale, means only that they are working for the overthrow of present-day conditions of production, and has nothing in common with establishing co-operative societies with state aid! But as far as present-day co-operative societies are concerned, they are *only* of value if they are independent creations of the workers and not creatures of the government or the bourgeoisie.

IV

I'll come now to the bit about democracy.

(A) '*The state's foundation in freedom.*'

According to section II, the German Workers' Party is striving above all for 'a free state'.

A free state – what's that?

It is not in any way a goal for workers, released from the limitations of servility, to make the state 'free'. In the German empire the 'state' is almost as 'free' as it is in Russia. Freedom consists in transforming the state from an agency superior to society into one thoroughly subordinated to it, and today, too, state forms are more or less free to the extent that they limit the 'freedom of the state'.

The German Workers' Party – at least if it adopts this programme – reveals that its socialism is not even skin-deep, for instead of treating existing society (and this holds good for any future one) as the '*basis*' of the existing state (or a future state, for a future society), it treats the state rather as an independent entity having its own '*foundations in ideas, morality and freedom*'.

And what a crazy abuse of the words 'present-day state' [and] 'present-day society' [are] in the programme, and the still crazier misunderstanding it has made of the state to which its demands are directed!

'Present-day society' is capitalist society, which exists in all civilised countries, more or less free of admixtures of medievalism, more or less modified through the historical development of each country, more or less advanced. By contrast, the 'present-day state' changes with each country's borders. It is different in the Prusso-German empire from the way it is in Switzerland, different in England from the way it is in the United States. '*The* present-day state' is thus a fiction.

Nonetheless the different states of different civilised countries, in spite of their various differences in form, all have something in common, namely that they are based on modern bourgeois society, just that it is only more or less capitalistically developed. Hence they also have certain essential characteristics in common. In this sense it is possible to talk of the 'present-day type of state', but in the future by contrast, its current basis, present-day bourgeois society, will have died off.

The question then arises: what transformation will the state undergo in a communist society? In other words, what social functions will remain there analogous to the functions of the current state? This question can only be answered scientifically, and one gets not a flea-hop closer to the problem by conjoining the words 'people' and 'state' a thousand times.

Between capitalist and communist society there is a period of revolutionary transformation of one into the other. There is also correspondingly a period of political transition, in which the state can be nothing else but *the revolutionary dictatorship of the proletariat*.

But the programme does not deal with this, nor with the type of state in a future communist society.

Its political demands are nothing but the democratic litany well known the world over: universal manhood suffrage, legislative initiative, civil rights, citizen militia, etc. They are but echoes of the bourgeois People's Party, [and] the League of Peace and Freedom.

So far as these have not been blown up into fantasies, they are public demands which have already been *realised*. Only the state to which they belong is not in the borders of the German Empire but in Switzerland, the United States, etc. A 'future state' of this kind is a '*present-day state*', but outside 'the bounds' of the German empire.

But something has been forgotten. Since the German Worker's Party expressly declares that it would work within 'the present-day national state', hence its own state the Prusso-German empire – else most of its demands would be meaningless, since you only demand what you haven't got yet – it should not have let the main point slip, that all these charming little trifles depend on the recognition of the so-called sovereignty of the people, since they are only appropriate in a *democratic republic*.

Because they lack courage – and wisely so, since the circumstances demand caution – to demand a democratic republic, as did the political programmes of the French workers under [King] Louis Philippe and [President then Emperor] Louis Napoleon – they should not have rushed to the subterfuge, which is neither 'honest' [as the Social Democratic Workers' Party was nicknamed] nor decent, of demanding things which only make sense in a democratic republic from a state that is nothing but a military despotism, embellished with parliamentary niceties, under the influence of the bourgeoisie but mixed up at the same time with elements of feudalism, bureaucratically structured and shored up by the police – and yet over and above all this to assure this state that they imagine they can impose these demands on it 'through legal means'!

Even the most vulgar democrats, who see the millennium in the democratic republic and have no inkling that it is in this last form of the state for bourgeois society that the class struggle will definitively be fought out – even they stand head and shoulders above a kind of democracy that keeps within the bounds of what is allowed by the police and disallowed by logic.

What they mean by 'state' is the governmental machine, or the state in so far as it constitutes an organisation in and of itself, distinguished from society through the division of labour, [and] this is revealed in the words:

'The German Workers' Party demands a unified progressive income tax etc. *as the economic basis of the state.*'

Taxation is the economic basis of the governmental machine and of nothing else. In the state of the future, already existing in Switzerland, this demand is nearly fulfilled. An income tax presupposes different sources of income for the different classes in society, hence capitalist society. Thus it is no surprise that the Liverpool financial reformers – a bourgeois group headed by Gladstone's brother [Robertson] – are making the same demand as the [Gotha] Programme.

(B) 'The German Workers' Party demands as the intellectual and ethical basis of the state:

(1) Universal and *equal elementary education by the state*. Universal compulsory attendance. Free tuition.'

Equal elementary education? What can these words mean? Do they think that in present-day society (and this is all they are dealing with here) education can be *equal* for all classes? Or are they also demanding that the upper classes should be reduced compulsorily to the modicum of education – the elementary school – which is all that is compatible with the economic relationships of wage-labourers and peasants alike?

'Universal compulsory attendance. Free tuition.' The first of these is in existence even in Germany, the second in Switzerland and the United States for elementary school. If in some states even 'higher' education is also 'free', this only means in practice that the upper classes can cover their costs of education from general tax receipts. And by the way this applies to the 'free administration of justice' demanded under A §5. Criminal justice is freely available everywhere; civil justice is almost exclusively concerned with property disputes, therefore almost exclusively it is the possessing classes that are affected. Should their lawsuits be funded from the public purse?

The paragraph on schools ought at least to have demanded technical schools (theoretical and practical) in conjunction with elementary schools.

'*Elementary education by the state*' is wholly objectionable. A general law defining the funding for schools, the qualifications of teachers, the subjects of instruction, etc., and monitoring these legal requirements through a state inspectorate as is done in the United States, is something quite different from appointing the state as people's educator! Instead church and state alike should be excluded from any influence on schools. In the Prusso-German empire in particular (and there's no help here from the lame excuse that we're dealing with a 'future state'; we have already seen what the matter is with that) the state could do with the contrary, some very rough-and-ready instruction from the people.

Despite the ring of democracy about it, the whole [Gotha] Programme is infested through and through with the Lassallean sect's servile belief in the state, or what is no better, by a faith in miracles of democracy, or rather it is a compromise between these two types of faith in miracles, both equally removed from socialism.

(2) *'Freedom for scientific inquiry'*, it says in the Prussian constitution. Then why [do we have it] here?

'Freedom of conscience!' If they wanted to remind liberalism of its old catch-phrases during this time of *Kulturkampf* [Bismarck's liberalising campaign against conservative Catholicism], then they should surely have done it in this form: everyone should be able to attend to their religious needs, just like their bodily ones, without the police sticking their noses in. But at this point the Workers' Party ought to have expressed its view that bourgeois 'freedom of conscience' is nothing other than the toleration of all possible types of *religious unfreedom of conscience*, and that on the contrary it strives for a conscience free from religious mystification. But they choose not to overstep the 'bourgeois' stage.

I have now got to the end, for the appendix is not a *characteristic* part of the [Gotha] Programme. So I can express myself very briefly here.

(2) [*sic*] *'Normal working day.'* In no other country has the workers' party limited itself to such an ill-defined demand, instead of fixing the length of the working day considered normal in the given circumstances.

(3) *'Limitations on female and child labour.'*

The standardisation of the working day must already include limitations on female labour so far as this refers to the length of the working day, breaks, etc.; otherwise this can only mean the exclusion of female labour from branches of labour which are particularly injurious to the female body or are morally objectionable to the female sex. If that is what they meant, then they should have said so.

'Prohibition of child labour!' It was absolutely essential to state the *age limit* here.

A *general prohibition* on child labour is incompatible with the existence of large-scale industry and hence an empty, pious wish.

Its implementation – if possible – would be reactionary, because with strict regulation of working hours for different age groups and other safety measures for the protection of children, an early combination of productive labour with instruction is one of the most powerful means for transforming present-day society.

(4) *'State supervision of industry in the factory, workplace and home.'*

Contrary to the position in the Prusso-German state, there should have been a demand that inspectors be removable only after due process; that every worker can take them to court for dereliction of duty; that they must belong to the medical profession.

(5) *'Regulation of prison labour.'*

A mean little demand in a workers' programme. In any case they should have made it clear that there is no intention to make common criminals competitive [as workers] by treating them like animals and in particular to deprive them of their only means of improvement, productive labour. That was the least we could expect from socialists.

(6) *'An effective law of liability.'*

What they mean by an 'effective' law of liability remains to be stated.

It might be noted in passing that with respect to the normal working day the section of the factory legislation that deals with health and safety regulations and accident prevention, etc. has been overlooked. The law of liability would only come into effect when these regulations were infringed.

In short, this appendix is also distinguished by slovenly editing.

Dixi et salvavi animam meam. [I have spoken and saved my soul; Ezekiel 3:18–19.]

'Notes' on Adolph Wagner[1]

(1) Herr Wagner's point of view is the *'socio-legal point of view'*. On that [he] finds himself in *'accord with [the political economists] [Johann Karl] Rodbertus, [Friedrich Albert] Lange, and [Albert Friedrich Eberhard] Schäffle'*. For the *'main, fundamental points'* he refers to *Rodbertus and Schäffle*. Herr Wagner himself speaks of *piracy* as 'illegal acquisition' by *whole peoples*, and says that it is only robbery, if *'a true international law* [jus gentium] is assumed to exist'.

Above all he is seeking the *'conditions of economic life in a community'*, and he *'defines, according to the same conditions, the sphere of the economic freedom of the individual'*.

> 'The "drive for satisfaction" . . . does not and should not operate, as a *pure force of nature*; rather it stands, like any human drive, under the guidance of reason and conscience. Any act resulting from it is consequently an *accountable* act and is always liable to a *moral judgement*, but that is itself, to be sure (!), subject to *historical* change.'

[1] In this text Marx quotes extensively from Adolph Wagner, *Allgemeine oder theoretische Volkswirthschaftslehre* [*General or Theoretical Economics*], Erster Theil, *Grundlegung* [*Foundations*], 2nd edn, Leipzig and Heidelberg, 1879; issued as vol. 1 of Karl Heinrich Rau, *Lehrbuch der politischen Okonomie* [*Political Economy*], new edn, ed. Adolph Wagner and Erwin Nasse. These quotations are enclosed in single quotes, whether in Marx's own text or set off as a separate paragraph. Marx used extensive emphasis, represented below with *italic* type. Words in neither English nor German, which were italicised in the original texts for emphasis, appear as foreign words in roman type for emphasis. Marx's insertions are in parentheses. Editorial insertions are in square brackets. The text here has been slightly adapted and simplified compared with the 1975 edition.

Under '*labour*' Herr Wagner does not distinguish between the *concrete character of each* [type of] *labour*, and the *expenditure of labour-power* common to all those concrete types of labour.

'Even the *mere administration of assets* for the *purpose of drawing revenue* always necessitates activities which belong *under the concept labour*, and it is the same with the *utilisation* of the income obtained, for the satisfaction of needs'.

The *historico-legal* [categories] are, according to Wagner, the '*social categories*'.

'In particular, *natural monopolies of location* have an effect, especially in *urban* relations' (! A natural monopoly – location in the City of London!) 'then, under the influence of *climate*, [there are,] for the *agricultural production* of whole countries, further *natural monopolies* of the *specific fertility of the land*, e.g. in especially good vineyards, and, indeed, even between different peoples, e.g. with the *sale of tropical products* to the countries of the temperate zone' ('*Export duties* on products in some sort of natural monopoly form a contribution – they are imposed in many countries (southern Europe, tropical countries) [Wagner's parentheses] in the safe assumption of throwing them on to foreign consumers'. If Herr Wagner deduces export duties in southern European countries from this, it indicates that he knows nothing of the '*history*' of those duties) – '[such] that *goods* at least *partially free by nature* are, on acquisition, requited in the highest possible degree for *purely economic* [goods]'.

The domain of *regular* exchange (*sale*) of goods is their *market*.

[Wagner includes] *under economic goods*: '*Relations to persons and things (incorporeal things)*, whose objective isolation [in political economy] is based on an abstraction: (a) *out of completely free commerce*: the cases of *goodwill*, *firms*, and the like, where profitable relations to other men, which are formed through human activity, can be acquired and sold *for payment*; (b) on the basis of certain *legal restrictions on commerce*: exclusive trading rights, real equities, privileges, monopolies, patents, etc.'.

Herr Wagner subsumes '*services*' under '*economic goods*'. What he really succumbs to here is his desire to present Privy Councillor Wagner as a '*productive labourer*'; for he says

'the response is prejudicial for a judgement on all those classes which exercise *personal services professionally*, hence on *servants*, on members of the *liberal professions,* and consequently even on the *state* [service]. Only if service is reckoned as an economic good, are the [above] mentioned classes *productive* in the economic sense.'

The following is very characteristic of the manner of thought of Wagner and associates:

[Karl Heinrich] *Rau* had remarked: it depends on the '*definition of assets,* and, in the same way, on the definition of economic goods', whether '*services* also belong there or not'. Then *Wagner: 'such a definition*' of '*assets*' – would have to '*be adopted,* which *includes services under economic goods*'.

But the '*decisive reason*' would be 'that the *means of satisfaction* could not possibly consist only in material goods, because *needs are not merely* related *to such* [things], *but to personal services* (in particular, those of the state, like *legal protection,* etc.) [Wagner's parentheses]'.

Assets:

1. '[taken] *purely economically* . . . the *supply of economic goods to hand* at a moment in time, *as real stock for satisfying needs*', '*assets as such*', 'parts of the total or national assets or the assets of a people'.

2. 'As an *historico-legal concept* . . .in the possession of, respectively, the property of one person, a fixed supply of economic goods', 'possession of assets'. The latter is an '*historico-legal, relative concept of property.* Property gives only a *certain authority for disposal* and a *certain authority for the exclusion* of others. The *extent* of this authority *changes*' (i.e. historically). 'Every asset in the second sense is an *individual asset,* the asset of a physical or legal person.'

Public assets,

'principally the *community-controlled economic* assets, hence particularly the *state, district,* [and] *communal assets.* These assets [are] defined for *general use* (like roads, rivers, etc.) and . . . property therein is assigned to the state, etc. as to the legal *representative of the whole* (people, inhabitants of a locality, etc.) or it is *state and communal assets* proper, particularly *administrative assets,* which serve for the establishment of state services, and *financial assets,* which are used by the state for the acquisition of revenue, as means for the establishment of its services'.

Capital, capitale, is a translation of κεφαλαιον, by which the debt of a sum of money was designated, in contrast [to the debt] of *interest* (τοκος). In the middle ages capitale, caput pecuniae came into use as the main thing, the essential, the primary [thing]. In German the word Hauptgeld was used.

> *'Capital, regular earnings, an interest-bearing stock of goods: a movable stock of the means of acquisition.'* On the other hand: *'stock for use*: a quantity of the movable means of gratification collected in any quantity'. [Wagner is quoting Rau.]

Circulating and fixed capital.

Value. According to Herr Wagner, Marx's theory of value is *'the cornerstone of his socialist system'.* Since I have never promulgated a *'socialist system'*, this is a fantasy of Wagner, Schäffle, and all such.

Furthermore: Marx

> 'finds the *common social substance* of *exchange-value*, which is solely what he has in mind here, in *labour*, [and he finds] the *quantitative measure of exchange-value* in socially necessary labour-time', etc.

Nowhere do I speak of *'the common social substance of exchange-value'*, but [I] say, rather, that exchange-values (*exchange-value* does not exist unless [there are] at least two of them) represent something *common to them* [commodities] which is wholly independent 'of their use-values' (i.e. here, of their natural form), namely *'value'*. This means: 'The common something, which is represented in the exchange-relation or the exchange-value of commodities, is therefore *their value.* The course of the inquiry will take us back to exchange-value as the necessary mode of expression or form of appearance of value, which is to be considered, at first, *however, independent of that form.'*

Therefore I do not say that the 'common social substance of exchange-value' is 'labour'; and since I deal extensively in that particular section [of *Capital*] with the *value-form*, i.e. the development of exchange-value, it would be strange to reduce that 'form' to a 'common social substance', labour. Also, Herr Wagner forgets that neither 'value', nor 'exchange-value' are my subjects, but the *commodity.*

Further:

> 'This' (Marxian) 'theory is, however, not so much a general theory of value as a *theory of costs*, connected *to* [that of] *Ricardo.'*

Herr Wagner [could] have acquainted himself with the difference between me and Ricardo from *Capital*, as well as from [Nikolai

Ivanovich] *Sieber's work* (if he knew Russian); in fact, he [Ricardo] concerned himself with labour only as the *measure of the quantity of value* and for that reason found no connection between his theory of value and the nature of money.

When Herr Wagner says that that would not be a 'general theory of value', then in his sense [of the term] he is quite right, since he understands by a general theory of value a musing over the word 'value', which enables him to stick with the traditional German academic confusion of 'use-value' and 'value', since both have the word 'value' in common. But when he says further that it is a '*theory of costs*', then either he runs to a tautology: commodities, so far as they are values, only represent a *social* something, labour, and, in particular, so far as the *quantity of value* of a commodity is specified, according to my account, through the *quantity of labour-time contained in it*, etc., then [it is specified] through the normal amount of labour which the production of an object costs, etc.; and Herr Wagner proves the opposite by asserting that his theory, etc. of value is not 'the general [theory]', because this is not Herr Wagner's view of the 'general theory of value'. Or else he says *something false: Ricardo* (following [Adam] Smith), lumps value and costs of production together; I have already in *A Contribution to the Critique of Political Economy* [1859] and likewise in the notes to *Capital* [German edns, 1867, 1872; French edn, 1872–5] expressly pointed out that *values* and *prices of production* (which merely express costs of production in money) do not coincide. Why not? I have *not* said [what he says I said] to Herr Wagner.

Moreover, I 'proceed' 'arbitrarily', if I

> 'reduce these costs only to the so-called productivity of labour in the strictest sense. That always presupposes a demonstration, which is lacking up to now [in Marx's work], that the process of production would be possible wholly without the mediating activity of *private capitalists* forming and utilising capital'.

Instead of burdening me with such future proofs, Herr Wagner would, on the contrary, have first to verify that a *social process of production*, to say nothing of the process of production generally, *did not exist* in the numerous communities which *did exist* before *the appearance of private capitalists* (the ancient commune of India, the family-commune of the southern Slavs, etc.). Besides, Wagner could only say: the exploitation of the working class by the capitalist class, in short, the character of capitalist production, as Marx presents it, is correct, but he errs by considering this economy as transitory, while, on the contrary, Aristotle erred by having considered the *slave economy* as *non*-transitory.

> 'So long as such a proof is *not* established' (alias, so long as the capitalist economy exists), 'then *in fact*' (here the club-foot or ass's ear makes its appearance) '*capital profit* is also a "constitutive" element of value, *not* merely a *deduction* or "robbery" on the labourer, as the socialists understand it'.

What a '*deduction on the labourer*' is, a deduction of his hide, etc., cannot be made out. In fact, in my presentation, capital profit is *not* 'merely a *deduction* or "robbery" on the labourer'. On the contrary, I present the capitalist as the necessary functionary of capitalist production and show very extensively that he does not only 'deduct' or 'rob', but forces the *production of surplus value*, therefore the deducting only helps to produce; furthermore, I show in detail that even if in the exchange of commodities *only equivalents* were exchanged, the capitalist – as soon as he pays the labourer the real value of his labour-power – would secure with full rights, i.e. the rights corresponding to that mode of production, *surplus value*. But all this does not make 'capital profit' into a '*constitutive' element* of value, but only proves that in the value not '*constituted*' by the labour of the capitalist, there is a portion which he can appropriate 'legally', i.e. without infringing the rights corresponding to commodity-exchange.

'That theory considers too one-sidedly only this one value-defining [conceptual] moment' (1. Tautology. The theory is false, because Wagner has a 'general theory of value' with which it does not agree; his 'value' is defined through 'use-value', as is proved by the academic salary in particular; 2. Herr Wagner substitutes for value the actual 'market price' or the commodity-price diverging from it, which is something very different from value), '[it considers] the *costs*, not the other [conceptual moment], the usefulness, the *uses*, the [conceptual] moment of *demand*' (i.e. it [Marx's own account] does not lump 'value' and *use-value* together, which is so desirable for a born muddle-head like Wagner).

'Not only does it not correspond to the *formation of exchange-value* in *present-day commerce*'

(he has in mind the *formation of prices*, which alters absolutely nothing in the *specification of value*: after all, the *formation of exchange-value* certainly *takes place in present-day commerce*, as any speculator, swindler, etc. knows; it has nothing in common with the *formation of value*, but has a sharp eye on value [already] 'formed'; anyway, I proceed, e.g. with the specification of the *value of labour-power*, from this [assumption], that its value is actually paid for, which, *as a matter of fact*, is *not the case*. Herr Schäffle is of the opinion, in [his book] *Capitalism*, etc., that it would be 'magnanimous' [to pay labour-power at its real value] or something similar. He only refers to a scientifically necessary procedure),

'but also, as *Schäffle* in the [books] *Quintessence* and particularly in the *Social Body* proves to perfection and indeed conclusively (!), [it does] not [correspond] to the relations, as *they would necessarily have to take shape, in the Marxian social state*'.

(Hence the social state which Herr Schäffle was so kind to 'shape' for me, is transformed into '*the Marxian*' [social state] (not the 'social state' falsely attributed to Marx in Schäffle's hypothesis).)

'This may be *strikingly* demonstrated, particularly in the example of grain and the like, whose *exchange-value* would necessarily have to be regulated *other* than *merely according to costs, even* in a system of "*social assessment*" ["Socialtaxen"], because of the influence of variable harvests with much the same demand.'

(So many words, so much idiocy. First, I have nowhere spoken of '*social assessment*', and in the *inquiry into value* I deal with bourgeois relations, not, however, with the application of that theory of *value* on the 'social state' never constructed by me, rather by Herr Schäffle for me. Secondly: if the price of corn rises after a bad harvest, then, in the first place, its *value* rises, because a given quantity of labour is *realised in less product*; in the second place, its *selling price* rises still more. What has this to do with my theory of value? To the degree that corn is *sold* above *its value*, other commodities, whether in their natural form or in their money-form, are, to the same degree, sold *below their value*, and, to be sure, even if their own money price does not fall. The *sum of values* remains the same, even if the expression of that total *sum of values* were to grow in money [terms], hence the sum of 'exchange-value' rises, according to Herr Wagner. This is the case, if we assume that the *fall in price* in the sum of the other commodities does not cover the *over-valued price* (excess price) of corn. But in that case the exchange-value of money has, to the same degree, fallen below its value; the sum of values of all commodities not only remains *the same*, it even remains the same in *monetary expression*, if money is reckoned among the commodities. Furthermore: the rise in the price of corn, as a result of the bad harvest, over its rise in value, is, in any case, smaller in the 'social state' than with present-day profiteering in corn. Then again, the 'social state' will direct production from the outset so that the yearly grain supply depends only to the very minimum on the variations in the weather; the sphere of production – the supply- and the use-aspects thereof – is rationally regulated. Finally, what is 'social assessment' to prove for or against my theory of value, supposing Schäffle's fantasies on that score were realised? As little as the rule of force encountered in the struggles for the means of life on board ship, or in a fortress, or during the French revolution, etc., which pay no attention to *value*; and how ghastly for the 'social state' to infringe the *law of value* of the 'capitalist (bourgeois) state', and hence also the theory of value! Nothing but childish twaddle!)

This same Wagner cites, with approval, from Rau:

> 'In order to eliminate misunderstandings, it is necessary to set down what is meant under *value pure and simple*, and *it is in conformity with German usage* to choose *use-value for* this.'

Derivation of the concept of value.

According to Herr Wagner, *use-value and exchange-value* are to be derived at once from the *concept of value*, not as with me, from a *concretum, the commodity*, and it is interesting to pursue this *scholasticism* in its latest '*Foundations*' [i.e. Wagner's book].

> 'It is a *natural* tendency of man to bring the relation in which intrinsic and extrinsic *goods* stand to his *needs*, into *clear consciousness* and *understanding*. This happens through the *assessment* (the *assessment of value*), whereby *value* is *ascribed* to goods, with respect to things in the external world, and is *measured*', and this signifies: 'All means for the satisfaction of needs are called *goods*.'

If in the first sentence we insert for the word 'good' its Wagnerian *conceptual content*, then the first sentence of the quoted passage reads:

'It is a *natural tendency* of *"man"* to *bring* the *relation*, in which the intrinsic and extrinsic' means for the satisfaction of his needs 'stand *to his needs*, into *distinct consciousness* and *understanding*.' We could simplify this sentence somewhat by dropping 'the *intrinsic* means', etc. as Herr Wagner does 'with respect to' in the sentence which immediately follows.

'*Man*'? If the category 'man' is meant here, then he has, in general, 'no' needs; if it is man who confronts nature as an individual, then he is to be understood as a non-herd animal; if it is man situated in any form of society – and Herr Wagner implies this, since, for him, 'man', even if he does not have a university education, has language at any rate – then the specific character of this social man is to be brought forward as the starting point, i.e. the specific character of the existing community in which he lives, since production here, hence his *process of securing life*, already has some kind of social character.

But with a schoolmaster-professor the relations of man to nature are not *practical* from the outset, that is, relations established by action; rather [for Wagner] they are *theoretical* relations, and two relations of that sort are interlocked in the first sentence.

First: since in the following sentence the *'external means for the satisfaction of his needs'* or *'external goods'* are converted into *'things of the external world'*, then the first interlocked relation takes the following form: man stands *in relation to the things of the external world* as means for the satisfaction of his needs. But on no account do men begin by 'standing in that theoretical relation to the *things of the external world'*. They begin, like every animal, by *eating, drinking*, etc., hence not by 'standing' in a relation, but *by relating themselves actively*, taking hold of certain things in the external world through action, and thus satisfying their need[s]. (Therefore they begin with production.) Through the repetition of this process, the property of those things, their property 'to satisfy needs', is impressed upon their brains; men, like animals, also learn to distinguish 'theoretically' from all other things the external things which serve for the satisfaction of their needs. At a certain stage of this evolution, after their needs, and the activities by which they are satisfied, have, in the meantime, increased and developed further, they will christen these things linguistically as a whole class, distinguished empirically from the rest of the external world. This happens necessarily, since they stand continually in the production process – i.e. the process of appropriating these things – in active association among themselves and with these things, and soon have to engage in a battle with others over these things. But this linguistic designation only expresses as an idea what repeated corroboration in experience has accomplished, namely, that certain external things serve men already living in a certain social connection (this is a necessary presupposition on account of language) for the satisfaction of their needs. Men assign to these things only a particular (generic) name, because they already know that they serve for the satisfaction of their needs, because they get hold of them through activity which is repeated more or less often, and they also seek to retain [them] in their possession; perhaps they call them 'goods', or something else which expresses the fact that they need these things practically, that these things are useful for them, and they believe that this useful character is possessed by the thing, although it would scarcely appear to a sheep as one of its 'useful' properties that it is edible by man.

Therefore: men begin, as a matter of fact, by appropriating certain things of the external world as the means for satisfying their own needs, etc. etc.; later they also come to designating *them linguistically* as what they [the things] are for them [men] in practical experience, namely, as *means for satisfying their needs*, as things which 'satisfy' them. If one calls this circumstance, that men do not only deal with such things practically as the means of satisfying their needs, but also that they designate them in ideas, and moreover in language, as things that are in themselves '*satisfying*' of their needs (so long as the need of man is not satisfied, he is in *conflict* with his needs, hence with himself); if one calls this 'ascribing' a '*value*' to them 'according to German usage', then one has proved that the general concept '*value*' arises from the behaviour of men towards the things found in the external world which satisfy their needs, and consequently that this is the *generic concept* of '*value*' and that all other sorts of value, as e.g. the chemical value of the elements, are only a subspecies.

It is 'the natural tendency' of a German professor of political economy to derive the economic category 'value' from a '*concept*', and he achieves this by re-christening what in political economy is commonly called 'use-value' as '*value*' pure and simple, 'according to German usage'. And as soon as 'value' pure and simple has been found, it serves in turn for *deriving 'use-value'* again from 'value pure and simple'. For that, one has only to replace the fragment 'use', which has been dropped, in front of 'value' pure and simple.

In fact, it is Rau, who says plainly that it 'is necessary' (for German schoolmaster-professors) 'to establish what is meant under *value pure and simple*', and who naively asserts: 'and for this it is *in accordance with German usage – to choose use-value*'. (In chemistry, the *chemical value* of an element means the number in which one of its atoms can be combined with the atoms of other elements. But the compound weight of the atoms also signified equivalence, the equivalent value of different elements, etc. etc. Hence one must first define the concept 'value pure and simple', etc. etc.)

If man relates himself to *things as 'means for satisfying his needs'*, then *he* relates *himself to them as 'goods'*, witness Wagner. He ascribes to them the attribute 'good'; the *content of this operation* is in no way altered by Herr Wagner's re-christening this in [the phrase] '*to ascribe value*'. His own addled consciousness comes forthwith 'to understanding' in the next sentence:

> 'This happens through the *assessment* (the assessment of *value*), by which *value* is *ascribed to the goods, with respect to* the *things of the external world*, and is measured.'

We do not want to waste words on Herr Wagner's derivation of *value* from the assessment of *value* (he himself adds to the word *assessment* the [phrase] 'assessment of *value*' in parenthesis, in order 'to bring' the matter 'to clear consciousness and understanding'). '*Man*' has the 'natural tendency' to do this, to 'assess' goods as '*values*', and this permits Herr Wagner *to derive* the result, promised by him, of the 'concept of *value* in general'. Wagner does not smuggle in '*with respect to*' the '*things of the external world*', under the word 'goods' for nothing. He sets out from this: Man 'relates' himself to 'things of the external world', which are the means for satisfying his needs, as '*goods*'. He *assesses* these things just by relating himself to them as 'goods'. And we have already had the earlier 'paraphrase' for this 'assessment', reading, for example:

> 'Man stands as a *needy* being in continuous contact with the *external world around him*, and discovers that in that external world lie *many conditions of his life and well-being*.'

This means nothing more than that he '*assesses* the things of the external world' so far as they satisfy his 'needy being', so far as they are the means for satisfying his needs, and for that reason, as we heard earlier, he relates himself to them as 'goods'.

Now, one can, particularly if one feels the 'natural' professorial 'tendency' to derive the *concept of value in general*, [do] this: to ascribe to 'the things of the external world' the attribute 'goods', even *to name* [them], [is] to '*ascribe value*' to them. One could also have said: Since man relates himself to the things of the external world, which satisfy his needs, as 'goods', he 'prizes' them, hence he ascribes '*Price*' to them, and then the derivation of the concept '*price* pure and simple' would be offered ready cut to the German professor through the methodology of '*man*'. Everything that the professor cannot do for himself, he lets '*man*' do, but he is in fact nothing but *professorial man*, who thinks to have conceived the world, when he arranged it under abstract rubrics. But so far as 'to ascribe *value*' to the things of the external world is here only another way of stating the expression to ascribe to them the attribute '*goods*', then, as Wagner wants to insinuate, 'value' is certainly not ascribed to the '*goods*' themselves as a definition different from their 'goodness'. It is only the word 'value' substituted for the word 'good'. (As we see, the word '*price*' could also be substituted. The word '*treasure*' could also be substituted; since '*man*' stamps certain 'things of the external world' as '*goods*', he 'treasures' them and relates himself to them as a '*treasure*'. Hence we see how the three economic categories *value, price*, [and] *treasure* can be conjured up at a stroke by Herr Wagner from 'the natural tendency of man' to offer the professor his blockheaded conceptual (imaginary) world.) But Herr Wagner has the hidden urge to escape from his labyrinth of tautologies and to obtain a 'further something' or 'something further' by false pretences. Hence the phrase: 'by which *value* is *ascribed* to the goods, *with respect to* the things of the external world, etc.' Since the stamping of 'things of the external world' as *goods*, i.e. ditto the *labelling* and *fixing* of them (in ideas) as the *means for satisfying* human needs, has been named by Herr Wagner: to '*ascribe value* to things', then he has just as little excuse to call this ascribing *value* to 'the *goods*' themselves, as he would have to speak of *ascribing value* to the 'value' of the things of the external world. But the somersault is made in the expression '*to ascribe value* to the *goods, with respect to* the things of the external world'. Wagner would have been obliged to say: the stamping of certain things of the external world as '*goods*' can also be *called*: '*to ascribe value*' to these things, and this is the Wagnerian *derivation* of the '*concept of value*' pure and simple, or in general. The *content* is not altered through this *alteration* of linguistic expression. It is always only the *labelling* or *fixing in ideas* of the things of the external world which are the means for satisfying human needs; in fact, it is only the *perception and recognition of certain things of the external world as means for satisfying the needs of 'man'* (who as such still suffers in fact from the 'conceptual need').

But Herr Wagner wants to make us or himself believe that he, instead of giving two names to the same content, has rather advanced from the definition 'good' to a *definition* 'value', [which is] developed and distinguished from it, and this happens simply by substituting the word 'goods' for 'things of the external world', '*with respect to*', a process which is 'obscured' again by substituting for 'the goods', '*with respect to*', the 'things of the external world'. His own confusion achieves the certain effect of making his reader confused. He could have reversed this pretty 'derivation' as follows: Since man *distinguishes* the things of the external world which are the means for satisfying his needs from the rest of the things of the external world, the means of satisfaction as such, and *labels* them, *appreciates* them, he ascribes *value to them* or gives them *the attribute 'value'*; this can also be expressed [by saying] that he ascribes to them the attribute '*good*' as a mark of character or considers or assesses them as 'good'. In that way the concept '*good*' is *ascribed* to '*values*', '*with respect to*', the things of the external world. And thus the concept '[economic] *good*' in general is 'derived' from the concept 'value'. With all such *derivations* it is simply a case of *being diverted* from the task, the solution of which is beyond us.

But Herr Wagner proceeds in the same breath from the 'value' *of goods* as quickly as possible to the '*measure*' of this value.

The content remains absolutely the same, were the term value not generally smuggled in. It could have been said: Since man stamps certain things of the external world, which etc., as 'goods', he comes by and by to compare these 'goods' with one another and, corresponding to the hierarchy of his needs, to bring [them] into a certain rank-ordering, i.e. if we want to call it something, 'to measure' them. Wagner may not speak at all of the development of the *real measure of these goods* here, i.e. of the development of their *measure of quantity*, since this would remind the reader too easily how little is in question here, [i.e.] what is normally understood under '*measure of value*'.

(Like Rau, Wagner could not only demonstrate from 'German usage' that the *labelling* of (pointing to) things of the external world, which are the means for satisfying human needs, as '*goods*', can also be *named*: 'to ascribe value' to these things, but: since the Latin word dignitas = *worth, merit, rank,* etc., which, ascribed to things, also means '*value*'; *dignitas* is derived from dignus, and this from dic, *point out, show, label, indicate*; therefore dignus means *pointed out*; hence also digitus, finger, with which one indicates a thing, points to it; *in Greek*: δεικ-νυμι, δακ-τυλος (finger); *in Gothic: ga-tecta (dico)*; *in German: indicate* [zeigen]; and we could take many more 'derivations' into consideration, that δεικνυμι or δεικνυω (make certain, bring to view, *point out*) has the fundamental stem δεκ (hold out, *take*) in common with δεχομαι.)

Herr Wagner accomplishes this much banality, tautological muddle, quibbling over words, [and] surreptitious manœuvres in fewer than seven lines.

After this trick it is no wonder that this obscurantist proceeds with great confidence:

> 'the much disputed *concept of value*, still *obscured* by many *only apparently profound inquiries*, is elucidated simply' (indeed) (rather 'is complicated'), 'if one, as was done hitherto' (namely by Wagner) 'starts out from need and the *economic nature* of man, and reaches the *concept of* [an economic] *good*, and *to that* concept – *connects the concept of value*'.

We have here the *conceptual* economy, whose alleged elucidation by the obscurantist runs to the '*connecting*' and, so to speak, to the '*disconnecting*' [i.e. a hanging].

Further derivation of the concept of value:

Subjective and objective value. Subjectively and in the *most general sense* of *the value of the* [economic] *good* = the *significance,* which 'is ascribed *to the good on account . . . of its usefulness . . . not* a property of thing in itself, even if it [value] has for a presupposition the objective usefulness of a thing' (hence [it] has *'objective' value* for a presupposition) '. . . In the *objective* sense we understand by "*value*", "*values*" [and] then also *value-bearing goods,* where (!) good and value, goods and values *become* in essence identical concepts.'

After Wagner has designated what is usually named '*use-value*' as '*value in general*', the '*concept of value*', pure and simple, he cannot fail to recall that 'the derived' (!) 'value' 'is therefore' (well, well!) '*use-value*'. After he has first designated 'use-value' as the 'concept of value' in general, as 'value pure and simple', he reveals that he has only drivelled on about 'use-value', hence he has 'derived' it, since for him drivelling and deriving are 'in essence' identical thought-operations. But at this point we learn what subjective content there is with the previous 'objective' conceptual confusion of pp. Wagner [i.e. Rau]. In particular, he [Wagner] reveals a secret for us. Rodbertus had written a letter to him, to be read in the *Tübinger Zeitschrift* for 1878, where he, Rodbertus, explains why 'there is only one kind of value', use-value.

> 'I' (Wagner) 'have endorsed this point of view, whose significance I had already stressed in the first edition.'

On what Rodbertus says, Wagner says:

> 'This is completely correct, and necessitates an alteration in the customary illogical "division" of "value" *into use-value and exchange-value,* as I had *proposed* it in §35 of the first edition',

and this same Wagner places me among the people according to whom 'use-value' is to be completely 'dismissed' 'from science'.

All this is 'drivelling'. In the first place I do not start out from 'concepts', hence I do not start out from 'the concept of value', and do not have 'to divide' these in any way. What I start out from is the simplest social form in which the labour-product is presented in contemporary society, and this is the '*commodity*'. I analyse it, and right from the beginning, in the *form in which it appears.* Here I find that it is, on the one hand, in its natural form, a *useful thing,* alias a *use-value;* on the other hand, it is a *bearer of exchange-value,* and from this viewpoint, it is itself 'exchange-value'. Further analysis of the latter shows me that exchange-value is only a '*form* of appearance', the autonomous mode of presentation of the *value* contained in the commodity, and then I move on to the analysis of the latter. 'When at the beginning of the chapter [in *Capital*] it was said in the customary way: the commodity is use-value and exchange-value, then this was, strictly speaking, false. The commodity is use-value or a useful object, and "value". It is presented as double what it is, as soon as *its value* possesses a *form of appearance* proper, that of *exchange-value, different* from its natural form', etc. Hence I do not divide *value* into use-value and exchange-value as antitheses into which the abstraction 'value' splits, rather [I divide] the *concrete social form* of the labour-product; '*commodity*' is, on the one hand, use-value, and on the other hand, 'value', not exchange-value, since the mere form of appearance is not its proper *content*.

Secondly: Only an obscurantist, who has not understood a word of *Capital*, can conclude: Because Marx, in a note to the first edition of *Capital*, overthrows all the German professorial twaddle on 'use-value' in general, and refers readers who want to know something about actual use-value to 'commercial guides' – therefore *use-value* does not play any role in his work. Naturally it does not play the role of its opposite number, of 'value', which has nothing in common with it, other than that 'value' appears in the term 'use-value'. He could just as well have said that 'exchange-value' is put aside by me, because it is only the form of appearance of value, but not 'value', since for me the 'value' of a commodity is neither its use-value nor its exchange-value.

If we have to analyse the 'commodity' – the simplest economic concretum – we have to withhold all relationships which have nothing to do with the present object of analysis. What is to be said of the commodity so far as it is use-value, I have said in a few lines, but on the other hand, I have emphasised the *characteristic form* in which use-value – the labour-product – appears here; namely: 'A thing can be useful and be the product of human labour, without being a commodity. Whoever satisfies his own need through his product, does create use-value, but not a commodity. In order to produce a commodity, *he must not only produce use-value*, but *use-value for others, social use-value.*' (This is the root of Rodbertus' '*social use-value*'.) So use-value itself – as the use-value of the 'commodity' – possesses an historically specific character. In primitive community-life, in which e.g. the means of life are produced in common and shared out among the communal associates, the common product satisfies the needs of life of each communal associate, of each producer directly; the social character of the product, of the use-value, lies here in *its (common) social character*. (Herr Rodbertus, on the other hand, converts the 'social use-value' of the *commodity* into 'social use-value' pure and simple, hence he talks drivel.)

Thus it would be pure drivel, as issues from the above, 'to connect' with the analysis of the commodity – since it is represented, on the one hand, as use-value or [economic] good, on the other as 'value' – 'to connect' on that occasion all kinds of banal reflections on use-values or goods, which do not fall into the realm of the commodity-world, like 'state-goods', 'communal goods', etc., as happens with Wagner and German professors in general, or on the [economic] good 'health', etc. Where the state itself is a capitalist producer, as with the exploitation of mines, forests, etc., its product is a 'commodity', and therefore possesses the specific character of any other commodity.

On the other hand, the obscurantist has overlooked [the fact] that my analysis of the commodity does not stop at the dual mode in which the commodity is presented, [but] presses forward, [so] that in the dual nature of the commodity there is presented the twofold *character* of *labour*, whose product it is: *useful* labour, i.e. the concrete modes of labour, which create use-values, and abstract *labour*, *labour as the expenditure of labour-power*, no matter in which 'useful' mode it be expended (the later presentation of the production process depends on this); that in the development of the *value-form of the commodity*, in the last instance, of its money-form, hence of *money*, the *value* of one commodity is presented in the *use-value* of another, i.e. in the natural form of another commodity; that *surplus value* itself is derived from a 'specific' *use-value of labour-power* which belongs to it exclusively, etc. etc., that hence with me use-value plays an important role completely different than [it did] in previous [political] economy, but that, *nota bene*, it only comes into the picture where such consideration [of value, use-value, etc.] springs from the analysis of given economic forms, not from helter-skelter quibbling over the concepts or words 'use-value' and 'value'.

For that reason, the definitions of 'capital' are not connected straight away with the analysis of the commodity, nor even with the discussion of its 'use-value', since it would have to be pure nonsense, so long as we are only at the stage of analysing the elements of the commodity.

But what worries (shocks) Herr Wagner in my presentation is that I do not do him the honour of following the 'tendency' of patriotic German professors, and of confounding use-value and value. Although German society is far behind the times, it is still, little by little, moving from a feudal, natural economy, or at least from its predominance, towards a capitalist economy; but the professors always stand with one foot in the old muck, which is natural. From serfs of the landed proprietors they have been converted into serfs of the state, in common parlance, the government. Hence our obscurantist, who has not once noticed that my *analytic* method, which does not start out from man, but from the economically given social period, has nothing in common with the academic German method of connecting concepts ('With words we can in heat debate/With words a system designate' [Goethe, *Faust*, I.1997–8]); for that reason he says:

> 'In agreement with *Rodbertus'* and *Schäffle's* point of view, I place the *use-value*-character of *all value* [at the head], and emphasise the assessment of use-value to such an extent, *because* the assessment of exchange-value is positively not applicable to many of the most important economic goods' (What is forcing him to these subterfuges? as the servant of the state he feels obliged to confound use-value and value!), '*hence not to the state and its services* or to other economic relations of the community'.

(This recalls the old chemists before the science of chemistry: because cooking butter, which in ordinary life means butter pure and simple (after the Nordic custom), may have a soft state, they called *chlorides zinc-butter, antimony-butter*, etc., buttery humours; they adhered, therefore, in order to talk with the obscurantist, to the *butter*-character of all chlorides, zinc, [and] antimony (compounds).) The flummery comes to this: because certain goods, especially *the state* (a good!) and its '*services*' (particularly the services of its professors of political economy), *are not* 'commodities', then the opposing characters (which also appear *explicitly* in the *commodity-form* of the labour-product), contained in the 'commodities' themselves, would have to be confounded with one another! Besides, Wagner and associates find it difficult to profess that they gain more if their 'services' are evaluated by their 'use-value', by their material 'content', than if they are evaluated by their '*salary*' (through 'social assessment', as Wagner expresses it), i.e. 'valued' by what they are *paid*.

(The one thing that is clearly at the basis of this German idiocy is that linguistically the words: *value* or *worth* were employed at first for useful things themselves, which existed for a long time just as 'labour-products', before they came to be *commodities*. But that has as much to do with the scientific definition of commodity-'value' as the circumstance that the word *salt* was employed by the ancients at first for cooking salt, and hence even *sugar*, etc. figure since Pliny as *kinds of salt* (indeed, all colourless solid bodies soluble in water, and peculiar in taste), so that the chemical category 'salt' includes sugar, etc.)

(Since the commodity is purchased by the buyer, not because it has value, but because it is 'use-value' and is used for specific purposes, it is completely self-evident, 1. that use-values are 'assessed', i.e. their *quality* is investigated (just as their *quantity* is measured, weighed, etc.); 2. that if different sorts of commodities can be substituted for one another in the same useful employment, this or that is given preference, etc. etc.)

In Gothic there is only one word for *value* and *worth*: *vairths*, τιμη (τιμαω – *to assess*, which is to estimate; to specify the *price* or *value*; to rate, to value metaphysically, to assess the value, to hold in esteem, to mark. τιμη – *assessment*, hence: the specification of value or price, an estimate, make an assessment. Then: *estimation of value*, also *value, price itself* (Herodotus, Plato), αι τιμαι – *expenses* in *Demosthenes*. Then: *assessment of value*, *honour*, regard, honorary post, honorary office, etc., *Greek–German Lexikon by [Valentin Christian Friedrich] Rost*.)

Value, price ([*Ernst*] *Schulze, [Gothic] Glossary*) Gothic: *vairths*, adj[ective], αξιος [worthy], ικανος [competent];

Old Norse verdhr, worthy, *verdh*, *value, price*; *Anglo-Saxon*: *verordh*, vurdh; English: *worth*, adj[ective] and subst[antive] *value* and *worth*.

> '*Middle High German*: wert, gen[itive] werdes, adj[ective] dignus and in the same way, pfennincwert.
>
> -wert, gen[itive] werdes, value, worth, excellence, aestimatio, *commodity of specific value* e.g. pfenwert, *pennyworth*.
>
> -werde: *meritum*, aestimatio, *dignitas*, valuable quality'. (*[Adolph] Ziemann, Middle High German Dictionary*.)

Hence *value* and *worth* are completely interrelated, according to etymology and meaning. What hides the matter is the *inorganic* (false) *mode of inflection* of value which became current in New High German: *Werth, Werthes*, instead of *Werdes*, for the High German *d* corresponds to the Gothic *th*, not *th* = *t*, and this is also the case in Middle High German (wert, gen[itive] werdes, the same). According to the Middle High German rule the d at the end of the word would have to become t, hence wert instead of werd, but genit[ive] werdes.

But this has just as much, and just as little, to do with the economic category 'value' as with the *chemical value of the chemical elements* (atomicity) or with the chemical equivalents or equivalent values (compound weights of the chemical elements).

Furthermore, we notice that even in the linguistic relationship – if from the original identity of *worth* and *value* it follows, as from the nature of the thing, that this word is applied to things, [to] labour-products in their natural form – it was later directly transferred, unaltered, to *prices*, i.e. to value in its developed value-form – i.e. exchange-value, which has as little to do with the matter as [the fact] that the same word was employed extensively for worth in general, for honorary office, etc. Hence there is no linguistic distinction here between use-value and value.

We come now to the obscurantist's [own] authority, to *Rodbertus* (whose essay is to be seen in the *Tübinger Zeitschrift*). What the obscurantist cites from Rodbertus is the following:

In the *text*:

> 'There is only *one type of value*, and that is use-value. This is either *individual* use-value or *social* use-value. The first stands over the individual and his needs, apart from considerations of social organisation.'

(This is sheer nonsense (see *Capital*), where it is said: that the *labour-process* as purposeful activity for the manufacture of use-values, etc. '*is equally common*' 'to all its' (human life's) '*social forms*' and '*is independent of any of them*'. In the first place, the word 'use-value' does not stand over the individual, rather *concrete use-values* [do so], and *which of these* 'stand over' him (with these men everything 'stands'; everything is 'standing'), depends wholly on the level of the social process of production, hence corresponds to 'a social organisation'. But if Rodbertus wants to state only the triviality that use-value, which actually stands over the individual as an object of use, stands over him as an individual use-value for him, then this is a trivial tautology or false, since for an individual, the need for a professorial title, or the title of privy councillor, or for a decoration, not to speak of such things as rice, maize or corn, or not to mention meat (which does not stand over the Hindu as the means of nourishment), is only possible in some quite definite 'social organisation'.)

> 'The second is the *use-value* possessed by a *social* organism, consisting of many individual organisms (respective individuals)' [Wagner is quoting Rodbertus].

What fine German! Does it deal here with the 'use-value' of the 'social organism', or with a use-value found in the possession of a 'social organism' (as e.g. land in primitive community-life), or with the specific 'social' form of use-value in a *social organism*, as e.g. where commodity-production is dominating, the use-value which a producer offers must be 'use-value for others', and in that sense, 'social use-value'? We want nothing to do with such windbaggery.

Hence to another proposition by Wagner's Faust [i.e. Rodbertus]:

> 'Exchange-value is only the historical covering and appendage of social use-value from a specific historical period. Since one stands an exchange-value over a use-value *as a logical opposition*, one puts a historical concept in logical opposition to a logical concept, which is not logical procedure'. 'That is', as Wagner exults, 'that is completely correct!'

Who is the 'one' who perpetrates this? Certainly Rodbertus has me in mind, since he has written a 'great fat manuscript' against *Capital*, according to R. Meyer, his servant. Who places in logical antithesis? Herr Rodbertus, for whom 'use-value' and 'exchange-value' are by nature two mere 'concepts'. In fact in every price-list every single sort of commodity goes through this illogical process of distinguishing itself from the others as a *good*, a *use-value*, as cotton, yarn, iron, corn, etc., of presenting an '[economic] good' [as] qualitatively different in every respect from the others, but at the same time presenting its *price* as qualitatively the same, [i.e.] presenting a quantitatively different thing *of the same essence*. It presents itself in its natural form for him who uses it, and in the thoroughly different *value-form*, 'common' to it with all other commodities, as *exchange-value*. We are dealing here with a '*logical*' antithesis only in the works of Rodbertus and German schoolmaster-professors allied to him, who start out from the 'concept' value, not from the 'social thing', the 'commodity', and let this concept divide (double) itself all by itself, and then argue about which of the two fantasies is the real Jacob!

But what lies in the murky background of these pompous phrases is simply the immortal discovery that in all circumstances man must eat, drink, etc. (one cannot go further all at once: to clothe himself, or to have a knife and fork, or bed and lodging, since this is not the case *under all circumstances*); in short, that he finds in all circumstances external things ready in nature for the satisfaction of his needs, and must take possession of them or must prepare them from what is found in nature; in this his actual conduct he always relates himself practically to certain external things as 'use-values', i.e. he always deals with them as objects for his use; hence use-value is, according to Rodbertus, a 'logical' concept; therefore, since man must also breathe, 'breath' is a 'logical' concept, but certainly not a 'physiological' concept. Rodbertus' complete vapidity comes forth, however, in his antithesis of 'logical' and 'historical' concepts! He understands 'value' (the economic value, in contrast to the use-value of the commodity) only in its form of appearance, in *exchange-value*, and because this only arises where at least some part of the labour-products, the objects of use, function as '*commodities*' – however, this does not happen at the beginning, but only in a certain period of social development, hence at a specific level of historical development – then *exchange-value* is a 'historical' concept. If Rodbertus – I will say further below why he has not seen it – had analysed the exchange-value of commodities further – for this exists simply where the *commodity* comes in the plural, [where there are] different sorts of commodities – then he [would have] found 'value' beneath this form of appearance. If he had inquired further into value, then he would have found that here the thing, the 'use-value', serves as the mere *objectification* of human labour, as the *expenditure of equal human labour-power*, and hence that this content is presented as an *objective* character of the *thing*, as [a character] which pertains *to it* materially, although this objectivity does *not* appear in its natural form (but [this is] what makes a special *value-form* necessary).

Hence he would have found that the 'value' of a commodity only expresses in a historically developed form, what exists in all other historical forms of society as well, even if *in another form, namely, the social character of labour*, so far as it exists as the *expenditure of 'social' labour-power*. If 'the value' of the commodity is only a specific historical form of something which exists in all forms of society, then so is the 'social use-value', as he characterises the 'use-value' of the commodity. Herr Rodbertus takes Ricardo's measure of the quantity of value; but just as little as Ricardo has he grasped or explored the substance of value itself; e.g. [he does not explore] the *'mutual'* character of the [labour-process] in primitive community-life as the community-organism of labour-powers that belong together and hence that ['mutual' character] of *their labour*, i.e. the expenditure of those powers.

At this point further discussion of Wagner's twaddle is superfluous.

Measure of the quantity of value. Herr Wagner has included me here, but finds to his regret that I have *'eliminated'* the *'labour of capital formation'*.

> 'In commerce regulated through social organs, the specification of *assessed values*, with respect to *assessed prices*, must proceed under the appropriate consideration of this [conceptual] *moment of cost'* (so he calls the quantum of labour expended, etc. in production), 'as also happened in principle in earlier assessment by authority and assessment through trade, and would happen again with a possible *new system of assessment'* (he means socialist!). 'However, in free commerce the *costs* are *not* the *exclusive* basis for specifying exchange-values and prices nor could they be in a *conceivable social condition.* For independent of costs, there would always be *fluctuations* of use-*value* and *demand*, whose *influence on exchange-value and prices* (contract-prices, like assessed prices) then modifies the *influence of costs* and must modify', etc. 'For the' (especially this!) 'penetrating correction of the socialist teaching on value . . . we are indebted to *Schäffle*' (!), who says: 'No kind of social influence on demands and productions can avoid the fact that *all demands* stay qualitatively and quantitatively each in balance with productions. But if that is so, then the *social quotients of cost-value cannot at the same time* function *proportionally as social quotients of use-value.*'

That this only amounts to the triviality of the rising and falling of *market-prices* over or under the value [of a commodity] and to the presupposition that his [Marx's] theory of value, developed for *bourgeois* society, *prevails* in the 'Marxian social state' – this is attested by Wagner's words:

'They' (the prices) 'will from time to time more or less diverge' (from costs), 'will rise with the goods whose use-value has become greater, fall with those whose use-value has become less. *Only in the long run* could costs be made continuously applicable as the deciding regulator', etc.

Law. One passage suffices for the fantasy of the obscurantist on the economically creative influence of *law*, although he patters on and on about that inherently absurd viewpoint:

'The individual economic system has at its head, as the organ of technical and economic activity . . . a *person* as the legal and economic subject. Again it is not a purely economic phenomenon, but it is, at the same time, dependent on the form of *law*. For this defines who counts as a person, and who can stand at the head of an economic system', etc.

Communication and *transportation*

Where the *'exchange in the (natural) components of the mass of goods'* (of an enterprise, alias with Wagner [it is] christened *'exchange of goods'*, for Schäffle's *'social exchange of material'* – at least one case of that is clarified; I have employed the word, however, for the 'natural' process of production as the material exchange between man and nature) [i.e. this term] is *borrowed* from me, where the material exchange appears at first in the analysis of C–M–C [commodity–money–commodity], and the interruptions of the formal exchange are later designated as interruptions of the material exchange.

Moreover, what Herr Wagner says on the *'inner exchange'* of the goods found in a branch of production (as he says, in an 'individual economic system'), partly in respect of their 'use-value', partly in respect of their 'value', I discuss with the analysis of the first phase of C–M–C, namely C–M, the example of the linen-weaver, where this is the conclusion: 'Hence our commodity-possessors discover that the same division of labour, which makes them into independent, private producers, [also] makes the social process of production and their relations in that process independent of them themselves, [and] that the independence of persons from one another is completed in a system of all-round material dependence.'

Contracts for the commercial acquisition of goods. Here the obscurantist gets mine and his upside down. With him there is, first, the law, and then commerce; in reality it's the other way round: at first there is *commerce*, and then a *legal order* develops out of it. In the analysis of the circulation of commodities I have demonstrated that in a developed trade the exchangers recognise each other tacitly as equal persons and owners of the goods to be exchanged respectively by them; they do this while they offer their goods to one another and agree to trade with one another. This *practical* relation, arising through and in exchange itself, only later attains a *legal form* in contracts, etc.; but this form produces neither its content, the exchange, nor the relationship, existing in it, of persons to one another, but vice versa. On the contrary with Wagner:

> '*This acquisition*' (of goods through commerce) 'necessarily presupposes a specific *legal order*, on the *basis of which*' (!) 'commerce is carried out', etc.

Credit. Instead of giving the development of money as the *means of payment*, Wagner makes the process of circulation, so far as it takes place in the form that the two equivalents are not opposed simultaneously in C–M, directly into the '*practice of credit*', whereby there is 'connected' [the fact] that this is frequently combined with 'interest'-payment; [this] also serves to establish the 'giving of trust' and hence 'trust' [itself] as a basis of 'credit'.

On the legal understanding of 'assets' of [Georg Friedrich] *Puchta* [the authority on Roman law], etc., whereby *debts* also belong there as *negative constituents*.

Credit is '*consumptive credit*' or 'productive credit'. The former is dominating in the lower level of culture; the latter, in the 'higher'.

On the *causes of indebtedness* (causes of pauperism: fluctuations in the harvest, war service, competition of slaves) in ancient Rome [Rudolph von] (Jhering, *Concept of the Roman State*).

According to Herr Wagner 'consumptive credit' rules in the 'lower level' [of culture] among the 'lower, servile' classes and the 'higher, prodigal' classes. In fact: in England, [and] America, *'consumptive credit' is generally dominating with the formation of the deposit-bank system!*

> 'In particular, *productive credit* ... is proved to be an economic factor of the national economy adhering to *free competition*, [and]

based *on private property in real estate and on movable capital*. It is connected with the *possession* of assets, not with the asset as a purely economic category', hence it is only an 'historico-*legal category*' (!).

Dependence of the individual economic system and of assets on the effects of the external world, especially on the influence of particular circumstances in the national economy.

1. *Alterations in use-value*: improved in some cases through the *course of time*, as a condition of certain natural processes (*wine, cigars, violins*, etc.).

'*Worsened* in the great *majority* [of cases] ... [use-values are] resolved into their material constituents, *accidents* of all kinds.' The '*alteration*' of exchange-value in the same direction, '*raising*' or '*lowering in value*', corresponds [to this]. *See the leasing of houses* in Berlin.

2. *Altered human knowledge of the properties of goods*; hence '*increased assets*' in the *positive case*. (*Use of hard coal for the smelting of iron* in England about *1620*, as the clearing of forests already threatened the continuation of iron works; chemical discoveries, as that of iodine (use of iodised sources of salt). Phosphorus as a means of fertilising. Anthracite as fuel. Material for gas lighting, for photographs. Discovery of dyes and pharmaceuticals. Guttapercha, india rubber. Vegetable ivory (from *Phytelephas macrocarpa*). Creosote. Paraffin-wax candles. Use of *asphalt*, of *pine-needles* (pine-needle wool), of gas in blast furnaces, hard coal tar for the preparation of aniline, woollen rags, sawdust, etc. etc.) In the *negative case*, the *diminution* of *usefulness and hence of value* (as with the discovery of trichina in pork, poisons in colourings, plants, etc.). Discoveries of *mineral products* in the earth, of new useful properties in its products, discovery of new employment for them increases the *assets of the owners of landed property*.

3. *Particular Circumstances.*

Influence *of all* the external 'conditions', which 'essentially codefine' 'the *provision of goods for commerce*, their *demand and supply*' ... hence their '*exchange-value*', also that '*of the single finished good*'; [this is] 'wholly or primarily independent' of the 'economic subject', 'with respect to the owner'. *Particular circumstances become* the '*decisive factor*' in the 'system of free competition'. The one [person] – 'by means of the *principle of private property*' – gains by 'what he has not *earned*', and thus the other suffers a '*forfeiture*', '*economically undeserved losses*'.

On *speculation. Price of housing. The coal and iron industry. Numerous alterations in technology* reduce the values of industrial products, as of instruments of production.

> With the 'national economy *advancing* in population and well-being there *prevail* … *favourable prospects*, even if there are also occasional temporary and local setbacks and fluctuations in *landed property, especially in cities* (great cities)'.
>
> 'So particular circumstances effect gains, particularly for the *landed* proprietor.' 'These, like most other *gains in value from particular circumstances* … [are] only *purely speculative gains*', to which correspond '*speculative losses*'.

Ditto on the 'corn trade'.

> Thus it must 'obviously be recognised: … the economic condition of the individual or family' is '*in essence*, too, a *product of particular circumstances*', and this 'necessarily detracts from the meaning of *personal economic responsibility*'.

Hence the '*present organisation* of the national economy and the *legal basis*' (!), 'for it, hence private property in … land and capital', etc., 'counts' 'as an *arrangement*, mainly *unalterable*', so after a lot of waffle, there is no means 'for combating … *the causes*' ([and] the evil conditions arising therefrom, as ever, stagnation of the market, crises, sacking workers, reduction of wages, etc.) 'hence *not* [a fight against] the evil itself', while Herr Wagner intends to combat the 'symptoms', the 'consequences of the evil', since he hits 'speculative *gains*' with 'taxes', [and] the 'economically undeserved' '*losses*', the product of particular circumstances, with a 'rational … *system of insurance*'.

This, says the obscurantist, is the result, if one takes the present mode of production with its 'legal basis' to be 'unalterable'; his investigation, however, which goes deeper than socialism, will go to the heart of the 'thing itself'. We shall see, eh?

The individual, principal [conceptual] moments which form the particular circumstances.

1. *Fluctuations in the harvest yield of the principal means of nourishment* under the *influence of the weather* and political relations, like

disturbances of cultivation through war. Producers and consumers influenced thereby. (On *grain dealers: [Thomas] Tooke, History of Prices;* for *Greece: [August] Böckh, Public Economy of the Athenians;* for *Rome: Jhering, Concept. Increased mortality of the lower orders* nowadays with each *small* rise in prices, '*certainly a proof of how little the average wage* for the mass of the working class *exceeds the amount absolutely necessary* for life'.) *Improvements in the means of communication* ('at the same time', it is called 'the most important presupposition of a speculative corn trade which equalises prices'), *altered methods of agriculture* ('*rotation of crops*', by means 'of the cultivation of *different* products, which are differentially increased or decreased through different weather conditions'); hence the *smaller variations in the price of grain within a shorter space of time* compared 'with the middle ages and antiquity'. But the fluctuations now are still very large.

2. *Alterations in technology. New methods of production.* Bessemer steel instead of iron, etc. *Introduction of machines in place of manual labour.*

3. Alterations in the means of communication and transport, which influence the *geographical* movement of men and goods: In that particular way . . . the *value of the land* and of articles of a *lower specific value* [are] affected; whole branches of production [are] pressed into a difficult transition to other methods of management. (*Rise in the value of land in the vicinity of good communications*, on account of the better sale of the products produced here; *facilitation of increased population* in cities, hence the *enormous rise in the value of land in cities* and of *value* in the vicinity of such places. *Facilitated export* from *regions with hitherto cheap prices for grain* and for other agricultural and forest raw materials, [and] for mineral products, into regions with higher prices; hence the straitened economic condition of all elements of the population with fixed incomes in the first regions, against protection of the producers and particularly of the landed proprietors there. For the contrary effect, the facilitated *supply (import!)* of grain and of other material of a lower specific value. Protected consumers, disadvantaged producers in the country where it is delivered; necessity to transfer to other productions, as in England, from growing corn to producing meat in the 1840s, on account of the competition of cheap East European corn in Germany. Difficult conditions for (present-day) *German farmers* on account *of the climate*, then [also] on

account of the *recent steep rise in wages* which they cannot slap onto products as easily as industrialists, etc.)

4. *Alterations in taste! Fashions*, etc., often quickly carried out in a short time.

5. *Political alterations* in national and international commerce (war, revolution, etc.); *trust and mistrust* thereby [become] *ever more important* with the growing division of labour, improvement of international commerce, etc., effects of the credit factor, terrible dimensions of modern warfare, etc.

6. *Changes in agrarian, industrial and commercial politics.* (Example: reform of the British corn laws.)

7. Alterations in the *geographical distribution* and in the *total economic condition of the whole population*, like the emigration from the countryside into the cities.

8. *Alterations in the social and economic condition of the individual strata of the population*, as through the granting of freedom [for labourers] to combine, etc. (The French 5,000,000,000 [franc reparations paid by France to Germany after the Franco-Prussian War of 1870–1]).

Costs in the individual enterprise. Under 'value'-producing 'labour', into which all costs resolve, 'labour' must particularly be taken in the correct *broad* sense, in which it 'comprises *all* that is necessary to human activity consciously directed towards securing a return', particularly also 'the *mental labour* of the director, and the activity through which capital is formed and employed', 'hence' the '*capital gain*' repaying this activity belongs to the 'constitutive elements of cost'. 'This point of view is in contradiction to the socialist theory of value and costs and the critique of capital.'

The obscurantist falsely attributes to me [the view] that 'the *surplus value* produced by the labourers alone was left to the capitalist employers in an *improper way*'. Well, I say the direct opposite; namely, that commodity-production is necessarily, at a certain point, turned into 'capitalist' commodity-production, and that according to the *law of value* governing it, 'surplus value' is properly due to the capitalist, and not to the labourer. Instead of yielding to such sophistry [i.e. the 'law of value' governing capitalist production], the character of the obscurantist as an academic socialist is proved by the following banality, that the 'unconditional enemies of the socialists' 'overlook the numerous cases of *exploitative relations* in which the nett profit is not divided rightly (!), the employers' *costs of production* for a *single enterprise* are diminished to the great disadvantage of the workers (also, of the loan capitalist) and to the advantage of those who provide work'.

National income of England and France.
The gross annual product of a nation:

1. Totality of the goods newly produced in a year. *Domestic raw materials* to be set down in entirety, according to their value; the *objects derived from such and from foreign material* (in order to avoid the double accounting of raw materials) [to be set down] for the *amount of the increase in value achieved by factory work*; the *raw materials* and *semi-manufactured* [goods] shifted and *transported in trade*, [to be set down] for the amount of the increase in value effected thereby.

2. *Import of money and commodities from abroad*, from the title to the income [received] from *secured claims* of the home country, from *extending credit*, or by the *capital investments* of citizens resident in foreign countries.

3. The *carrying of freight* by the *domestic shipping business* in *external trade and mutual commerce*, paid for in real terms by means of the importation of foreign goods.

4. *Cash or commodities* from abroad *imported as remittances for resident foreigners*.

5. *Importation of uncompensated gifts*, as with *continuing tribute* from a foreign land to the home country, *continuing immigration, and hence regular* [import of the] *assets of immigrants*.

6. *A surplus of value from the import of money and commodities, resulting from international trade* (but then to be deducted, 1. *export[s]* to foreign countries).

7. *Amount of value [received]* from the utilisation of useful assets (as of dwelling houses, etc.).

To be deducted for the *nett product* among other things, the 'export of goods as payment for the *carrying of freight by foreign ships*'. (The matter is not so simple: The *price of production (domestic) + freightage = selling price*. If the home country exports its own commodities in its own ships, then the foreign countries pay the costs of freight, if the market price prevailing there, etc.)

'Regular payments to *foreign subjects abroad*, to be reckoned as part of continuing tribute' (bribery, as from the Persians to the Greeks, *salaries of foreign scholars* under Louis XIV, Peter's pence).

Why not the *subsidies* which the German princes regularly derive from France and England?

See the naive sorts of *divisions for the income of private persons*, which consist of 'state and clerical services'.

Individual and national assessment of value.

In his *Researches into the Mathematical Principles of the Theory of Wealth*, 1838, [Augustin] Cournot calls the *distribution of a part of a stock of commodities*, in order to sell the rest more dearly, 'a true creation of wealth in the commercial sense of the word'.

Compare the decline of *stocks* for consumption by private individuals, or *as Wagner calls it, their 'use-capital'*, in our cultural period, especially in *Berlin*; for that, [there is] too little money or proper *working capital in the business of production* itself.

Relatively greater significance of foreign trade nowadays.

Index

Aristotle, 232
art, 137, 155–7

Barrot, O., 49–50, 54, 66, 67, 68, 76, 89, 97, 105
basis, real, *see* foundations, material
Bastiat, F., 129
Bebel, A., xviii
Bismarck, O., 165, 169, 170, 173, 186, 193, 195, 205, 217–18, 225
Blanc, L., 31
Blanqui, A., 113, 175–6, 178
Bonaparte, Emperor Napoleon xii, 31–2, 64, 80, 115–23, 124, 127, 169, 191
Bonaparte, Louis (Emperor Napoleon III): and Society of 10 December, 77–80, 111, 124; capture of, xvi, 165; career of, xii; *coup d'état* of, 34, 105–10, 114–15, 183; government of, 124–7, 186, 191–2; imperial ambitions of, 64–7, 69–76, 80–4, 90–3, 100–1; presidency of, 35, 47, 49–50, 54, 60, 182, 190, 197–8, 223; relation to Napoleon, 31, 33, 41; swindler, 85–6
bourgeois society, *see* society, bourgeois
bourgeoisie, history of, 1–7, 10

capital, concept of, 14, 145, 153, 154, 158, 229–30
Capital, xiv, 14, 242, 246
Carey, H., 129, 131
Caussidière, M., 31
Cavaignac, L.-E., 42, 46, 47, 54, 90, 101, 109, 204

Changarnier, N., 50, 51, 54, 60, 64, 65, 79–81, 83, 86–9, 92, 98, 100, 105, 109, 177
Chartists, 29
Civil War in France: context of, xv–xviii; text of, xxvi
class, social, x–xi
class struggle, xii, xiv, 1–4, 6–12, 18–20, 55–6, 182
Cohen, G. A., xv
commodity, 158, 241–4
Commune, Paris: and civil war, 175–80; and democracy, xvi–xvii, 184–7; and hostages, 204; and national defence, 163–72; disarmament of, 172–3; fall of, 195–207; proclamation of, 163; reaction against, 192–5
communism: and classless society, xiv; and political institutions, xvi–xviii; and political theory, xi; and production, xi, 214–15; and women, 17; principles of, 1, 13, 187–8; relation to other parties, 29–30, 40; rights in, xix; transformation of the family in, 16–17
Communist League, x
Communist Manifesto, see Manifesto of the Communist Party
Communist Party, *see* Communist League
communist revolution, *see* revolution, proletarian
Constant, B., 33
A Contribution to the Critique of Political Economy, xiii; *see also* 'Preface' to

Cousin, V., 33
Critique of the Gotha Programme: context of, xviii–xix; text of xxvi
Cromwell, O., 33, 109

Dante, 162
Danton, G., 31, 32
democracy: and constitutionalism, ix, x, xi; and 'free state', 221–3; failure of, xi, xvi, 59–66, 86–90, 93–105, 111–13
Desmoulins, C., 32
dictatorship of the proletariat, xviii

education, public, 16–17, 20, 224
Eighteenth Brumaire of Louis Bonaparte: context of, xi–xiii; political analysis in, xiv; text of, xxvi–xxvii
Elster, J., xix
Engels, Friedrich: and *Manifesto of the Communist Party,* x, 161; and newspaper editorships, xii; and Paris Commune, xvii; and 'Preface' to *A Contribution to the Critique of Political Economy,* xiv; and socialist politics, xviii; edits Marx, xxvii; publishes *Critique of the Gotha Programme,* xviii

Favre, J., 164–6, 169, 172, 175, 178, 193, 199
feudalism, *see* society, feudal
foundations, material, 56, 159–60, 251; *see also* superstructure
Fourier, C., 27
freedom, bourgeois, 225–6
French revolution, *see* revolution of 1789, revolution of 1848

Gambetta, L., 164
Goethe, J., 36, 218, 244
Grundrisse, xiv; *see also* 'Introduction' to
Guizot, F., 1, 33, 96, 97, 113, 114, 126, 159

Hegel, G., 31, 146, 147, 159
Hugo, V., 67
human nature, *see* political theory

International Working-Men's Association (First International), 163, 206, 210, 217, 218
internationalism, 217–18; *see also* nationalism

'Introduction' to the *Grundrisse:* context of, xiii, 158; text of, xxvi

labour: concept of, 149–51, 208–10; emancipation of, 211–12, 215–16; means of, 210–11; Wagner's concept of, 228; *see also* wage-labour
Lamartine, A., 91
Lange, F., 218–19, 227
Lassalle, F., xviii, 208 n., 210–12, 216, 218–20, 224
League of the Just, *see* Communist League
Ledru-Rollin, A., 42, 55, 60, 63
Liebknecht, W., xviii
Locke, J., 33
Louis Philippe, king of the French, xii, 36, 37, 38, 40, 41, 42, 47, 49, 54, 65, 66, 77, 95, 96, 98, 112–13, 116, 166–9, 175, 186, 197, 220–1, 223
Louis XIV, king of France, 118
Louis XV, king of France, 126
Louis XVIII, king of France, 33
lumpenproletariat, 11, 38, 77–8, 84, 111, 124; *see also* Bonaparte, Louis, and Society of 10 December

Malthus, T., 219
Manifesto of the Communist Party, context of, ix–xi, xiv; text of, xxvi–xxvii, 216, 217
Marrast, A., 33, 51
Marx, K.: and partnership with Engels, x; career of, 158–9; editor, xxvii; *see also Civil War in France, Critique of the Gotha Programme, Eighteenth Brumaire of Louis Bonaparte,* Engels, 'Introduction' to the *Grundrisse, Manifesto of the Communist Party,* 'Notes' on Aldoph Wagner, 'Preface' to *A Contribution to the Critique of Political Economy*
Masaniello, T., 108
Metternich, K., 1, 55
Mill, J. S., 131, 132
Montesquieu, C., 186

nationalism, 17–18, 41; *see also* internationalism
'Notes' on Adolph Wagner, context of, xix–xx

O'Malley, J., ix
Oudinot, N., 51, 63
Owen, R., 27

Paris, siege of: in 1848, 46–7; in 1870, 164–5
Paris Commune, *see* Commune, Paris
Paris proletarians, *see* proletariat, in Paris
peasantry, 47, 116–23, 189–91
political theory: and determinism, xiii, xiv; and human nature, xix; and ideal society, xvi; and reductionism, xiii; starting with 'man', xx, 235–6
Popper, K., xv
'Preface' to *A Contribution to the Critique of Political Economy:* and *Capital*, xiv; context of, xiv–xv; text of, xxvi
production; concept of, 128–33, 231–2; relation to other economic concepts, 133–45, 154–5
proletarians: and communists, 12–20; class politics of, 1–2, 7–12; in Paris, 37, 38–9, 74–5, 113–14, 163, 181
proletariat, *see* lumpenproletariat, proletarians, *see also* dictatorship of; revolution, proletarian
property: expropriation of, 19; forms of, 56, 160–1; private, xi, 13–16, 251–2; 'question', xii; rights to, xviii–xix; *see also* rights; superstructure
Proudhon, P.-J., 26, 63, 129–30, 153, 161, 169

Rau, H., 227, 229, 234, 237, 240, 241
revolution, bourgeois, 3, 35
revolution, proletarian, 11–12, 19–20, 30, 188–9
revolution of 1789, 32, 46, 52
revolution of 1848, 32, 47; periods in, 36, 48, 52–3, 110–11
Ricardo, D., 128–9, 141, 142, 230–1
rights, 'equal' or 'bourgeois', 42–3, 55, 211–14
Robespierre, M., 31
Rodbertus, J., 227, 241, 244, 246–8

Rousseau, J.-J., 128, 209

Saint-Just, L.-A., 32
Saint-Simon, H., 27
Say, J.-B., 33, 139
Schäffle, F., 227, 230, 233, 244
Shakespeare, W., 156
Sieber, N., 230–1
Sismondi, J., 22
Smith, A., 128–9, 131, 149–50, 231
social class, *see* class, social
social-democratic party, in France, 54–5, 58–9
socialism: conservative forms of, 25–6; reactionary forms of, 20–5; state aid to, 220–1; utopian forms of, 26–9
society, bourgeois: concept of, 2, 3, 6–7, 32–3, 128–9, 151–2; economic analysis of, xiii, 145–54, 158; feudal, 2, 3, 6, 12, 32, 160; *see also* bourgeoisie
state: form of, 34, 159–60; French, 67–8, 115–16, 181–3
Steuart, J., 129
Storch, H., 139
Sue, E., 73–4
superstructure, 57, 159–60; *see also* foundations, material
surplus value, *see* value, surplus

Thiers, A., 58, 60, 73, 97–109, 164–89, 193–206
Tocqueville, A., 97
Trochu, L., 163–5, 170, 174, 176, 203

value, and external circumstances, 252–7; concept of, 230–4, 236–41, 244–50; surplus, 232; *see also* capital; commodity
Voltaire, F., 69, 179

wage-labour: and subsistence, 7, 14; definition of, 218–20; women's, 8; *see also* labour
Wagner, A.: career of, xix; theory of, 227–56

Cambridge Texts in the History of Political Thought

Titles published in the series thus far

Aristotle *The Politics and The Constitution of Athens* (edited by Stephen Everson)
0 521 48400 6 paperback

Arnold *Culture and Anarchy and other writings* (edited by Stefan Collini)
0 521 37796 X paperback

Astell *Political Writings* (edited by Patricia Springborg)
0 521 42845 9 paperback

Augustine *The City of God against the Pagans* (edited by R.W. Dyson)
0 521 46843 4 paperback

Austin *The Province of Jurisprudence Determined* (edited by Wilfrid E. Rumble)
0 521 44756 9 paperback

Bacon *The History of the Reign of King Henry VII* (edited by Brian Vickers)
0 521 58663 1 paperback

Bakunin *Statism and Anarchy* (edited by Marshall Shatz)
0 521 36973 8 paperback

Baxter *Holy Commonwealth* (edited by William Lamont)
0 521 40580 7 paperback

Bayle *Political Writings* (edited by Sally L. Jenkinson)
0 521 47677 1 paperback

Beccaria *On Crimes and Punishments and other writings* (edited by Richard Bellamy)
0 521 47982 7 paperback

Bentham *Fragment on Government* (introduction by Ross Harrison)
0 521 35929 5 paperback

Bernstein *The Preconditions of Socialism* (edited by Henry Tudor)
0 521 39808 8 paperback

Bodin *On Sovereignty* (edited by Julian H. Franklin)
0 521 34992 3 paperback

Bolingbroke *Political Writings* (edited by David Armitage)
0 521 58697 6 paperback

Bossuet *Politics Drawn from the Very Words of Holy Scripture*
(edited by Patrick Riley)
0 521 36807 3 paperback

The British Idealists (edited by David Boucher)
0 521 45951 6 paperback

Burke *Pre-Revolutionary Writings* (edited by Ian Harris)
0 521 36800 6 paperback

Christine De Pizan *The Book of the Body Politic* (edited by Kate Langdon Forhan)
0 521 42259 0 paperback

Cicero *On Duties* (edited by M. T. Griffin and E. M. Atkins)
0 521 34835 8 paperback

Cicero *On the Commonwealth and On the Laws* (edited by James E. G. Zetzel)
0 521 45959 1 paperback

Comte *Early Political Writings* (edited by H. S. Jones)
0 521 46923 6 paperback

Conciliarism and Papalism (edited by J. H. Burns and Thomas M. Izbicki)
  0 521 47674 7 paperback
Constant *Political Writings* (edited by Biancamaria Fontana)
  0 521 31632 4 paperback
Dante *Monarchy* (edited by Prue Shaw)
  0 521 56781 5 paperback
Diderot *Political Writings* (edited by John Hope Mason and Robert Wokler)
  0 521 36911 8 paperback
The Dutch Revolt (edited by Martin van Gelderen)
  0 521 39809 6 paperback
Early Greek Political Thought from Homer to the Sophists (edited by Michael
Gagarin and Paul Woodruff)
  0 521 43768 7 paperback
The Early Political Writings of the German Romantics (edited by Frederick
C. Beiser)
  0 521 44951 0 paperback
The English Levellers (edited by Andrew Sharp)
  0 521 62511 4 paperback
Erasmus *The Education of a Christian Prince* (edited by Lisa Jardine)
  0 521 58811 1 paperback
Fenelon *Telemachus* (edited by Patrick Riley)
  0 521 45662 2 paperback
Ferguson *An Essay on the History of Civil Society* (edited by Fania Oz-Salzberger)
  0 521 44736 4 paperback
Filmer *Patriarcha and Other Writings* (edited by Johann P. Sommerville)
  0 521 39903 3 paperback
Fletcher *Political Works* (edited by John Robertson)
  0 521 43994 9 paperback
Sir John Fortescue *On the Laws and Governance of England* (edited by Shelley
Lockwood)
  0 521 58996 7 paperback
Fourier *The Theory of the Four Movements* (edited by Gareth Stedman Jones and
Ian Patterson)
  0 521 35693 8 paperback
Gramsci *Pre-Prison Writings* (edited by Richard Bellamy)
  0 521 42307 4 paperback
Guicciardini *Dialogue on the Government of Florence* (edited by Alison Brown)
  0 521 45623 1 paperback
Harrington *A Commonwealth of Oceana* and *A System of Politics*
(edited by J. G. A. Pocock)
  0 521 42329 5 paperback
Hegel *Elements of the Philosophy of Right* (edited by Allen W. Wood and
H. B. Nisbet)
  0 521 34888 9 paperback
Hegel *Political Writings* (edited by Laurence Dickey and H. B. Nisbet)
  0 521 45979 3 paperback

Hobbes *On the Citizen* (edited by Michael Silverthorne and Richard Tuck)
0 521 43780 6 paperback
Hobbes *Leviathan* (edited by Richard Tuck)
0 521 56797 1 paperback
Hobhouse *Liberalism and Other Writings* (edited by James Meadowcroft)
0 521 43726 1 paperback
Hooker *Of the Laws of Ecclesiastical Polity* (edited by A. S. McGrade)
0 521 37908 3 paperback
Hume *Political Essays* (edited by Knud Haakonssen)
0 521 46639 3 paperback
King James VI and I *Political Writings* (edited by Johann P. Sommerville)
0 521 44729 1 paperback
Jefferson *Political Writings* (edited by Joyce Appleby and Terence Ball)
0 521 64841 6 paperback
John of Salisbury *Policraticus* (edited by Cary Nederman)
0 521 36701 8 paperback
Kant *Political Writings* (edited by H. S. Reiss and H. B. Nisbet)
0 521 39837 1 paperback
Knox *On Rebellion* (edited by Roger A. Mason)
0 521 39988 2 paperback
Kropotkin *The Conquest of Bread and other writings* (edited by Marshall Shatz)
0 521 45990 7 paperback
Lawson *Politica sacra et civilis* (edited by Conal Condren)
0 521 39248 9 paperback
Leibniz *Political Writings* (edited by Patrick Riley)
0 521 35899 x paperback
The Levellers (edited by Andrew Sharp)
0 521 62511 4 paperback
Locke *Political Essays* (edited by Mark Goldie)
0 521 47861 8 paperback
Locke *Two Treatises of Government* (edited by Peter Laslett)
0 521 35730 6 paperback
Loyseau *A Treatise of Orders and Plain Dignities* (edited by Howell A. Lloyd)
0 521 45624 x paperback
Luther and Calvin on Secular Authority (edited by Harro Höpfl)
0 521 34986 9 paperback
Machiavelli *The Prince* (edited by Quentin Skinner and Russell Price)
0 521 34993 1 paperback
de Maistre *Considerations on France* (edited by Isaiah Berlin and Richard Lebrun)
0 521 46628 8 paperback
Malthus *An Essay on the Principle of Population* (edited by Donald Winch)
0 521 42972 2 paperback
Marsiglio of Padua *Defensor minor* and *De translatione Imperii*
(edited by Cary Nederman)
0 521 40846 6 paperback
Marx *Early Political Writings* (edited by Joseph O'Malley)
0 521 34994 x paperback

Marx *Later Political Writings* (edited by Terrell Carver)
0 521 36739 5 paperback
James Mill *Political Writings* (edited by Terence Ball)
0 521 38748 5 paperback
J. S. Mill *On Liberty*, with *The Subjection of Women* and *Chapters on Socialism* (edited by Stefan Collini)
0 521 37917 2 paperback
Milton *Political Writings* (edited by Martin Dzelzainis)
0 521 34866 8 paperback
Montesquieu *The Spirit of the Laws* (edited by Anne M. Cohler, Basia Carolyn Miller and Harold Samuel Stone)
0 521 36974 6 paperback
More *Utopia* (edited by George M. Logan and Robert M. Adams)
0 521 40318 9 paperback
Morris *News from Nowhere* (edited by Krishan Kumar)
0 521 42233 7 paperback
Nicholas of Cusa *The Catholic Concordance* (edited by Paul E. Sigmund)
0 521 56773 4 paperback
Nietzsche *On the Genealogy of Morality* (edited by Keith Ansell-Pearson)
0 521 40610 2 paperback
Paine *Political Writings* (edited by Bruce Kuklick)
0 521 66799 2 paperback
Plato *The Republic* (edited by G. R. F. Ferrari and Tom Griffith)
0 521 48443 x paperback
Plato *Statesman* (edited by Julia Annas and Robin Waterfield)
0 521 44778 x paperback
Price *Political Writings* (edited by D. O. Thomas)
0 521 40969 1 paperback
Priestley *Political Writings* (edited by Peter Miller)
0 521 42561 1 paperback
Proudhon *What is Property?* (edited by Donald R. Kelley and Bonnie G. Smith)
0 521 40556 4 paperback
Pufendorf *On the Duty of Man and Citizen according to Natural Law* (edited by James Tully)
0 521 35980 5 paperback
The Radical Reformation (edited by Michael G. Baylor)
0 521 37948 2 paperback
Rousseau *The Discourses and other early political writings* (edited by Victor Gourevitch)
0 521 42445 3 paperback
Rousseau *The Social Contract and other later political writings* (edited by Victor Gourevitch)
0 521 42446 1 paperback
Seneca *Moral and Political Essays* (edited by John Cooper and John Procope)
0 521 34818 8 paperback

Sidney *Court Maxims* (edited by Hans W. Blom, Eco Haitsma Mulier and Ronald Janse)

  0 521 46736 5 paperback

Sorel *Reflections on Violence* (edited by Jeremy Jennings)

  0 521 55910 3 paperback

Spencer *The Man versus the State* and *The Proper Sphere of Government* (edited by John Offer)

  0 521 43740 7 paperback

Stirner *The Ego and Its Own* (edited by David Leopold)

  0 521 45647 9 paperback

Thoreau *Political Writings* (edited by Nancy Rosenblum)

  0 521 47675 5 paperback

Utopias of the British Enlightenment (edited by Gregory Claeys)

  0 521 45590 1 paperback

Vitoria *Political Writings* (edited by Anthony Pagden and Jeremy Lawrance)

  0 521 36714 X paperback

Voltaire *Political Writings* (edited by David Williams)

  0 521 43727 X paperback

Weber *Political Writings* (edited by Peter Lassman and Ronald Speirs)

  0 521 39719 7 paperback

William of Ockham *A Short Discourse on Tyrannical Government* (edited by A. S. McGrade and John Kilcullen)

  0 521 35803 5 paperback

William of Ockham *A Letter to the Friars Minor and other writings* (edited by A. S. McGrade and John Kilcullen)

  0 521 35804 3 paperback

Wollstonecraft *A Vindication of the Rights of Men* and *A Vindication of the Rights of Woman* (edited by Sylvana Tomaselli)

  0 521 43633 8 paperback